Human Resource Development

*The Prentice Hall Series
on Human Resource Development*

R. WAYNE PACE, EDITOR

Human Resource Development: The Field

❦ ❦

R. WAYNE PACE
PHILLIP C. SMITH
GORDON E. MILLS

BRIGHAM YOUNG UNIVERSITY

PRENTICE HALL, Englewood Cliffs, New Jersey 07632

Library of Congress Cataloging-in-Publication Data

Pace, R. Wayne.
    Human resource development, the field / R. Wayne Pace, Phillip C.
Smith, Gordon E. Mills.
        p.   cm.
    Includes bibliographical references and index.
    ISBN 0-13-446394-3 (pbk.)
    1. Personnel management.   2. Employees, Training of.   3. Career
development.   I. Smith, Phillip C.   II. Mills, Gordon E.
III. Title.
HF5549.P215   1991
658.3'124—dc20   90-40754
                                                    CIP

Acquisitions editor: Alison Reeves
Cover design: Mike Fender
Prepress buyer: Debra Kesar
Manufacturing buyer: Mary Ann Gloriande

Printed in the United States of America
2 4 6 8 10 9 7 5 3 1

ISBN 0-13-446394-3

Prentice-Hall International (UK) Limited, *London*
Prentice-Hall of Australia Pty. Limited, *Sydney*
Prentice-Hall Canada Inc., *Toronto*
Prentice-Hall Hispanoamericana, S.A., *Mexico*
Prentice-Hall of India Private Limited, *New Delhi*
Prentice-Hall of Japan, Inc., *Tokyo*
Simon & Schuster Asia Pte. Ltd., *Singapore*
Editora Prentice-Hall do Brasil, Ltda., *Rio de Janeiro*

Contents

CHAPTER 2
The History of Human Resource Development   **19**

Editor's Foreword

The Prentice-Hall Series on Human Resource Development seeks to define and give direction to the theory and areas of application involved in developing human beings—employees, managers, executives—who work in organizations.

Although the concern for and the practice of human resource development has long had a place in organizations, the systematic formulation of perspectives, views, knowledge, and methods is just now coming into focus.

The prospects, opportunities, and visions of the future are grounded in the dogged yet exciting work of a generation of writers and practitioners who saw very early that organizational competitiveness and productivity are closely tied to employee knowledge, attitudes, and skills.

The content of each volume in this series will focus on a specific role or area of application and will review the theory, principles, research, and skills involved in understanding, appreciating, and performing the role or working in the area.

The books in the HRD series may be used by both practitioners and academicians who have an interest in the field. Since each book has a strong application dimension that is buttressed by theory and research, employees who work in personnel development, management development, employee development, technical development, professional development, sales development, and personal skills development will find each book useful and enlightening.

College and university faculty who prepare students for careers in HRD will discover that the books in this series provide compact and detailed statements of the critical knowledge and competencies that a prospective practitioner needs in order to perform effectively.

Students will recognize that the materials represent real practices in the field, and HRD professionals will recognize that the information and procedures are theoretically sound.

The books in this series may be used as the primary texts in HRD courses in programs such as adult and vocational education, personnel/human resources and industrial relations, behavioral and social sciences, human and educational services, organizational communication and corporate media, and curriculum/instruction and educational psychology.

They may also be used as supplementary textbooks in courses in related programs where students are preparing for careers in training and development. Departments such as communication, organizational/industrial psychology, instructional science, organizational behavior, marketing, and administrative sciences are more and more offering courses that lead to careers in human resource development. These books provide the fundamentals of the field and build very nicely on theoretical foundations in related disciplines.

The books in this series may be used in both undergraduate and dual-level (graduate and undergraduate) courses. They are especially appropriate in courses where working professionals are enrolled. The authors and editors recognize that some courses prepare students in more than one role. The compactness of the books in this series allows them to be mixed and matched to meet the specific needs of HRD students, faculty, and courses.

R. WAYNE PACE

Preface

The basic objective of this book is to introduce readers to the field of human resource development. Almost from the first conference of professors of HRD/T&D in 1979, it was evident that students and practitioners alike needed a single, manageable volume explaining what the field of human resource development consists of, and what people do who work as HRD practitioners. Since that time, more and more literature has become available, but the need for such a brief, compact book is still apparent.

Human Resource Development: The Field provides a "big picture" of its subject, including a definition of the concept of HRD, the future of the field, a history of HRD, its structure, the major roles taken by practitioners, the program areas, the international setting of HRD, and careers and career preparation.

This book is based on the assumption that human resource development is a professional area of practice whose major goal is to develop the skills of employees at all levels in the organization. Thus, HRD appropriately encompasses the activities and programs designed to improve technical and operations employees, staff support personnel, and sales forces, as well as supervisors, managers, and executives.

Professionals in human resource development should be involved in planning, implementing, and managing both training and career and organization development activities and programs offered for all employees in the organization. HRD functions should be staffed by professionals who have been prepared to assume responsibilities in this area.

This book attempts to delineate and differentiate the field of HRD from other areas of study while acknowledging that HRD academic programs may be administered by an amazingly wide array of scholarly departments. This book identifies what is central to HRD, but shows how HRD professionals may be located and function in diverse organizational settings, ranging from personnel to marketing/sales and manufacturing. The book occasionally argues for ideal positioning and ideal ways of functioning relative to HRD, but it also accepts a philosophy of "best fit" in which local circumstances dictate the most reasonable accommodation between the "ideal" and the actual work circumstances.

Some topics and the manner in which they are treated were suggested by the work of the competency and standards projects of the American Society for Training and Development, in which the authors have been involved, but the responsibility for unique interpretations and ways of organizing the ideas rests with the authors. Nevertheless, every effort has been made to provide standard, normative definitions and classifications that can be used across disciplines.

Explanations of what HRD professionals do are based, to a large extent, on visits to hundreds of organizations and the information provided by representatives of those organizations during the process of placing hundreds of HRD majors in internships. Over a period of ten years, the authors have placed human resource development interns in over 500 organizations in all sectors of the economy, contacting and visiting the organizations, negotiating placements, coordinating student efforts, receiving and reviewing reports, and evaluating the work of both students and organizations.

As might be expected, practices reported in the book are composites of organizations and employees rather than reports of specific individuals and organizations. Any resemblance of the illustrations used to actual (historical) organization situations is purely coincidental. On the other hand, all activities discussed have some basis in organizational practices and what working professionals do.

We are deeply indebted to those who have shared information with us, but especially to colleagues and associates in the American Society for Training and Development, and especially the Brigham Young University Chapter of ASTD (Provo, Utah) and the Society for Human Resource Development (Laie, Hawaii) in which our students have held membership. Warm friends and stalwart members of the Professors' Network of ASTD have played a strong role over the years in shaping our thinking about human resource development.

Our families have been small organizations in which we have tried out some of the ideas about developing individuals. Gae Pace, Ruth Ann Smith, and Joan

Mills accepted the challenge of being author-spouses and read and pondered and, mostly, kept clear on those bad days. They are our first choices with whom to walk the beach, think about, and enjoy life. May they find a way to reap the rewards of writing a book.

R. WAYNE PACE, *Orem, Utah*
PHILLIP C. SMITH, *Laie, Hawaii*
GORDON E. MILLS, *Spanish Fork, Utah*

CHAPTER 1

❧ ❧

The Concept of
Human Resource Development

INTRODUCTION

It's not playing in the World Series, but the pure satisfaction and enduring excitement of working in an intellectual environment in a business setting is nearly unequaled as a career: rush to a meeting with managers in manufacturing and discover that they are frantic about lagging production, then run back to the office and do some reading; crank up the computer and dash off a few pages that may represent a new, creative way of energizing employees; do an on-site inspection of the way in which a product is being assembled; go down to the audio-visual lab and video tape a role play for use as a problem in a seminar later in the month; back to the computer to work up a questionnaire to find out what is bothering engineering; meet with the divisional manager about an executive seminar; write a set of recommendations for more efficient use of career center materials; conduct a workshop for new supervisors; and stop by the community college to talk about after-hours courses for secretaries.

There is no routine in this job! It challenges you with a variety of work assignments as you make significant contributions to the business objectives of the organization. The range of weekly activities of HRD professionals is as wide as a college curriculum and as intense as a downhill ski run. What you don't need to know could be put on the head of a pin. What you do need to know and be able to do is so expansive that it is a bit scary. Only in the last decade have we begun to fully understand the scope of what it takes to build a great work

1

force, to help make individuals, groups, and organizations quality contributors in creating products and providing services.

Human resource development (HRD) is the professional field that uses *developmental practices* to bring about more quality, higher productivity, and greater satisfaction among workers, managers, and other organization members. Human resource development is defined by its philosophy of *development*. HRD professionals are dedicated, educated, and prepared to assist employees, their managers, and others in the organization to increase the cost-effectiveness of individuals, groups, and systems.

Human resource development professionals have discovered that productivity is a function of both an *individual's knowledge, skills, and attitudes* and *the policies, structure, and management practices* that constitute the *system* in which the individual works. HRD professionals seek to strengthen both the individual and the work system in which the individual is employed to achieve both short-range and long-range individual and organizational goals.

Human resource development professionals take an integrated approach to development so that changes are made at the least cost and for the optimum benefit of organization members. The goal of HRD is to achieve the highest quality of work life for the employee and to produce the highest quality of products and services possible in the environment and context of the organization in which development is occurring.

HRD has been described as "the integrated use of [individual] training and development, organization development, and career development to improve individual, group, and organizational effectiveness" (McLagan, 1989, p. 52). HRD leads to the achievement of greater efficiency and contributes value to products and services.

Human resource development is also a field of academic study in which colleges and universities offer degrees and students enroll in programs of study to prepare to work as professionals. If you are interested in learning how to help people (the human resources) acquire the knowledge, skills, and attitudes to do their jobs better (the development part), then HRD may be the field for you. In this chapter, we shall look at what makes up the field of human resource development, including the professional field as well as the academic preparation of practitioners.

❦ Value

Human resource development can be understood more clearly when you can draw upon both work-related experience and the systematic knowledge provided by theory and research. We shall start this book with the concept of HRD and its accompanying definitions in order to lay a foundation and establish a way of thinking about HRD that should make it much easier to both understand what the field is about and to work more effectively in the profession.

❦ *Chapter Organization*

This chapter provides an overall, initial picture of the field of human resource development. It defines HRD and explores each of the roles that characterize HRD as an integrating, interdisciplinary field of study and practice. We shall also look at some assumptions underlying the field. This chapter touches on HRD in the organization, its position as a staff function, and its reporting relationships in organizations. Last, this chapter describes briefly what HRD practitioners do and how HRD activities might be combined in various organizational work settings.

❦ *Learning Objectives*

After studying this chapter, you should be able to:

1. Identify the human resource activity areas that may exist in organizations and create a diagram showing their relationships to one another.
2. Explain what is meant by human resource development and how it is distinguished from other human resource activities.
3. Describe where the human resource development function fits in organizations and how it relates to other functions.
4. Describe what HRD practitioners do and how the HRD roles might be combined to constitute different types of jobs.

HUMAN RESOURCE ACTIVITY AREAS IN ORGANIZATIONS

Most organizations work with three types of resources: (1) physical resources, which include materials and equipment; (2) financial resources, which include capital and credit; and (3) human resources, which include workers and managers. Virtually all organizations—business, educational, governmental, or service—make optimum use of these types of resources to compete effectively.

The focus of our discussion is on the resources of human capital. Human resource activities in an organization have three somewhat different goals: (1) creating, (2) maintaining, and (3) improving the system, portrayed in Figure 1.1 as the human resource activity areas or HRAAs of an organization. People who wish to work in the human resources functions of an organization often need quite different academic preparation in different areas. Employees who work in

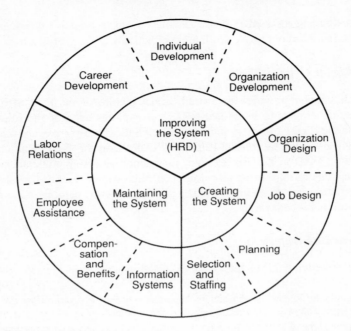

FIGURE 1.1
Human Resource Activity Areas Wheel

information systems, for example, may require very different preparation from employees working in organization development, even though the activities are both part of the human resources field.

At the core of the wheel are the goals of "creating," "maintaining," and "improving" the system. They are accomplished by one or more of the HR activity areas in the organization, represented in the outer circle of the wheel. For an organizational system to function, for instance, it must identify and hire employees (often called the selection and staffing activity area), the system is maintained by providing employees with salaries or wages and health benefits (frequently referred to as the compensation and benefits activity area), and it improves the system by training individuals (called the individual development area). As you can see, each of the human resource activity areas has an important function to fulfill in making certain that the organization is fully operational.

Let us look at the three goals and the activity areas that provide services to achieve each of the goals.

🎗 Creating the System

Some of the HRAAs focus on the organization itself (how it is designed, structured, and implemented); activities such as organization and job design, theoretically, precede all other activities, since it would be almost impossible to have a functioning organization without the system itself. Equally obvious is the fact that jobs must be identified for people to be able to carry out job tasks. Human resource planning and human resource selection and staffing tend to be most concerned with matching people with the organization and its jobs and attracting people to the organization. These activities tend to share a common base in *creating the system*.

🎗 Maintaining the System

Once the system is organized and staffed, the next concern is keeping the system functioning. To that end, some of the HRAAs focus on working with and providing services to the human resources after the organization is operating and the policies and strategies are established; such areas as compensation and benefits, employee assistance, information systems, and labor relations are dedicated to maintaining an active work force and sharing a common base in *maintaining the system*. Most of the traditional personnel activities in an organization are designed to help maintain the system, a critically important function if the company or agency is to be effective in accomplishing its mission.

🎗 Improving the System

Three of the HRAAs focus on improving individual and organizational productivity and the quality of performance in the organization so that the goals of the organization and organizational effectiveness can be achieved without sacrificing personal goals; the areas of individual training and development, career development, and organization development are dedicated to improving the quality of performance and work life and share a common base in the concept of *improving the system*.

This book is concerned with the human resource activity areas represented in the wheel that contribute to improving the system. The principles and methods of human resource development are embodied in the content of individual training, career, and organization development roles.

Three basic ways are usually used to improve an organization. One, focus on changing and refining the organization's structure. Two, identify and recruit the best possible individuals to fill the positions in the organization. Three, train the people who hold organization positions to be more skillful. These three approaches represent how human resource development accomplishes the goal of improving the system.

DEFINITION OF HUMAN RESOURCE DEVELOPMENT

Human resource development takes as its primary domain the improvement of individual, group, and organizational effectiveness. HRD involves the integrated use of individual development methods, career development methods, and organization development methods to provide a comprehensive approach to improving the system.

Individual development (*ID*) involves helping employees identify their strengths and weaknesses, build on those strengths, work at correcting their weaknesses, and use their full potential to contribute to the effectiveness of the organization while achieving their own personal goals. Individual development is achieved through the skillful implementation of several roles that are discussed in later chapters, such as needs analyst, program designer, and instructor/facilitator.

Organization development (*OD*) focuses primarily on the system—its structure and functioning—and the processes of change that produce effective intraunit and interunit relationships. The organization change agent role encompasses and implements OD activities.

Career development (*CD*) focuses primarily on the match between the individual and organization jobs and how the worker performs and shapes work roles and positions. The individual career development counselor role makes CD a vital force in the organization and contributes immensely to the development of its human resources.

We therefore define *human resource development* as *the integration of*

HRD:
IMPROVING THE SYSTEM
BY HELPING EMPLOYEES TO:

- **Perform current jobs more effectively**
- **Assume a variety of different jobs in the organization**
- **Move into jobs not yet identified and defined**

*individual development, career development, and organization development
roles to achieve maximum productivity, quality, opportunity, and fulfillment for
organization members as they work to accomplish the goals of the organization.*

HRD practitioners around the world are particularly interested in the
growth and expansion of the talents, skills, and abilities of individuals in all
countries so that they can, in turn, contribute to the ultimate goal of creating a
good life for everyone, not only in organizations, but also in all aspects of the
global community.

Former Secretary of State George Shultz asserted, for example, in his
address on economic cooperation in the Pacific Basin, that "human resource
development [was] chosen as a focus because it encompasses all nations in the
region, big and small" (U.S. Department of State, *Bureau of Public Affairs,*
February 21, 1985).

Great strides are being made in Japan, Taiwan, China, Singapore, and India
even today. Productivity is the single most discussed issue, for example, relative
to the emergence of East Asia and part of Southeast Asia as economic powers;
the question is whether or not Western nations can compete with these emerging
nations. HRD efforts in Singapore illustrate this commitment. Singapore's
National Productivity Board is intensively involved in helping employees
become more productive. The government of Singapore realizes, as do others
in these areas, that the long-term success of any business enterprise depends on
increasing the productivity of its employees. From an international competitive
perspective, therefore, the work of HRD practitioners in helping employees
enhance productivity is of prime importance.

Individual talents are being developed through extensive training programs. The accomplishment of national goals depends on how quickly quality
HRD practitioners can be prepared to lead the assault on ignorance and incompetence.

Systematic human resource development lies at the heart of success in all
areas of organized life. As Szilagyi (1988) writes,

> In today's complex and dynamic environment, it is no longer necessary to debate
> whether training and development [human resource development] activities are
> luxuries in which only large organizations can indulge in prosperous times. Most
> organizations—large and small—have come to realize that developing an effective
> work force is no more a luxury than having a sales or accounting department. It is
> an accepted fact that training and development are necessary for the spirit, survival,
> and performance of an organization—it must develop those who will manage the
> organization in the years to come. (p. 382)

HRD can also contribute to the ultimate goal of creating a good life for
every individual citizen, not only in business organizational settings, but also in

family, religious, and community relations. No area of human life is without the need to help individuals achieve a higher quality of living.

As important as human skills are, proficiency in financial planning, evaluation, and computer skills are, on the other hand, also important for working effectively in organizations.

HRD ASSUMPTIONS

Seven basic assumptions undergird the effective development of human resources and provide the philosophical perspective that impels the contribution HRD makes to people's lives.

1. *Worth of the Individual.*   Human beings are important in their own right. Individual worth, however, goes beyond this seemingly simple statement to suggest that an organization's quality is judged by how well this worth and each individual's contribution to the organization is recognized and taken into account in the work situation.

2. *Employees as Resources.*   Employees, regardless of their status in the organization, are capable of helping to meet the present and future human resource needs of the organization. This means that a pool of skilled employees who are involved in acquiring new skills, learning new ideas, and preparing to occupy new positions in the organization must be available.

3. *Quality Work Environment.*   The quality of work life is a legitimate and valuable concern of human beings in all areas of the organization. Employees have a right to safe, clean, pleasant surroundings in which to do their work. A development approach to employee relations means that organizations should constantly seek to improve the quality of their work environments.

4. *Employee Satisfaction.*   Human beings have the right to be satisfied and feel good about the ways in which they contribute to the organization. Fulfill-

---

HRD ASSUMPTIONS

- **Worth of the individual**
- **Employees as resources**
- **Quality work environment**
- **Employee satisfaction**
- **Continuous learning need**
- **Change opportunities preparation**
- **Broad scope of HRD concern**

---

ment on the job comes from a deep-seated satisfaction with the work that one is doing. Organizations should constantly seek to redesign work so that it is suited more for mature human beings than it is for robots. Jobs should provide intrinsic work satisfaction so that a person's work represents a good fit between technology and talent.

5. *Continuous Learning Need.* The training and development of employees is not a one-time effort. Individuals do not come to the organization with all the knowledge and skills they need to fulfill every demand initially placed upon them. Although employees should be selected on the basis of their competence to work at specific jobs, talents and skills must be refined and adapted, and new skills must be acquired. Any organization that fails to help its employees prepare for the future will find that it may not have a future. There is a need for continuous learning.

6. *Change Opportunities Preparation.* Changing conditions, environment, markets, and resource demands necessitate the continual preparation of human beings to assume different positions in the organization. Every day, every week, every month, every year conditions arise that create potential change opportunities for individuals.

7. *Broad Scope of HRD Concerns.* HRD constitutes more than technical training. The field involves an understanding of human behavior, how people respond and relate to one another, and how human beings contribute to organizational productivity as well as to their own well-being. That is to say, human beings must know more than what is necessary to do a specific task assigned to the organization. An understanding of and competence in a wide range of human skills is important at all levels in the organization.

POSITIONING HRD IN THE ORGANIZATION

So far in this chapter, we have defined HRD and described the philosophical assumptions that underlie it. In the remainder of this chapter, we shall position HRD in the organization. This will be accomplished by emphasizing the need for HRD, highlighting its importance in organizations, elaborating on the nature of staff and line functions with regard to HRD, commenting briefly on reporting relationships, and introducing the roles performed by HRD practitioners.

❦ *The Need for HRD Specialists in the Organization*

HRD practitioners are in demand when an organization wants to increase its effectiveness through individual, career, or organization development. Human resource development, when properly positioned, pervades and permeates all aspects of the organization. Where people exist, HRD should also exist. Where people lack the knowledge, skills, and attitudes to contribute effectively to accomplishing goals, HRD specialists should be involved. Where employees seek to move into new positions or assume new, greater, or broader responsibilities, an HRD specialist is needed. Where the environment, technology, and markets for products come into existence or change, HRD specialists are needed to help prepare employees for the changes. HRD programs teach employees to manufacture, operate, and sell new products.

Human resource development is "an asset-developing function" (Zemke, 1981) that thrives on creative problem solving to ensure a work force of qualified, enthusiastic, achieving individuals. HRD specialists assist employees in acquiring both technical and "human" skills.

Business India, for example, reported that the

> development of workers is to help them to acquire new skills—both work skills as well as human skills . . . [which] include skills of collaboration, communication, group work, confrontation, collective action, positive assertion, empathy, helping skills and organizing groups, etc. These are as necessary as technical skills, if not more so. (Khandelwal, 1985)

❦ *The Importance of HRD in the Organization*

Human resource development can take place in any context and at any level, on an individual basis or in small groups; however, most formal HRD work takes place in an organizational setting. The development of human resources in an organization should be the central part of all employee activities. Everyone should be concerned about the development of their employees; executives should be concerned about the development of managers. The more skillful the work force, the greater the likelihood that employees—from operators through managers and executives—will be more productive.

A knowledgeable, informed, work force is more powerful than a group of uninformed employees. A work force with positive perceptions of the organization and their role in it is a happier, more willing work force. Human resource development is that function within an organization that assists employees to understand, to appreciate, and to contribute both to the organization and to their own lives.

Fest (1979) suggests that the challenge of human resource development is to "help workers become contributing human beings, and human beings to become committed workers" (p. 86). He reasons, also, that the cause is just and important and that

> human resource development is emerging from an incidental, peripheral and uncertain status to one that is central and essential. We need trained professionals to

conceive, manage and conduct the development programs within the total organizational framework and in consonance with both individual and organizational needs and goals. (p. 83)

These perspectives and illustrations emphasize the fundamental importance of human resource development to organization survival and competitiveness. The most successful organizations are those that give high priority to HRD and act vigorously on that priority. Even when organizations are able to identify and recruit the most outstanding, skilled personnel available, changes in technology, environmental conditions, and the knowledge base itself mandate a continued effort in employee development. HRD practitioners should never be far from the mainstream of organizational life.

❦ *HRD as a Staff or a Line Function*

Most organizations distinguish between employees who are involved directly in the design, production, and distribution of goods and services (called "line" personnel) and employees who provide advice, policy, and technical guidance to the line (usually called "staff" personnel). In an ideal setting, staff employees provide expertise about how tasks might be done and look after specialized problems, and in other ways support employees involved directly in manufacturing and marketing products, disseminating information, and providing services to customers.

Human resource development is a staff function, since it focuses its expertise on helping the line do a better job of production and sales, rather than on production itself. HRD specialists are not involved directly in producing or furnishing products for the organization's clients, but they assist employees at all levels in the organization to develop the skills and perceptions essential to doing their jobs and making progress in the organization.

❦ *HRD Reporting Relationships*

Because HRD specialists work with operators in technical training programs and with executives in executive development programs, the HRD

HRD AS A STAFF FUNCTION

LINE: Planning and producing goods and services
STAFF: Support line work: planning, research, training

HRD REPORTING RELATIONSHIPS

Separate, but Connected to Organization Policymakers

---

function is not restricted to any particular segment of the organization. Since the development function relates directly to organization productivity and the ultimate survival of the organization, it is advantageous for the HRD manager to report as directly as possible to the executive-in-charge of the organization, either the corporate president or chief executive officer, the divisional manager or the supervisor of a strategic business unit. In all cases, regardless of how the position is defined, the person in charge of the organizational unit overseeing employee performance should be the person and position to which the HRD manager reports.

Although some companies continue to have HRD report to the Personnel or Human Resources Department, the emerging pattern today is toward separating personnel from HRD and having a vice president for human resource development. Since Personnel and Human Resource Development have such different sets (maintenance versus improvement), those organizations that still have HRD report to Personnel risk having an unsuccessful HRD program.

Odiorne (Zemke, 1981) expressed the argument a few years ago when he said:

> I still think I can make as strong a case as ever for having personnel report to human resources development and not the other way around. . . . HRD is an asset-developing function and personnel is a bookkeeping function. . . . You don't ask production planning or manufacturing to report to maintenance. It doesn't make sense. HRD is where the action is, not personnel. (p. 67)

WHAT HRD SPECIALISTS DO

Human resource development is a professional area of employment. Professionals are individuals who have acquired the skills, competencies, and analytical abilities to work independently. The work done by professional people is usually described in terms of the roles they perform. The term "role" refers to a set of closely related behaviors encompassed within the scope of a single concept.

A "job," on the other hand, may encompass a number of different roles. A role may or may not describe an entire job. For the HRD practitioner, the ability to perform the key roles is of first priority; thus, this text concentrates more information and details on what it takes to execute critical roles than on any other single aspect of HRD.

The 1988 Competency and Standards Project of the American Society for Training and Development (McLagan) identified 11 roles that fall within the scope of human resource development. An HRD professional should be able to perform most of the 11 roles, although no particular HRD position or job encompasses all roles.

The 11 roles (listed alphabetically) that emerged from the work are defined as follows:

1. *Administrator.* The role of providing coordination and support services for the delivery of HRD programs and services.
2. *Evaluator.* The role of identifying the impact of an intervention on individual or organizational effectiveness.
3. *Individual Career Development Advisor.* The role of helping individuals to assess personal competencies, values, and goals and to identify, plan, and implement development and career actions.
4. *HRD Manager.* The role of supporting and leading a group's work and linking that work with the total organization.
5. *Instructor/Facilitator.* The role of presenting information, directing structured learning experiences, and managing group discussions and group process.
6. *Marketer.* The role of marketing and contracting for HRD viewpoints, programs, and services.
7. *Materials Developer.* The role of producing written and/or electronically mediated instructional materials.
8. *Needs Analyst.* The role of identifying ideal and actual performance and performance conditions and determining causes of discrepancies.

WHAT HRD PRACTITIONERS DO:
THE ROLES

Administrator	Marketer
Evaluator	Materials Developer
Individual Career Development Advisor	Needs Analyst
	Organization Change Agent
Instructor/Facilitator	Program Designer
HRD Manager	Researcher

9. *Organization Change Agent.* The role of influencing and supporting changes in organization behavior.
10. *Program Designer.* The role of preparing objectives, defining content, and selecting and sequencing activities for a specific intervention.
11. *Researcher.* The role of identifying, developing, or testing new information (theory, concepts, technology, models, hardware) and translating these into implications for improved individual or organizational performance.

HRD ROLE COMBINATIONS IN REAL JOBS

Advertisements about job openings often describe the requirements and job qualifications required to do a job. Two job announcements for positions in the field of human resource development, one from a government agency and the other from a manufacturing company, illustrate how organizations combine HRD roles in different ways to create professional positions. Study these descriptions to see how they have combined HRD roles in different ways.

Example 1: Government

• Participates in overall planning with senior administrator to provide effective training, staff development, and continuing education programs for agency personnel.
• Advises on current status of specialized training projects for professional, technical, and administrative personnel, and new training needs. Implements, directs, or conducts agency orientation training for key staff, administrators, and other personnel groups as assigned.
• Schedules, assists, or conducts cooperative training programs for field or community operations within the policies of the agency. Designs curricula and course outlines; develops instructional methods, training aids, manuals and materials appropriate to the conduct of specific agency staff development.
• Conducts trainer courses for other staff development specialists or agency staff and skills training for subordinate staff.
• Maintains necessary records, accounts, and inventories, administers designated funds for training projects, manages all correspondence and information dissemination appropriate to the assigned areas of responsibility within the policies and procedures of the agency.
• Assists in the review and assessment of effectiveness for specific staff development programs and proposes modifications to improve effectiveness.
• As assigned, represents the agency at meetings related to training, staff development, and continuing education.
•

Example 2: Business

• Manages all training for market-related functions, including sales management, sales representation, field office, home office personnel who are involved in the sales of products and services; customer service, including home office and field personnel who provide direct customer service; and marketing, as it relates directly to the sale of our product, designing implementation packages for the new sales tools produced.

- Develops, with resident experts, a basic training curriculum by defining areas of training need, identifying experts who can supply needed knowledge, developing training modules or packages of skills and knowledge to be trained, creating training tools to see that each skill or unit of knowledge is mastered by defined individuals, such as tests, audio-visual, work books, policies and procedures, and selects supplementary materials from outside vendors, such as audiocassettes, VCRs, and motion pictures.
- Develops a training faculty by defining the terms, requirements, and compensation; administers the system, including a system of rotation among functions.
- Administers training by staging seminars, scheduling personnel for on-the-job training, supervising field office training visits by internal staff, and identifying and scheduling outside conferences for skill development.
- Measures and reports training results.

ROLE COMBINATIONS IN WORK SETTINGS

Government	*Business*
Planning, Advising	**Managing, Administering**
Scheduling, Training	**Develop Training**
Record Keeping	**Develop Curriculum**

The responsibilities of the two positions just described differ in terms of the types of roles the employees are required to perform, but both ask employees to identify development needs, to design programs, to develop materials, and to conduct and administer training sessions. Although the second position was in a marketing department, neither it nor the first position explicitly required the employee to market training materials. Neither position seemed, from the way the descriptions read, to include the roles of researcher, organization change agent, or individual career development advisor, although skills in these role areas could be inferred from the job descriptions. The role of manager of the human resource development department was described in one and implied in the other.

From the somewhat informal analysis of these two positions, we may conclude that different jobs may require the performance of different roles; however, professionals in the field should be able to perform the key roles in either type of organization, even if they are not directly specified in current job descriptions.

SUMMARY

In this chapter we have provided a description and definition of organization activities that focus on the individual employee. Three groups of activities were identified:

1. .Activities involved in the creation of the organizational system—organization and job design, planning, selection and staffing.
2. Activities involved in the maintenance of the human resource system—information systems, compensation and benefits, employee assistance, and labor relations.
3. Activities involved in improving the human resource system—organization development, career development, and individual development.

The creative and integrated use of individual, career, and organization development methods to achieve individual, group, and organizational effectiveness was described as the primary goal of HRD. Seven basic assumptions on which human resource development in organizations is based were discussed.

A few paragraphs were devoted to discussing where HRD should be located in an organization, given its overriding interest and charge to develop all employees in the organization. It was concluded that HRD should report as directly as possible to the officer-in-charge of the unit.

Eleven roles of HRD specialists were listed and defined, and a distinction was made between the job held by someone working in HRD and the range of knowledge and skill to be acquired by someone learning to perform all 11 roles. Two job descriptions were analyzed to illustrate how organizations combine different roles to make a position in HRD.

HRD PROFESSION: MAIN COMPONENTS
AND REMAINDER OF BOOK

The chapters in the remainder of this book tend to elaborate upon elements of the HRD profession model (Figure 1.2). Except for the immediately following chapters (2, 3, and 4), which provide historical, conceptual, and structural background, and Chapter 10, which provides an introduction to the international

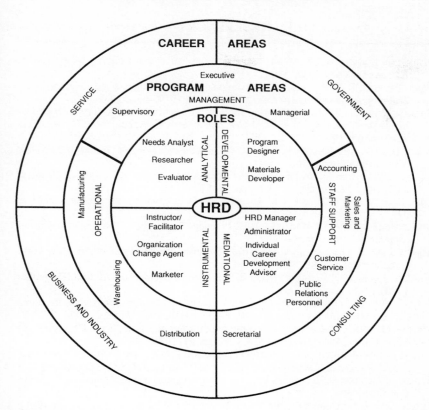

FIGURE 1.2
Human Resource Development Profession

setting in which many HRD activities take place, the remaining chapters systematically explore the three main components of the HRD profession: HRD roles, HRD program areas, and HRD careers.

HRD roles (the inner circle of the model) are discussed in Chapter 5 (Analytical Roles Cluster), Chapter 6 (Developmental Roles Cluster), Chapter 7 (Instrumental Roles Cluster), and Chapter 8 (Mediational Roles Cluster). HRD program areas (the middle circle) are discussed in Chapter 9, and HRD careers (the outer circle) are described in Chapters 11 and 12.

REFERENCES

AMERICAN SOCIETY FOR TRAINING AND DEVELOPMENT. *Serving the New Corporation.* Alexandria, VA: ASTD, 1986.

FEST, THORREL B. "HRD within Organizational Settings: Contexts and Relationships." *Training and Development Journal,* 33 (March 1979), pp. 80–86.

FRENCH, WENDELL L., CECIL H. BELL, JR., AND ROBERT A. ZAWACKI (EDS.). *Organizational Development: Theory, Practice, and Research,* rev. ed. Plano, TX: Business Publications, 1983.

KATZ, DANIEL, AND ROBERT L. KAHN. *The Social Psychology of Organizations.* New York: John Wiley, 1966.

KHANDELWAL, ANIL K. "A Development Approach to Industrial Relations." *Business India* (July 29–August 11, 1985), pp. 94–99.

KUR, C. EDWARD. "OD and HRD." *Training and Development Journal* (April 1981), p. 34.

MCLAGAN, PATRICIA A. "Models for HRD Practice." *Training and Development Journal* (September 1989), pp. 49–59.

MINER, JOHN B. *Organizational Behavior: Performance and Productivity.* New York: Random House, 1988.

NADLER, LEONARD. "Defining HRD." *Training and Development Journal* (December 1980), p. 68.

PACE, R. WAYNE. *Organizational Communication: Foundations for Human Resource Development.* Englewood Cliffs, NJ: Prentice Hall, 1983; 2nd ed., 1989.

SHULTZ, GEORGE C. "Economic Cooperation in the Pacific Basin," U.S. Department of State, Current Policy Number 658, February 21, 1985.

SREDL, HENRY, AND WILLIAM J. ROTHWELL. *The ASTD Reference Guide to Professional Training Roles & Competencies,* Vols. I and II. Amherst, MA: HRD Press, 1987.

SZILAGYI, ANDREW D., JR. *Management and Performance,* 3rd ed. Glenview, IL: Scott, Foresman, 1988.

ZEMKE, RONALD. "George Odiorne: Father of MBO." *Training/HRD* (October 1981), pp. 66–67.

CHAPTER 2

❦ ❦

The History of Human Resource Development

INTRODUCTION

Whether it is, as Voltaire said, that "history is little else than a picture of human crimes and misfortunes," or as Tolstoy speculated, merely "a tissue of disconnected accidents" or "the life of peoples and humanity," the special work of groups of individuals has a history. Shakespeare claimed that "there is a history in all men's lives," and Emerson asserted that "man is explicable by nothing less than all his history."

History's value lies in using the rich resource of the past in order to see where we have been (Roethlisberger, 1977), how we got there, and where we are going (Smith and Steadman, 1981). Thus, tracing the strands of thought and action that appear antecedent to and form a foundation for recognizing human resource development as both a field of professional application and a field of scholarly study may be yet another explication of, another history of, an important dimension of the human family.

This account will examine only a few major historical eras within which HRD developments took place, and the key benchmarks appearing during each era. Out of these eras and benchmarks has developed the field of human resource development, both as an academic discipline and a career field.

❦ *Value*

Knowing the history of an academic discipline and its related career areas has value for those interested in not only the life of a practitioner, but also what it takes to prepare for a career in HRD. A feeling for the history of the career field may help practitioners better understand the skills and attitudes that new employees bring into the field. Historical perspectives may help practitioners see that they can influence what happens to them and what they do for others, such as the shift from worker satisfaction to worker enhancement did in the years following World War II. The history of the field may also help practitioners discover that newness does not necessarily mean progress since a number of the earlier ways of doing things may be more suited than contemporary ones to meeting some of the challenges faced by HRD practitioners today.

Most important, history shows us that HRD professionals can come to see not only the great potential of employees, but also to recognize that the employees themselves are both more productive and contented when their total enhancement, as individuals and as workers, is taken into account.

As a student, the events leading to the emergence of the field of HRD should provide a natural tie to other history courses encountered as part of general education programs in most colleges and universities. HRD acquires greater meaning when one recognizes that the field did not spring full-blown from some professor's imagination, but that it has roots in a variety of real events.

Since history has its romantic side, one may, perhaps, even see oneself through the eyes of earlier practitioners realizing, for example, that Michelangelo's pupils stood in somewhat the same relationship to him professionally as students of today do to those who seek to prepare them to take their place in the world of work.

Another value comes from seeing that HRD roles are not performed exclusively in modern business corporations, but that they are found across both time and space in virtually every type of human organization.

Possibly the most important principle to learn, from the standpoint of the future HRD practitioner, is that history tells us about the value of work. Self-esteem is tied to work, to seeing that those involved in jobs of almost any kind are making an important contribution to society. Health, that other important dimension of happiness, also depends on feeling productive and useful in some kind of work setting. Looking at the history of HRD provides a way of seeing just how societies became aware that employees are the most important asset of an organization. Accordingly, the most effective means of both organization and societal progress comes from understanding the history of our efforts to develop individuals, which, in turn, may improve all of society.

❦ Chapter Organization

This chapter analyzes four theoretical explanations for how academic disciplines and career fields emerge. It also charts those events that seem to be benchmarks in the progress of the field to achieve an identity separate from other fields.

❦ Learning Objectives

After studying this chapter, you should be able to:

1. Recognize and explain four ways that new fields of study and practice come into existence.
2. List and characterize the four stages through which HRD has passed in the process of achieving its current professional status.
3. Illustrate, with specific examples, each of the benchmarks that are prominent in the history of HRD.

THEORETICAL EXPLANATIONS FOR HRD DEVELOPMENT

Determining just how a given academic discipline and/or career field came into existence is not always easy. Experts frequently have different opinions about what brings new materials or conditions into a given society. Most experts generally agree that changes come from either other cultures or subcultures by diffusion, or they simply evolve within a culture as an independent invention. However, different theoretical explanations of social and technological change may account for and help identify truly antecedent benchmarks of HRD and what caused these benchmarks to develop.

In the discussion here, four different explanations are presented as they relate to the field of HRD. These theoretical approaches attribute change to one or a combination of the following four patterns: (1) cyclicalism, (2) evolutionism, (3) functionalism, and (4) conflictism.

❦ Cyclicalism

Cyclical views suggest that career fields and supportive, related academic disciplines tend to follow a fluctuation pattern. That is, ideas and approaches apparently related to the development of a particular career and/or academic field come onto the scene, are seized upon as the answer to some societal challenge or problem, stay in vogue for awhile, and then disappear only to reoccur at a later date, often in the same form and order as they previously occurred. This approach seems particularly adept at explaining the emergence of many of the "new" ways for improving productivity, which in retrospect look suspiciously like an updated version of earlier techniques.

One area where the cyclical view seems weak is in its application to new technology. How can a "new cycle" be another, perhaps even updated, version of an old pattern when, for example, something different, like personal computers, comes on the scene? Since human resource training and development must be on the cutting edge of progress, much of what is new is likely to differ from the old in some significant ways.

❦ *Evolutionism*

The evolutionary view is based on the premise that an earlier idea or practice is refined and improved, leading to a new version, which in turn is modified and becomes a new and better idea or practice. An evolutionary approach assumes that people are becoming more knowledgeable and wiser, that technology is providing an increased potential for higher productivity, and that people can learn new lessons while avoiding the mistakes of the past. Looking back with evolutionary "glasses," one can organize history to show how each refinement built on past ones, essentially moving humans from less advanced to more advanced types of behaviors.

An illustration of this approach is the emergence of computer-based instruction, with its great possibilities for individualized training. Computerized interaction with instructional materials is indeed a refinement. Look at the advantages that accrue to airlines by using, for example, computer-controlled flight simulators in pilot training. American Airlines reduced pilot training by 50 percent, an estimated savings of $30 million in fuel by using computer-based training and simulators (Whrenberg, 1985).

An evolutionary approach implies that teachers will be surpassed, at some time, in their levels of performance by their students. If this perspective is valid over time, HRD will become even better as a discipline and more rewarding as a career than it is now. We will all learn from the past and from the systematic developments of the discipline.

❦ *Functionalism*

The functionalist view, as defined by social scientists, is that, as changes occur in society, new or formerly unimportant elements arise to counterbalance the new features. Thus, as new organizations and demands arise, along come new solutions set up to meet the demands. Functionalism argues that things may not be better, but they are in balance and working properly to meet the present needs of a society, a discipline, or a career. This approach leaves open the possibility that some choices may not work, that they may even be dysfunctional, and may temporarily set an organization back, although in the long run, problems will be solved to produce smooth functioning organizations.

❦ *Conflictism*

In the conflict view, no particular direction or pattern is evident in past events, except the eternal cycle of thesis-antithesis-synthesis—action, reaction, merger. The present may be no better than the past, but the present has emerged from the resolution of differences. Conflict can, in this view, be the process whereby new ways of improving productivity emerge. The right person being on the scene at the right time can and does, in line with this theoretical approach, respond to the competitive environment by recombining existing and perceived elements into new and different configurations. Logical steps are often ignored, and the connection of the new condition to the past is obscured.

Applying these theoretical approaches to past events can serve to help explain more accurately just how it was that HRD emerged as both an academic discipline and a career field. Elements of all strategies seem to be appropriate for understanding the emergence of the HRD field. At times benchmarks seemed to develop in response to each change strategy. See if you can recognize which philosophy seems to explain the emergence of each era and set of benchmarks in the history of human resource development.

ERAS AND BENCHMARKS

With these various strategies in mind, consider those "benchmark" events that appear, in hindsight, as being the major precursors of the present state of human resource development, as both a career field and an academic discipline. We will not suggest, in any definitive way, that earlier developments necessarily "caused" later ones, since there is often insufficient evidence to draw those kinds of conclusions.

What is important for our purposes here is that these benchmarks did occur and that they have had an impact on the form and content of the HRD career field and its related academic disciplines.

It is not possible to touch on all the events which have contributed, in one way or another, to the present state of the field. Here we will deal briefly with those benchmarks which appear most important to this development, indicating what these are, approximately when they began, and what type of relationship to employees each benchmark represents.

Employee Skillfulness (to 1800)	→	Employee Efficiency (1800–1920)	→	Employee Satisfaction (1920–1945)	→	Employee Enhancement (1945–present)

Placing all these events into some kind of coherent framework is challenging. Since HRD focuses, primarily, on the individual, on individual productivity and long-term development, past HRD-related events are grouped according to the importance and emphasis attributed to individuals in the world of work. Given the variety and diversity of events related to development of individuals in organizations, this type of perspective allows for a fairly good classification of the history of HRD under four eras:

1. *Employee Skillfulness* (emphasis until about 1800). During this era, the worker's skills were usually developed informally, in a context in which the worker was seen, in a qualitative sense, as both producer and valued family member; work activities took place in or near the home, with some emphasis on productivity but with little concern for efficiency.

2. *Employee Efficiency* (emphasis from about 1800 to about 1920). At the turn of the century, the focus changed. During this era, workers were viewed, essentially, as producers, in which the concern of managers was to have the highest efficiency in the performance of job skills, with only secondary concern for the satisfaction or well-being of workers.

3. *Employee Satisfaction* (emphasis from the 1920s to about 1945). As we moved into the postwar era, development activities focused more on achieving worker satisfaction, primarily by altering and improving the conditions in the work environment. The famous Hawthorne studies, for example, demonstrated that concern for employee satisfaction contributed to improved productivity.

4. *Employee Enhancement* (emphasis from 1945 to the present). Today, development is geared to foster the enhancement and worth of the individual employee as a valued human being regardless of the kind of work done or position held in the organization.

The stages described here represent events more in terms of degrees of difference rather than as differences in kinds of events. The correspondence between stages and specific events may not be perfect, although a strong case can be made (particularly during employee satisfaction and employee enhancement periods) that both the academic disciplines and the career area attempted to change the focus of their activities to more clearly achieve the goals of those eras (Table 2.1).

TABLE 2.1
Eras in the Evolution of Human Resource Development

Era	Employee Emphasis	Benchmark	Beginnings
1	Skillfulness	Informal example	Before 3500 B.C.
		Apprenticeship	2100 B.C.
		Guilds	About 1100 A.D.
		Craft training	About 1750 A.D.
2	Efficiency	Early training and education programs	About 1800
		Factory schools	By late 1800s
		Government efforts	Late 1800s
		Management and labor	Late 1800s
		Training associations	Early 1900s
		Corporate schools	1913
3	Satisfaction	Executive training	1919
		Correspondence schools	1920s
		Government welfare/work-force programs	1930s
		World War II programs	Early 1940s
4	Enhancement	American Society of Training Directors	1945
		Training as education in organizations	1950s
		HRD as an academic discipline	1970s
		Cooperative efforts of ASTD and HRD academic community	1980s

ERA 1: EMPLOYEE SKILLFULNESS

Until the beginnings of the industrial revolution, agricultural workers generally worked in or near their own homes, and craftsmen usually had their shops in back of or near their houses. The family, both immediate and extended, was usually the work group. The use of the term skillfulness in this context is meant to suggest that work was to be done at a high level of proficiency, but that there was no particularly strong focus on just how efficiently the work itself was carried out. Primary emphasis was not directly on workplace performance, but on the end product.

HRD, as we know it today, was not generally present in these work situations. Training that occurred, except possibly for the military, was usually on a small scale and conducted within some type of family structure. Most learning was informal and by imitation or oral direction, since the employer-employee relationship was intensive and over a long duration, and literacy among workers was relatively rare. Although our historical information about earlier times is far from complete, it appears that four particular types of events comprised training activities that occurred during this time period, namely, (1) informal example, (2) apprenticeship, (3) guilds, and (4) craft training.

❦ *Informal Example*

Although informal examples were used, and have a pervasive influence in all the subsequent events to be discussed here, much of the early effort devoted to training may have been nothing more than one person watching another person perform a task and then simply imitating what was seen. In a way this seems to fit with the apprenticeship benchmark discussed next, except that informal examples are usually without much conscious attempt to structure and "teach" an employee to do a task. The earliest civilizations, therefore, probably trained new members in most situations in a matter-of-fact fashion, by doing the tasks themselves and expecting the newer workers to learn by observation and imitation. Exceptions were present when it came to keeping records, especially genealogies, where accuracy of repetition was mandated.

An example of this benchmark might be that of a young man watching his father and older brothers build a house, picking up skills by observation, and then pitching in to be of service.

❦ *Apprenticeship*

At some point, it became more important to pass on increasingly varied and complex sets of skills. A given culture recognized that the transmission of these skills could not be left to chance, but that each learner or apprentice needed the opportunity to receive some kind of systematic training. Such training usually took place in or near one's own living area, with children being trained by their parents or by other members of their extended family.

As the variety of skills became too numerous and the level of skill development too advanced to be taught by the father or mother alone, it became desirable to send the aspiring professional to a person with more extensive and detailed backgrounds. Thus began the practice of placing the "novice" with a "master" to learn a skill or trade. For example, young men worked under Michelangelo, helping with the production of his great artistic masterpieces. They were used not only for much of the heavy work, but they were also taught by this great master in technique, color, and materials preparation.

These two methods of training (informal example and apprenticeship) were virtually the only ones used for most of recorded history. In nearly all cultures, only a small number of individuals, usually the elite, had anything approaching formal education. The great majority of the population were in agriculture or the crafts or, at times, "fodder" conscripts in the military. Although careers were available in religion and government, only a few professional practitioners had the level of technical expertise expected nowadays in all areas of work.

❦ Guilds

The next major level of training in occupational areas came when, for the first time, two or more skilled craftsmen banded together to try and control access to the commercial use of their skills. With the introduction of guilds, individuals with marketable skills could pressure those who wanted to learn the skills to join the guild as an *apprentice*. The status of *journeyman* required years of work, but could be earned with true persistence and some luck. A chosen few could eventually even gain the status of *master*.

❦ Craft Training

As economic competition increased, and the guilds wanted to compete successfully in a growing market, the issue of quality training for workers became much more important. The seeds of what would later be vocational education appeared in the United States in the 1700s, as groups such as the Moravian brothers and the Methodists established and carried out more formal training programs (Steinmetz, 1976). Formal programs were set up to train individuals to perform select work skills.

ERA 2: EMPLOYEE EFFICIENCY

With the advent of the industrial revolution, the production of goods shifted from the home to the factory, from rural areas to urban areas, from small-scale production to mass production. The desire of owners and employers was to achieve high productivity with minimal costs. This goal is achieved usually by producing the most possible in the least amount of time.

The major significant change in the world of work occurred with the onset of the industrial revolution. Where individuals had previously worked in small family groups, the industrial revolution meant the eventual demise of any kind of extensive home industry. In 1790 in the United States, about 90 percent of all Americans lived and worked on farms, usually small family ones, whereas

100 years later, fewer than 50 percent still lived and worked on small farms, and today the number is less than 5 percent of the population.

The industrial revolution led, as well, to the decline of small-scale craft activities. As large machinery was invented so that materials could be produced much less expensively in factories rather than in shops, small family enterprises were often forced out of business. Factories became the new centers of work activity, making it possible to turn attention to large-scale efficiency.

This emphasis on efficiency, with few exceptions, essentially held sway from the beginnings of the industrial revolution (around 1800) until shortly after World War I. Creating efficient employees was the major goal of training and development activities during this era.

Changes in work environments, from home to factory settings, created a need for training on a larger scale. Employers, particularly, were looking for ways to train the increasingly large numbers of workers needed to operate the machinery in large factories. These efforts can be classified and understood in terms of six benchmarks: (1) early program efforts, (2) factory schools, (3) government efforts, (4) management versus labor, (5) professional associations, and (6) corporate schools.

❦ Early Training and Education Programs

With the great influx of workers from rural areas and craft settings into factories, and with continuing ease in replacing workers by those eager to benefit from increased economic rewards, at least in comparison to what they knew before, employers did not see the immediate need for training. As machines became more complex and competition keener, however, beginning about 1800, *training institutes* of various kinds were established. These institutes were the forerunners of schools for adults, which are a major part of present-day HRD efforts (Nadler, 1984). Those who were already skilled upgraded their competence, and basic education was offered for those hoping to become mechanics and tradesmen. Along with training institutes came the development of *industrial education,* a forerunner of vocational education. The Franklin Institute of Philadelphia, for example, was set up to "teach the principles of science to mechanics and to encourage inventions and manufacturing improvements" (Eurich, 1985).

❦ Factory Schools

As time went by, factory owners and operators recognized that they were unable to find an adequate supply of skilled workers, so they provided technical schooling in their own workplace. Employers selected those already working for the company to provide instruction to others. Factory schools, as they were called, thus became a part of the industrial economic scene.

❦ *Government Efforts*

A major step in the historical development of training took place with the passage of the Morrill Land Grant Act in 1862. This significant piece of legislation led to the establishment of dozens of *agricultural and mechanical colleges* where the primary emphasis was, as the names suggest, initially on teaching agricultural and mechanical skills. Land-grant colleges, as they were called, took the idea of the smaller-scale training institutes and made them a major focal point on a much larger scale. Publicly-funded institutions, in conjunction with industry, provided much of the basic training for those who eventually moved into the more complex occupations. The Morrill Act helped give rise later to the development of the *extension service,* where today government employees provide job-related training and expertise. Subsequent legislation, such as the Smith–Hughes Act of 1917, provided funds for vocational education in home economics, agricultural trades, industrial skills, teacher training, and other *emergency training programs* needed for the war effort.

❦ *Management Versus Labor*

The growth of industry in the United States accelerated rapidly near the end of the nineteenth century. The drive for efficiency came, in a significant way, to pit management against labor. This ongoing struggle, for not only the control of efficiency on the job but also for the training of workers coming to the job, is epitomized by the efforts of Frederick Taylor and others who introduced *scientific management* into the workplace (Taylor, 1911). Tasks were analyzed and redesigned so as to squeeze the greatest amount of efficiency out of the workers.

The labor movement opposed these efforts, which in the eyes of many people appeared to dehumanize workers, and began in earnest in the early 1900s to set up its own training guidelines and programs. *Union learning and training programs* were the first efforts by workers, since the beginnings of the industrial revolution, to control the content, methods, and efficiency with which work was performed.

❦ *Professional Associations*

The early years of the twentieth century saw the beginnings of efforts to professionalize the training field. Those involved in industrial training saw the need for cooperation and mutual assistance. This need led, in 1913, to the formation of the National Society for the Promotion of Industrial Education. The Smith–Hughes Act of 1917 also gave an impetus to the training movement and helped to shift the emphasis from industrial to vocational education.

❦ *Corporate Schools*

Concurrent with the development of associations for professionals in HRD, the National Association of Corporate Schools, a forerunner of the present-day corporate classroom, was established in 1913. Although corporate schools had their beginnings as early as 1872, they grew during the ensuing century to become a fixture in business and industry. An offshoot of the corporate school was the idea of *executive training,* which first appeared in 1919. With this development came a shift in the emphasis from "schools" to "training" to reflect a broader view of the total process; current definitions of "training" and "schools" tend to reverse the earlier conceptions, making schooling broad and training narrow.

ERA 3: EMPLOYEE SATISFACTION

With the end of World War I and the return to "normalcy" during the 1920s came a shift in emphasis from employee efficiency to employee satisfaction. Much of the impetus for this effort came from the famous Hawthorne studies. The initial effort of the Hawthorne research was to see if productivity could be increased by improving the physical work environment. A major but unanticipated finding of the research was that an increase in worker satisfaction was associated with increased productivity. These studies made a significant contribution to the development of the field of industrial psychology (Miller and Form, 1951), which in turn influenced the emergence of organizational development (OD) as an area of academic study. Four benchmarks also appeared during this era: (1) management training, (2) correspondence schools, (3s) government programs, and (4) World War II programs.

❦ *Management Training*

The first movement focused on executive and managerial training. It was a precursor to the American Management Association and subsequent efforts to provide a wide range of training experiences for managers. Management training was an outgrowth of corporate schools, with a focus on helping those at the top levels become more effective and productive.

❦ Correspondence Schools

The prosperity of the 1920s led to a deemphasis on training in industrial settings and an increase in learning technical skills through correspondence schools. Some employers, when the demand for products was high and the labor pool large, cut back on company-sponsored training. Correspondence schools arose to fill the needs of those who wanted to develop skills, but who had difficulty since they lacked access to on-the-job training.

❦ Government Work-Force Programs

The onset of the Depression produced a marked decrease, across the board, in industry-based training efforts. There was no labor shortage because of the layoff of millions of workers, in the early and middle 1930s. To provide employment for this large supply of workers, a large number of government-funded and -supported programs (CCC, WPA) were established.

Concurrent with these programs was the recognition that training on a large scale was needed for potential workers, which represented the beginning, in 1938, of government support for human resource development. This support expanded tremendously during World War II and led, after the war's end, to the first clear indications that a new field, human resource development, was soon to emerge as a distinct entity.

❦ World War II Programs

World War II led to a recognizable need for training related to the war effort, similar to that noted during World War I, but on a much larger scale. Due to the drafting of young, able-bodied males from the labor force into the armed services, women and older citizens were being recruited to enter the labor market. Most of these individuals needed training and needed it in a hurry.

Many industrial, job, and program development training activities were begun. On-the-job training became a mammoth undertaking. For the first time job instructor training (JIT) programs were established, which was the first strong indication of the value of training trainers.

Early trainers were generally selected from individuals who were already supervisors in the organization. Their preparation as trainers was limited. In addition, they had to learn how to train those who had not been gainfully employed before or had been out of the labor market for some time. Their lack of preparation to lead training activities was apparent.

ERA 4: EMPLOYEE ENHANCEMENT

The end of World War II heralded another significant shift in emphasis in the training of individuals. Job satisfaction had generally meant a pleasant work environment and the type of "hygiene" benefits Herzberg, Mansner, and Synderman (1959) said were important so that workers would not be unhappy.

Employee enhancement, on the other hand, is a holistic approach, encompassing not only the work environment and employee benefits, but also efforts to help individual employees become more productive, both on and off the job. The latter part of this era, dubbed the "human resource development" period, highlighted the growing training industry and concerns of the academic community in preparing individuals with the skills to engage in employee enhancement and improvement (HRD). Three benchmarks appeared during this era: (1) HRD as education in organizations, (2) HRD as an academic discipline, and (3) cooperation between professionals and the academic community.

❦ American Society of Training Directors

As early as 1942, the seeds for a society for those doing training in organizations were planted, and in 1945 such a society was officially established. From the beginning, members of the society consisted of people from both academia and industry. Several name changes have taken place since the 1940s, but practitioners and academicians finally settled on the title *American Society for Training and Development (ASTD)*. During the 1980s, ASTD recorded a membership of over 25,000 representing more than 50,000 dedicated professionals.

❦ HRD as Education in Organizations

During the postwar years, in spite of a temporary lull in growth, organizations of all types have come slowly but increasingly to see the value and importance of having trainers as permanent, full-time staff specialists. Nearly all successful companies now have human resource development departments, and other types of organizations are concerned with upgrading the skills of their employees and professionals. Those doing such training are drawn from a body increasingly made up of those who have been or are being educated in human resource development academic programs.

❦ HRD as an Academic Discipline

The development of new academic fields that endure and are recognized as legitimate contributors to the education of students do not come easily. Many academicians trained in other fields have difficulty reorienting their thinking to respond to changes in the world of work. The last 20 years have seen, however, an increasing number of HRD programs in colleges and universities. The form of these programs is and may continue to evolve as HRD finds compatible and comfortable academic quarters.

❦ Cooperative Efforts Between ASTD and the HRD Academic Community

In December 1979, the first conference on the academic preparation of practitioners of human resource development was held in Washington, D.C. Thirty-four professors representing 26 institutions of higher education met to share information about the academic programs of their institutions and to make recommendations for continued cooperative efforts.

In May 1980, a group of approximately 25 professors met at the ASTD national conference in Anaheim, California, to renew associations and to discuss continuation of the conference idea.

In February 1981, the first *Directory of Academic Programs in HRD/T&D* was published by ASTD and the second conference on the academic preparation of practitioners was held in Williamsburg, Virginia, with 67 professors in attendance. Twenty faculty members presented papers describing their models for curriculum design. At the 1981 annual conference of ASTD in Boston, a professor's "special interest group" was formed.

In October 1982, 55 professors from 48 colleges and universities attended the third conference on the academic preparation of practitioners of HRD held in Kansas City, Missouri.

During 1983, ASTD adopted a new governance structure and the Professor's Special Interest Group became the Professor's Network. As part of the new structure, an Academic Relations Committee was created, providing formal, institutional liaison in support of academic programs. During 1984, a new *Directory of Academic Programs* was published, with entries from 113 colleges and universities. By 1988, more than 250 schools were offering programs in human resource development.

SUMMARY

A number of major benchmarks contributing to the present-day emergence of the academic discipline and career field of human resource development have been discussed. Four theoretical approaches for explaining the emergence of formal training and development practices in organizations were described. Finally, four main eras in the history of HRD were presented and key benchmarks within each era were identified.

As it becomes more apparent that little change is possible unless individuals change, the field of HRD should increase in importance and opportunity. The progress of society depends more on the character, quality, and skill level of its members than on perhaps any other single condition. The future of human society may depend in great measure on how well the upcoming generations are trained to be productive and to contribute to the betterment of human life.

REFERENCES

EURICH, NELL P. *Corporate Classroom, the Learning Business*. The Carnegie Foundation for the Advancement of Teaching, Lawrenceville, NJ: Princeton University Press, 1985.

HERZBERG, F., B. MANSNER, AND B. SYNDERMAN. *The Motivation of Work*. New York: John Wiley, 1959.

MILLER, DELBERT C., AND WILLIAM H. FORM. *Industrial Sociology*. New York: Harper & Row, 1951.

NADLER, LEONARD (ED.). *The Handbook of Human Resource Development*. New York: John Wiley, 1984.

ROETHLISBERGER, FRITZ J. *The Exclusive Phenomena*. Cambridge, MA: Harvard University Press, 1977.

SMITH, C. D., AND L. E. STEADMAN. "The Value of Corporate History." *Harvard Business Review,* 59 (November–December 1981), pp. 69–76.

STARK, RODNEY. *Sociology,* 3rd ed. New York: Wadsworth, 1987.

STEINMETZ, CLOYD S. "The History of Training." In Robert L. Craig, ed., *Training and Development Handbook,* 2nd ed. New York: McGraw-Hill, 1976.

TAYLOR, FREDERICK W. *The Principles of Scientific Management*. New York: Harper & Brothers, 1911.

WHRENBERG, S. "Is the Computer the Ultimate Training Tool?" *Personnel Journal,* 64 (April 1985), pp. 95–98.

CHAPTER 3

❦ ❦

Human Resource Development
in the 1990s

INTRODUCTION

While history shows us where we have been and, often, helps us to understand where we are now, futuring gives us a vision of what we must do to prepare to meet challenges that accompany our entry into the next era.

Peering through a glass darkly lit may not seem like the best of circumstances for getting a glimpse at what the future holds. Nevertheless, dusty crystal balls provide even less clarity than informed opinions for guessing future directions of a field. At the outset, we need to make clear, however, that mere mortals cannot predict the future. If the future could be predicted accurately by humans, that would mean that the future is inevitable, that we would be unable to make independent decisions and affect what happens after today.

❦ *Value*

Futuring involves detecting trends in events. Trends represent patterns that appear to be cohesive, have meaning, and point in some general direction. The

---

This chapter is based on a presentation prepared and delivered by Patricia A. McLagan, president, McLagan International, Inc., St. Paul, Minnesota. All rights reserved.

detection of trends increases the predictability that certain courses of action are more probable in the future.

The purpose of looking at trends is to get a picture of what could happen *if* circumstances did *not* change. Because we can affect our own futures, we are the best people to forecast or predict our own futures. As members of the HRD profession, or as individuals preparing to enter the profession, we are part of the trends and scenarios; we can do much to build our own futures.

❦ *Chapter Organization*

This chapter considers seven forces that may shape HRD in the coming years. In addition, it introduces eight critical issues that HRD professionals must be prepared to cope with during the coming decade. Finally, the chapter points out some broad implications that these forces and issues have for HRD professionals and those preparing to enter the HRD field in the future.

❦ *Learning Objectives*

After studying this chapter, you should be able to:

1. Identify and explain seven forces that are shaping the way in which HRD functions.
2. Describe and discuss eight issues that may be critical in the professional life of people working in HRD.
3. Recognize three zones of influence within organizations that may come within the purview of HRD professionals in the future.

AN UNCERTAIN FUTURE

What will the human resource development profession look like in the 1990s and beyond? Although there may be very exciting times ahead, many business and professional people are asking whether human resource development is going to have any role in business in the future. Some people say that there will be only a limited role for HRD professionals. Some people say that our role will be greater. Some people believe that our role will be much different from what it is today. The changing role of HRD is the topic of this chapter.

The rate at which change occurs is something that we do not understand very well. Although we may have experienced change, we often do not relate it directly to what is happening to our personal lives. To illustrate this point, Alvin Toffler, author of *Future Shock,* conducted an exercise with his college classes that provides insight into how we relate change to our circumstances. In the first few weeks of class, he asked students to draw a time line for the world, from the present to as far into the future as they could imagine. The students generally drew time lines ending in the year 2000 or 2010 with a nuclear explosion.

Later in the class, he asked the same individuals to draw time lines for themselves, to project their own lifeline out as far as they could. When students drew their own lifelines and talked about events that might happen, Toffler found that his students projected themselves moving into significant positions in their organizations in the year 2010. Some predicted that they would be company president in 2035, and others had retired in 2040 and were living a great life in retirement. Toffler concluded that people often do not link their lives with what is actually going on around them. How could the world, for example, be blown up in 2010 and still find people continuing in their careers beyond the year 2030?

Perhaps we do not have a habit, in this country, and maybe elsewhere also, of thinking about our lives as inextricably connected with what is going on in the world around us. It may be that we need to become more sensitive to the forces that are shaping our lives to understand fully what the future may be like.

SEVEN FORCES SHAPING HRD

Before we plunge into a discussion of the seven major forces that may shape the work of HRD professionals, let us briefly comment on a few features that may characterize the general work force during the 1990s.

The average age of the U.S. work force in 1975 was 28 years; in the 1990s, the average will be closer to 40 years. It is projected that 70 percent of the work force will be from 25 to 55 years of age.

Trends indicate that 75 percent of the 1990s work force will be high school graduates, 33 percent college graduates, and 9 percent will have advanced degrees, but 18 percent will be functionally illiterate. For the 15 million college graduates of the 1990s, there will be no more than 13 million jobs available that require a college education. Although 55 percent of the work force will have white-collar jobs, there will be 30 applicants for every middle-management job available. Most experts anticipate having more job sharing, multiple job holders, permanent part-time employees, and frequent leaves of absence.

❦ *Force No. 1: New Communication Vehicles*

Within the context of a changing work environment, several forces will exercise considerable influence over HRD activities. The first of these is called "communication vehicles" or the technology that will be the driving force of the information economy. Technology enables communication to be decentralized on a massive scale; thus, learning, management, and work may also be decentralized. We should not underestimate the incredible impact of this force. Visionary people project that by the early 1990s, the average home in America will have two VCRs, a personal computer, and ready access to satellite communication.

What are the effects of these new communication vehicles on business? What are the implications for HRD professionals? First, they have the potential to decentralize learning and information management. Second, decentralization makes it possible for learners to manage their own training and development.

Although we have talked about self-management and participation for a long time, the tools have not been available on a large enough scale to be meaningful in our day-to-day work. Finally, we are able to move information—through communication vehicles—to the point of contact between the organization and the user. Control of communication vehicles at the point of user contact is a key challenge for HRD professionals.

❦ *Force No. 2: New Structures*

The second force affecting business and the HRD profession is new structures found in organizations and business communities. Some people are talking about this phenomenon using terms that are unfortunate, such as "downsizing" or "flattening." Those words reflect the old paradigms, the old model of hierarchical organizations.

The move, however, is toward more useful conceptual terms, toward creating forms of organizational structure that are more responsive to the interests of consumers of HRD services. The need is to respond more quickly than competitors. The hierarchical format for organizations simply does not make quick response possible. There is a move toward multiskilled work designs with the accompanying and compatible organization structures. Most people, however, do not yet know how to operate in these new structures.

The Nordstrom, a West Coast department store chain, experiment is an example of new structures. In their stores, sales representatives are assigned to customers rather than to departments. They serve customers to the point that if a customer wants something that the store does not carry, the employee has authority to go out and buy it someplace else, just to keep the customer happy.

Another manifestation of this force in action is seen in manufacturing organizations where workers move from one line to another, depending on where they are needed. Union work rules, which prevent people from doing parts of each other's jobs, are falling away bit by bit. Movement is away from traditional organization structures which put people in narrowly defined jobs and toward more flexible use of skills. More broadly defined jobs are appropriate because more work today is knowledge work. It cannot be easily proceduralized, and the boundaries between one job and another are often not clear.

What are some of the implications of the new structures for HRD professionals? For one thing, they need to help people become more accountable for their work, to feel empowered to take responsibility for doing their work well. For another, HRD professionals need to become very good at working with flexible job designs and at scrutinizing the appropriateness of the systems being used now to describe and analyze work. This is the beginning of a new age for job analysis, for job evaluation, and for all those processes that are based on some very different assumptions than have operated in the past. New ways need to be found to describe work that is continually changing and that cannot be easily proceduralized.

Another implication is that most of our systems need to become more individualized. We should not be running employees through training just as we take cars to a car wash. People have different needs, different capabilities, and do different jobs. It is going to be important for HRD professionals to figure out how to get to the users, the customers of their products, the learners in programs so that what they learn is actually meeting their needs.

HRD professionals need to become better at helping employees manage their own learning process. Researchers have discovered that people learn most of what they learn on the job. They learn most of what they learn through a self-managed process. And yet, the process of on-the-job learning, the process of self-learning, is often not very efficient because employees may not realize that the job offers significant learning opportunities.

Allen Tough, a Canadian who began research on this topic many years ago, discovered that when he asked adults how much they learned in the last year, many would say, "Well, I really have not had time to learn." He soon realized that he was asking the wrong question. What he discovered when he asked the question more obliquely was that the average adult spends over 800 hours a year in deliberate learning—learning aimed at picking up a new skill, or a new capability, or a new attitude, whether for leisure or work. He discovered that most people do not have a self-concept of themselves as learners (Tough, 1979).

Honeywell also did a very interesting study a number of years ago. They found that 50 percent or more of what people learned was learned on the job. They also found that learning was often very inefficient and created an aversion to risk, plus it was costly to the organization.

There are many people managing their own learning processes, but they are doing it unconsciously and often without using the best learning skills. In this age of individualization, ways must be found to bring the power, responsibility, and skills for learning to those who have the most control over it:

individuals themselves. Supporting self-managed learning is one of the major challenges facing HRD in the 1990s.

❦ *Force No. 3: Shifting Population Characteristics and Values*

The third force that is going to have a major impact on business and the HRD profession is shifting population characteristics. The concentration of people and power in the world is shifting. North America, Japan, and Western Europe account for 15 percent of the world's population and 66 percent of its income. By the year 2000, the population growth in these more "developed" countries is likely to decline, or, at least, it will not increase at the same rate as in other parts of the world. Countries dominated by white and, often, male ethics will be in the minority.

Add to the shifts in population the fact that our society is aging. The American work force is aging. It is a work force with a unique set of values and goals, often described as "me" generation values. Its focus is often not on contribution and optimizing production. Rather, the emphasis of "me" values is often on consumption. Countries that are beginning to gain in productivity have a producer ethic, not a consumer ethic.

The consumer ethic has had the general effect of exacerbating environmental problems, fostering enormous trade and budget deficits, and increasing the disparity between "have" and "have-not" countries. Future prosperity depends on facing and resolving these challenges, and at the same time developing a greater balance of economic power around the world. America must sell to other countries to keep the trade balance up. Residents of other countries may not be able to afford American goods unless they, in turn, achieve a much higher level of economic prosperity than they now enjoy.

The signs of a decline in United States influence in global markets are evident, and of much concern to those in the HRD profession. Productivity growth in the United States is progressing at a slower rate than it is in most other countries in the Western world. Japan will assume, very soon, the position as the number one economic power in the world. No country that has ever been number one in the past and lost that position has regained it. Egypt, Greece, Italy, Spain, England, all fell from the favored, first position. The United States, if definite changes in productivity do not take place soon, will likely join that illustrious list.

It is time for new values in the workplace. This will require a new conscience to guide ethics and goals. HRD professionals are in a unique position to stimulate this new consciousness. They can help organizations to focus on a higher purpose. They need to look at the consequences of the actions of organizations and organizational members and help them see the consequences and the implications of their behavior. HRD professionals can play the role of activist for ethical behavior.

In sum, HRD professionals have a responsibility for helping organizations focus on production rather than consumption, in effect to reenthrone the production ethic. The efforts that many organizations are making toward quality and productivity improvement are steps in that direction. HRD professionals need to be quality and consumer advocates. They need to stand for ethical behavior, for professionalism, for productivity, and for the development of strong internal assets.

HRD professionals can also be activists for transcultural values. Hispanic, Oriental, and other groups are increasing as a percentage of the total work force. Finding ways to bring alternative, new, and diverse values into the predominantly Western work force is a challenge for HRD professionals.

❦ Force No. 4: A Competitive and Global Marketplace

Another force to be reckoned with in the 1990s is that of a competitive and global economic marketplace. Communication technology has made information available on a worldwide basis. Increases in information have fueled the fire of competition. As recently as the 1970s, international competition was not a particularly threatening factor for most United States businesses. International competition was thought about, but often only in an academic sense; nowadays it is a major factor, and both the HRD profession and organizations in general are affected by it.

Three factors are important in a highly competitive environment: (1) quality, because consumers tend to invest in products that provide the greatest value; (2) productivity, because high producers are able to provide merchandise and services to meet the demand on time and at a favorable cost; and (3) innovation, because the creative application of resources makes producers more responsive to consumer needs and, therefore, more competitive.

If quality, productivity, and innovation become predictable emphases in an organization, they, also, have some distinct implications for HRD professionals:

- Creativity becomes much more important. Thus, everything possible ought to be done to identify and aid people in developing creative skills and using them to be innovative.
- Anticipation becomes critical in a fast-paced, competitive environment. Life cycles of some products are shorter than the development cycles. As Rosabeth Moss Kanter has suggested, the mean time between surprises is often less than the mean time between decisions. Corporate leaders must be thinking ahead, since organizations and people who look to the future will probably have the edge.
- Integration becomes very important. Many of us grew up in organizations that segmented responsibilities. Most of the time, marketing, sales, engineering, and

manufacturing rarely, if ever, got together to coordinate activities. Organizations can no longer afford the waste that occurs with segmentation.

• Employee participation becomes essential, for it is the only way to assume that all the best ideas and human energy are available to the organization and its customers.

Human resource development professionals need to help create a culture that is anticipatory, competitive, globally oriented, and focused on the future. Job design, performance management, training and development, and staffing and career management must all be done with these values in mind. If we can help people focus on the future, rather than on the past, the process will be helped along. A lot of people set goals based on what they learned last year instead of on what needs to happen next year. The focus must be on the future.

Another way HRD professionals can respond is to help people learn how to exercise good judgment. In training sessions, for example, instead of using cases where we know what happened and what the answer is, the focus should be on today's real problems, the ones for which we do not have the answers, since the entire scenario has not been played out. HRD professionals can be more supportive of their organizations by helping people think about problems and opportunities rather than about the "right" answers.

❦ *Force No. 5: Technology Evolution*

The issue of technology and its effects is very important to the HRD profession. New technology gives organizations the capacity to automate routine and dangerous tasks. The whole lower end of the work scale is being phased out of organization systems. What that leaves, of course, is more judgment work. The net effect is an increase in the quality of judgments that people are expected to bring to their jobs. This expectation applies no matter where one is in the organization, whether a floor sweeper or an executive.

The use of quality circles is a statement, for example, to the organization saying that we expect everybody to bring judgment to their work. No matter where they are, good ideas, new ideas, better ideas, and continuous improvement is the stuff that is going to make our organizations grow. Ideas for increased quality are expected from everyone.

The force of technology evolution has some major implications for HRD professionals because most of our practices evolved out of the Industrial Age. The kinds of job analyses that many of us use assume more stability in work and less judgment than actually exists. Many human resource systems are form and procedure driven, and, yet, forms cannot begin to capture the judgment component of work. Many managers would love to see an appraisal system that runs on its forms because they are uncomfortable talking to people. One employee reported that the only appraisal he had ever received was one where his boss had written an appraisal on a piece of paper, then turned it into an airplane and sailed it into his office.

Some people say, "Can't we fix this rating scale so that it has more finely tuned points that I can circle?" The real point is, "What does it matter if the rating is a 9.6 or an 8.7?" The main thing is that ratings are judgment calls that should not be left to forms and procedures. Valid appraisals involve talking to people and they require credible performance management processes. No form will ever suffice.

A major challenge is to design systems that are going to be viable in a high judgment-oriented work environment. We may need to rethink such concepts as management by objectives (MBO), which are often totally measurement driven. The premise is that objectives should not be used unless they can be measured. On the other hand, objectives that meet customer needs should probably be used, whether or not they can be measured. The customer ought to be the factor that drives an objective or goal, not just its measurability.

Another challenge along these same lines concerns career ladders. Thinking of career progress in terms of movement from one job to another job to still another job may be obsolete in this day and age. Maybe we ought to be thinking of types of career experiences or competencies that enable us to prepare for specific kinds of positions. A whole new way of thinking may be required for HRD professionals to generate new systems for thinking about careers.

Now is a wonderfully exciting time because of the need for even more creativity in the area of HRD. People need help to make better judgments. Ways need to be adopted to support better judgment methods in organizations. These are key issues surfacing as a result of changes in technology.

❦ Force No. 6: General Turbulence

Another force to consider is that of general turbulence. We are clearly involved in a shift from the industrial age to the information age. This shift is producing what one observer (Weisbord, 1987) calls a state of permanent "white water." The analogy from canoeing and rafting suggests that we are living in a time when many things are contributing to a general turbulence.

First, many products being sold nowadays often contain more knowledge than they do material or energy; many of our products are "services," and services contain more knowledge than tangible assets. Also, boundaries between organizations and their environments are blurring. People looking ahead at the new economy are saying that American organizations need to become better at creating relationships among various groups, such as vendors and companies.

Many companies' best customers are their competitors. Boundaries between large and small organizations are becoming more flexible, and managing the resulting permeability is a very tricky business.

Power is also shifting, which appears to be a continuing trend. The growth in the number of mergers, acquisitions, and shifting relationships between large and small companies is the current expression of this turbulence.

Another challenge faced in this age of turbulence is that of finding new models for reaching higher levels of stability. Higher stability means finding common values on which to base decisions. Changing tasks and activities must be accompanied by a core of common values creating a "stability zone" around which to rally. Organizations need to organize such stability zones to counter the fluctuations caused by constant restructuring. One area of stability is the job element, although the elements of many jobs are being reallocated to different people. If stability can be seen in the job elements themselves rather than in the way in which the elements are organized, life might seem less frenzied.

The job of the HRD professional is to help organizations find the new stabilities, whatever they may be. One source of stability is the "process" skills of the people themselves. For example, people who are versatile and self-managing will be more adaptable (i.e., "stable").

If you have tried to implement quality teams or productivity circles, you know that putting people into situations where they have power is just not enough. They need skills in conflict management, communication, creativity, and other related skills. Employees need to be equipped with the fundamental skills critical to enacting the key roles that they are asked to take.

On another tack, "higher stability" requires flexible systems, flexible approaches to job design, and flexible goal-setting processes. Many goal-setting methods, for example, no longer have credibility. People feel that goal setting is something they have to do, then they put the goals in a drawer, dust them off at the end of the year, and explain that they were not accomplished because things changed.

Why do we persist in using systems that have no credibility? If the system lacks credibility, we ought to figure out how to fix it. One way to fight deteriorating credibility is to adopt an ethic of continuous learning. In perpetual white water, learning must be continuous. And yet, many HRD professionals work in organizations where leaders are not visible on a regular basis as learners. If executives do not model continuous learning, other employees are not likely to become learners themselves. Learning is something that must be done better; HRD professionals must find ways to increase the prestige of learning in their organizations.

One CEO announced recently, in a strategic planning meeting, that he had learned a lot during his last three years as chairman. This admission of "humanness" led to an improvement in the outlook of the entire organization. Continuous development and learning, on a personal level, are key to establishing an atmosphere where HRD professionals can become better facilitators and counselors themselves.

❦ *Force No. 7: Systems Perspective*

A systems perspective is the final force discussed here that we predict will have an effect on the shape of the work of an HRD professional. A systems perspective is interesting and exciting because of the many new opportunities that it affords the HRD professional. The main point here is that people in organizations are beginning to think more in terms of organization interdependencies.

The concept of interdependency is becoming a more prominent focus. Words like "just-in-time" inventory processes, quality processes, sociotechnical design, the customer chain, and global plans are evidence that more people are beginning to talk in systems language.

A systems perspective is permeating business organizations today. The implications are profound for HRD. First, the HRD professional must help people in organizations to think beyond their jobs. Many organizations, in fact, are expressing interest in rotating employees from one part of the organization to the other. Rotation is a response to the need to have "big-picture thinkers" and more flexible and skilled employees. HRD professionals can help people think beyond their jobs, and they, themselves, must be thinking at least one level above where they are in the organization.

Another implication that affects HRD is the tendency that we have had to think of training as a strategy. When we develop a training strategy, the assumption is that training is the solution, but that is not a systems way of thinking. HRD professionals must realize that training is a tactic rather than a strategy. Training is a tactic that supports larger business and human resource strategies.

Here is yet another interesting implication of systems thinking. The more that line managers think in terms of systems, the more they realize how important people are—the development of people, the rights of people, and the movement of people. Human resource development is becoming a more critical issue for line managers. They are taking a more personal interest in it, and, as they do, they move into the HRD professional's turf. That presents some interesting opportunities for us, as well as some challenges, particularly if we continue to think of the development of human resources as some type of "turf." We need to approach the development of human resources from a systems point of view and broaden our thinking about the issue.

In summary, seven forces affecting the role of HRD in the 1990s have been identified and described:

1. New communication vehicles—putting pressure on organizations to decentralize.
2. New structures—putting pressure on organizations to individualize.
3. Shifting demographics and values—putting pressure on organizations for more activism.
4. Competitive, knowledgeable global markets—putting pressure on organizations to focus more on development than control.
5. Technology evolution—putting pressure on organizations to focus more on developing the judgment of people rather than on developing the routine side of work.
6. General turbulence—putting pressure on organizations to be more flexible.
7. A systems perspective—putting pressure on organizations to help people look at what is happening from a broader point of view.

EIGHT CRITICAL ISSUES
FOR HUMAN RESOURCE DEVELOPMENT

The first part of this chapter has emphasized societal, cultural, and organizational trends that may have a distinct impact on the future of the HRD field. These trends have evolved somewhat independently of the field, but they may have wide ranging implications for all kinds of organizations and for all levels in organizations.

In light of these forces, eight critical issues to be faced by HRD professionals can be identified. We shall summarize the essence of each issue.

Empowered Work Force. The first critical issue involves helping to create an empowered work force in our organizations. Organizations must have leaders who lead, followers who take responsibility for following, and others who can shift from one role to another. Empowered people can take charge and use their energies to further the best interests of the organization.

Aligned Values and Commitment. The second critical issue concerns aligned values and commitment. This issue is expressed in such questions as, "Are people in your organization moving in the same direction? Are individual goals aligned with larger organizational priorities?"

Available Talent and Competencies. The third critical issue centers on the availability of talent and competencies in the organization. If skills are not available when positions open up, then the human resource development professionals are not doing as good a job about the bottom line as they could.

Productive Interpersonal Environment. The fourth critical issue concerns fostering a productive interpersonal environment. By this we mean that the environment of the organization ought to have as little waste as possible created by conflict, nondisclosure, noncommunication, and all of the detrimental attitudes that make it impossible to get work done or that can delay progress toward goals. HRD professionals can make a major impact on the productivity of the interpersonal environment, whether it is through training, through communication, through staffing, or through other creative ways.

Efficient Creation and Adoption of Change. The fifth critical issue has to do with the efficient creation and adoption of change. If the organization is slow to respond to change, if it lacks a high incidence of innovation, then something is not working in the human resource development system.

Goal Ownership and Accomplishment. The sixth critical issue involves goal ownership and accomplishment. The basic question is, "Do people own their goals?" At appraisal time, do employees say, "I couldn't accomplish that goal because someone else did not do what they were supposed to do!"? If so, that probably means that they did not own their goals. Otherwise, they would have brought the problem up earlier. If the organization is accomplishing its goals, then that is a sign that people are being developed and managed well.

Quality and Customer Focus. The seventh critical issue has to do with quality and customer focus. Internal and external customers should reign as highly important factors in decision making. Quality should be urgent for every employee in the company. If it is not, the human resource function needs to be examined.

Quality of Work Life. The eighth and final critical issue has to do with the quality of work life, especially in terms of challenge, respect, and balance between the individual and the organization. When the quality of work life is low, human resource development is not having the impact that it should.

INDICATORS OF HRD EFFECTIVENESS

The eight critical issues just discussed must be dealt with in order for human resource development to improve and retain its credibility as a professional area. HRD professionals can use many tactics, such as training, career planning, OD techniques, and performance management assistance, and they may be beautifully done with slick materials, but if they fail to deal with the critical issues, then HRD is not going to be effective. In addition, several other indicators may be used to measure the effectiveness of human resource development.

First, we can look at the ratio of managerial costs to worker costs. If the work force is empowered, if people own their own goals, relatively fewer managers should be needed to direct worker efforts.

Second, we can look at the revenues and costs per employee. Organizations that have the best ratio of income to costs over time are making the best use of the human resource—all resources.

Third, we can look at the speed at which vacant positions are filled. Keeping track of how long it takes to fill the positions can be a major indicator of whether the talent and competencies are available.

Fourth, we can look at the results of organizational climate surveys. High ratings of employee satisfaction and fulfillment are signs of good HR management.

Fifth, we can examine the innovation track record of the organization. Many annual reports have direct statements about the number of innovations per period of time, which is a reflection of the extent to which organizations encourage risk and entrepreneurship. One can also look at the time it takes for an idea to appear and come to fruition. To be competitive, organizations must have a short development cycle for idea implementation. Each month it takes to bring a new idea to maturity can mean millions of dollars in costs and revenues for organizations today.

Sixth, we can look at customer satisfaction. We need to find new ways to measure customer satisfaction. We need to ask customers how to rate us, and then we need to learn from the results.

There are many other indicators that can be used to evaluate the effectiveness of human resource development. Market share is an obvious indicator; reactive health care costs is an indicator of quality of work life. Finally, goal accomplishment indicates that things must be working.

BEYOND COMPETENCE TO QUALITY

What, now, is the HRD role in the 1990s and beyond? How can we help move our organizations from competence to quality? Although these ideas may seem a little abstract, there appear to be some major indicators that can add clarification. First, we need to become confident in some subject matters in which we have not been confident in the past, such as in business and economics. Nevertheless, our analytical skills, our conceptual skills, our ability to see the big picture, our ability to move from tactics to strategies, are all strengths that enable us to contribute strongly to the process. Our leadership and visionary capabilities enable us to become activists. Interpersonal skills, political skills, psychological understanding, and self-understanding are tools for effective change that lead to strong abilities in facilitating and counseling and being creative, which are all strengths that are becoming more important.

Some of the old processes are cracking and crumbling. We need to respond by creating new approaches. We need to become more collaborative. Since things are moving toward line management, we need to get out of our offices and go where the people are. We need to work together and to support line management in playing a larger role in managing and developing people. It is a very exciting time to be in human resource development.

Human resource development professionals must be committed. Although we are heading in new directions, the mechanisms for support are not yet in place. When we start moving in some of the new directions, others in the organization might think we are just another force trying to take more power. In reality, we are all learning to share power. Even though we are committed to the new directions, our organizations may not be, making the road ahead not quite as easy as we might hope.

Finally, we need to be courageous. If we are going to really provide value-added service in the future, we must be strong activists. We usually do not think of ourselves as activists. In fact, our organizations may resist the concept of activism. But, if we can make the critical issues clear, our organizations will see the changes that need to be made.

We do not know all about what is ahead for business or for human resource development. When asked what we might suggest to individuals preparing for careers in HRD, we might not have a "right" answer, but if we take our potential seriously, look at those critical issues, move to a more strategic role, and act with creativity, confidence, collaboration, commitment, and courage, we have a very exciting future ahead. The issue is not whether human resource development will have a bigger role or a smaller role, but it is an issue of how to assume a very different role, a role that will take us and our organizations into the 1990s and beyond.

SUMMARY

This chapter has focused on where the HRD profession is going into the 1990s and beyond. Seven key forces were identified and explored with respect to their influence on the field of human resource development. Within the framework of these forces, eight critical issues or challenges were discussed. In addition, several indicators of the effectiveness of HRD efforts during the coming years were noted. Last, the challenge of moving HRD from competence to quality was presented.

REFERENCES

TOUGH, ALAN. *The Adult's Learning Projects: A Fresh Approach to Theory and Practice in Adult Learning,* 2nd ed. Toronto: Ontario Institute for Studies in Education, 1979.
WEISBORD, MARVIN R. "Toward Third-Wave Managing and Consulting." *Organizational Dynamics,* 15 (Winter 1987), pp. 4–24.

CHAPTER 4

❦ ❦

The Structure of Human Resource Development

INTRODUCTION

John Galsworthy rightly observed that "the beginnings and endings of all human undertakings are untidy." He applied this generalization to building a house, writing a novel, and finishing a voyage. Creating an organization is also likely to be a bit untidy. In fact, many good ideas are never acted upon because the structure of the organization makes it difficult to implement them. Organizations are able to achieve their goals to the extent that their structures permit employees to function effectively.

By structure, we mean the arrangement of reporting relationships in the organization; that is, the structure of an organization is represented by the idea of who reports to whom.

Some of the questions that should be answered, with regard to the organization of HRD, are: How should the HRD program be structured? Where should HRD be located in the organization? To whom should the manager of HRD report in the organization? The answers to these questions are the focus of this chapter.

These are important questions to answer because the value of the contribution of the HRD program to the goals of the organization may be affected positively or negatively depending upon where HRD is located in the organizational structure.

❦ *Value*

Understanding some of the alternatives for organizing the HRD function in a company will give you a broader grasp of issues associated with how to create more effective organizations. Optimum structuring should provide a foundation on which the HRD program may build to accomplish its goals, produce the development needed, and fulfill its mission more effectively. Where the HRD function is located and to whom it reports are two of the most critical decisions an organization can make if it wants to have a cost-effective HRD function. Although the executive and management teams have a direct impact on the quality of performance elicited from the HRD staff, where that staff is situated in the structure of the organization is strongly related to performance quality.

❦ *Chapter Organization*

This chapter seeks to provide information about ways in which the HRD function can be structured and positioned in an organization so as to achieve maximum and optimum output and productivity from its professionals. Where the HRD function should be located for best results, alternatives for how it might be structured, what kinds of positions are most helpful to have, and what kinds of resources are needed to manage a quality HRD function are discussed.

❦ *Learning Objectives*

After studying this chapter, you should be able to:

1. Explain where the HRD function should be placed in an organization to get the most out of the HRD department.
2. Diagram and explain several alternative ways in which an HRD department might be organized.
3. Identify the staff and their respective responsibilities for operating an effective HRD department.
4. Make a list of the physical resources needed to provide quality HRD services for improving productivity in an organization.

LOCATION OF THE HRD FUNCTION

Since the goal of HRD is to monitor, maintain, and help to improve the productivity of members of the organization at all levels, the top HRD manager should be located so as to have direct access to those who make the key decisions that affect productivity goals (Robbins, 1987, Chap. 9). In effect, the HRD manager should report as directly as possible to the chief executive in the organization. In large organizations, the HRD function might be represented by a vice president, whereas in small organizations, a manager might be the leader. Nevertheless, in all cases, the person over the HRD function should be able to meet with top executives relative to personnel and productivity policies and strategy decisions (Stephan et al., 1988).

Executive-type decisions have to do with the mission of the organization. In business and industry, producing and selling a product are manifestly important, for without the proper completion of these functions, the organization goes out of business. The same is true, but to a lesser degree, for not-for-profit organizations. If the clients are not served properly, administrators raise questions which might lead to a reduction in, or even an end to, budget allocations for particular aspects of the organization.

Not seen as clearly, perhaps, is the fact that the most important element in successfully developing a product (as in business) or providing a service (as is typical of nearly all organizations) is the quality of performance of individual employees. In this day of rapid change, those already working for the organization must respond to changes in markets, technology, and budgetary conditions.

For this reason, those in positions to help employees respond qualitatively with human resource development programs need to be involved in executive decision making, so that they can plan ways to bring employees up to peak performance levels. Without a close relationship between mission accomplishment and improvements in employee productivity, responses to change may be slow or nonexistent. The surge of Japanese industry in recent years is a function, in part, of the concern they have for making sure that employees are trained and developed on a continuing basis.

As a general rule, therefore, the HRD function should be situated so that its staff can work with the line or production units of the organization, as well as with all levels of management. As shall be described later, the programs of the HRD unit are created to respond to productivity needs. This means that HRD staff need to have a strong working relationship with all key units in the organization.

Organizational relationships that meet these basic requirements may be portrayed in a simple organization chart as shown in Figure 4.1.

In this model, the HRD executive reports directly to the executive vice president over human resources, with the executive vice president reporting to the CEO of the company and serving as part of the executive committee of the organization. This arrangement helps the HRD function to maintain a constant awareness of the mission, goals, and needs of the organization so that it can focus human resource development efforts on the real concerns of the company. Ideal situations, such as the one just described, may not always be the case in

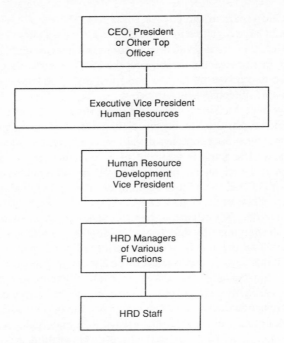

FIGURE 4.1
Simple HRD Organization Chart

organizations. Tradition, rather than common sense or effectiveness, often governs where units are located and who reports to whom.

All too frequently, HRD staff lack the power to decide where they are to be located, leading, for example, to placement in a personnel administration unit. Personnel departments often include sections that administer compensation, safety, benefits, labor relations, employment, and training. Unfortunately, the philosophical and theoretical base of personnel functions is different from, and, often contradictory to, development functions. Personnel is more firmly grounded in business fundamentals whereas human resource development is based on concepts of communication, learning, and change.

As Camp, Blanchard, and Huszczo (1988) explain, an "increasingly popular option is to staff an HRD department separate from personnel and reporting directly to a member of top management" (p. 10), as illustrated in Figure 4.2.

Rather than working with compensation, safety, and benefits, the HRD function absorbs human resource planning, recruitment, selection, orientation, employee and management development, organization development, and quality of work life programs. Hellriegel and Slocum (1978), when discussing the

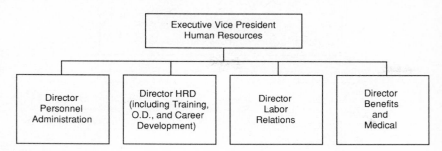

FIGURE 4.2
Organization Chart Showing HRD as a Separate Department

complexities of strategic planning, argue strongly for having the human resource development function closely associated with those involved in corporate planning.

🐝 *Departmental Organizational Patterns*

The precise organizational plan for an HRD department depends on the *type* of organization in which it is located and the *size* of the organization. Governmental organizations are usually structured differently from heavy manufacturing; banking and financial organizations are likely to have a structure that is different from health care or educational organizations. The most common way, regardless of type and size considerations, is to organize the HRD function around the clusters of people to be developed.

Industrial organizations have distinct ways of structuring, based on the philosophy that company products should be made both properly and efficiently, resulting in both cost-effective and profitable operations. For example, a major high-tech manufacturer organizes around the following units:

Engineering training
Executive education
Management, staff, and support training
Manufacturing and material training
Sales and marketing training

The vice president of human resource training and development has managers over each of the major functions just cited. In addition, a special section provides organization development services on a contract basis. The organization chart looks something like that in Figure 4.3.

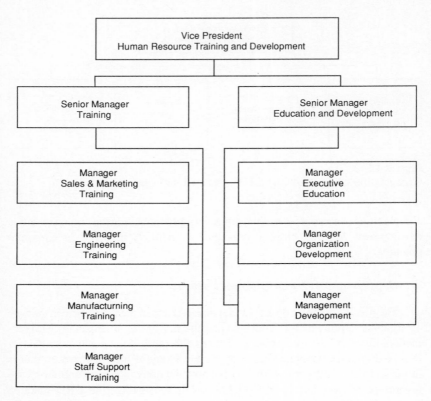

FIGURE 4.3
Large Company HRD Organization Chart

The organization chart for the HRD function in a *business* organization, in contrast, may look considerably different, although the structure may be based on the same general principles. A national financial institution, for example, has a structure like portrayed in Figure 4.4. Levels in this structure include a vice president over human resources, a director over training and development, managers over specialized areas within the human resource development function, and supervisors over program areas. Each supervisor has a staff of professionals who carry out the programs.

Larger corporate structures, those sufficiently large to have regions or major divisions, have HRD requirements which may be more extensive and complex. In an organization such as that portrayed in Figure 4.3, the corporate staff sets policy, designs and develops training and development programs and materials,

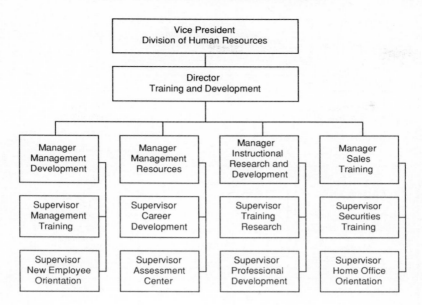

FIGURE 4.4
National Financial Institutions

trains training staff, and evaluates and maintains records of training activities. When training comes from corporate headquarters to divisions in a number of different geographical areas, in contrast, the regional staff members may be involved primarily in coordinating and conducting training programs coming from corporate headquarters. The HRD structure in this type of situation may be like the one shown in Figure 4.5.

A division of a company, in some instances, may organize in order to integrate human resource training and development into functional rather than geographical areas. An organization chart showing the integrated structure might look like Figure 4.6.

Weaknesses of this structure are a lack of unity in direction and difficulty maintaining quality training. Without a divisional director of human resource development, each functional area sets its own policies and operating guidelines. In the long run, a great deal of duplication and inefficiency may occur. Design of programs, production of materials, and maintenance of facilities and equipment may, in fact, require more coordination than time allows. Although the training function is close to bottom-line areas, the structure does not allow the HRD function to be coordinated and directed by a person close to the executive in charge.

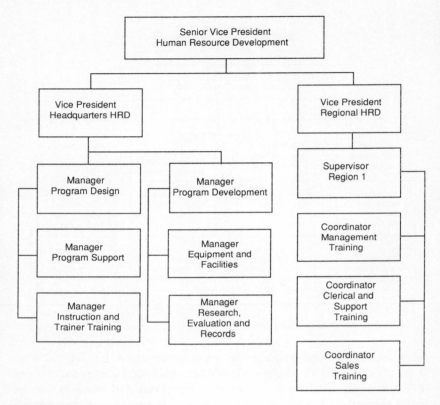

FIGURE 4.5
National/Regional HRD Organization Chart

The impact of department structure on HRD activities in an organization may be illustrated by the following example. A major high-tech company with a considerable number of government contracts organizes its rather extensive human resource development function around four divisionwide needs: management and professional development; data processing; industrial training; and environment, health, and safety training. A divisional staff is responsible for the design, production, and delivery of divisionwide programs. Within the division, each organization has a training coordinator who serves as the source of information about training for the manager of the organization by helping identify training needs, by being the initial contact for managers wishing to enroll employees in training programs, by scheduling courses and maintaining

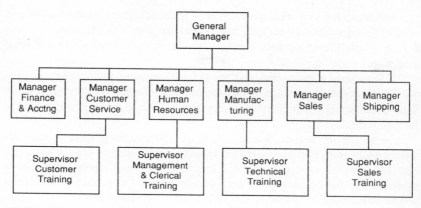

FIGURE 4.6
Integrated HRD Organization Chart

enrollment records, and by serving as the liaison between the line department and the management and professional development organization.

Each training coordinator is assisted by a training representative assigned to departments within the division in order to help meet specific training needs and to consult with employees of the department. Training representatives are assigned, for example, to departments such as administrative services, contracts, engineering, facilities, finance, human resources, logistics support, central manufacturing, planning and control, production readiness, marketing, material, pricing, and quality assurance.

The management and professional development staff design, develop, and deliver courses in management development and general skills development. All enrollments for the courses are processed by the department training coordinator, while confirmation notices are distributed by the divisional training administration.

Management development courses include decision making, time management, clear writing, goal setting, interviewing, performance feedback and coaching, and the role of management. General skills development includes courses such as customer relations, effective presentations, oral communication skills, professional skills for secretaries, speed reading, technical writing, and telephone dynamics.

Data processing training includes courses such as microcomputer literacy, IBM PC and Apple fundamental operations; using Lotus 1-2-3, BASIC, Symphony I and II, dBase, Terminal Operations, and FORTRAN; a systems development series; and numerous other technical computer courses.

Industrial training includes courses such as adhesives, metal burnishing, special fastener installation, sealant applications, wire splicing, electrical soldering, graphite epoxy repair, pressure testing, and overhead crane and hoist operation.

Environmental protection, safety, and health training offers courses such as accident prevention, management safety, new hire employee safety orientation, warehouse storage, shipping and receiving of hazardous materials, and respirator training.

Some internal organizations, such as quality assurance, offer courses designed to develop skills unique to the organization. Employee improvement, for example, offers a course for quality circle facilitators and supervisory training in manufacturing operations. Finance has its own training room and offers a course in journalistic writing skills for newsletter representatives.

The organization and administration of such a wide-ranging human resource training and development program is a complex and monumental task involving dozens of staff members and thousands of employees. The exact structure must attempt to match the needs of the company and its employees and the unique mission of the organization. Simple answers are not likely to deal with the enormity of the challenge.

HRD PHYSICAL RESOURCES

Many corporations have their own training centers that surpass in sophistication those of many colleges both in terms of range of course offerings and in the technology available to deliver the courses (Eurich, 1985). Even at that, the marvelous corporate training facility may not be able to accommodate the training and educational demands placed upon it. At Du Pont, for example, their magnificent training facility accommodates only about three-fourths of the training needs of the 18,000 management staff (Murray, 1979).

Nearly all small and medium-sized companies also have physical facilities assigned to them to carry out their responsibilities. Although they may not have the elegance of the Coca-Cola USA Training Center in Atlanta, Georgia, the expansiveness of McDonald's Hamburger University in Oakbrook, Illinois, or the beauty and detail of Arthur Andersen's (accounting firm) professional development center in St. Charles, Illinois, they have some elements in common with all of the great training centers around the world.

State-of-the-art HRD facilities occupy a space that has an environment suited for a variety of training approaches ranging from straight technical work based on behavioral theory, to highly personal management training based on experiential theory, to action-oriented group and team building based on role theory, to powerful success-oriented sales training based on achievement theory, to intense executive training based on rational theory. The space should allow for movement among trainees, formal presentations, a multitude of configurations for chairs and tables, and the use and storage of a wide variety of media equipment.

Equipment for an ideal training facility has been described by Gelbach (1982), a summary of which appears in Table 4.1. The training facility should consist of one or more training rooms with appropriate equipment. At one end of each room should be a projection booth with an access corridor leading to it and a raised 5-foot platform. A storage area should be included with the projection space so that the entire training room consists of a space approximately 40 × 50 feet and 14 feet high, with 8 feet taken by projection and storage. In addition, each room should have a refreshment center. At least four break-out rooms seating ten people each should be included in the facility. Double-door entries should be used to accommodate the handicapped and to permit movement of people and equipment easily and quickly. Walls and ceilings should be properly insulated and the floors should be covered with a small-patterned loop or cut-pile carpet.

TABLE 4.1
Equipment for an Ideal Training Room

Equipment	Cost
Prewired floor space: 1,520 square feet @ $50 per sq. ft. (est.)	$75,000
Tables and chairs	$11,300–$20,600
Lectern	$400–$1,200
Rear-projection screen: 128 sq. ft. (est.)	$13,000
Front-projection screen: 48 sq. ft., with built-in sound system	$4,000
Dual-image slide projection system with remote controls	$5,550
Long-range opaque projector	$2,300
Stop-frame 16mm movie projector	$1,450
Stereo sound-presentation and cordless voice-enhancement system with tuner and 14 speakers (est.)	$2,500
Hard-copy display boards, framed	$500
Five microcomputers with accessories, ($2,500 each)	$12,500
Five videodisk training machines	$11,250
High-powered video projector	$10,000
Two half-inch video cameras and recorders with accessories and editing units	$12,000
Electronic opinion counter and consensus analyzer	$14,000
Electronic teletraining blackboard	$6,000
Optical fiber communication and satellite linkup system (est.)	$25,000
Three overhead projectors ($300 each)	$900
Six flip charts with newsprint ($100 each)	$600

A studio for producing videotapes is also common now, especially with the ability to distribute multiple copies to locations across the country quickly and conveniently.

Administrative offices for managers, training specialists, and support personnel, as well as workspace, storage, and word-processing areas are essential.

Although many other aspects of facilities for an HRD department might be discussed, such as office decor and building design, the primary issues of positions, people, space, and equipment have been outlined to provide a glimpse of the structure of HRD in organizations.

STAFFING A HUMAN RESOURCE DEVELOPMENT FUNCTION

Staffing in human resource development depends on identifying and hiring individuals who have expertise in one or more of several critical skills. Human resource development is carried out through the performance of role behaviors. Each role is comprised of select competencies involving skills, abilities, information, and attitudes. Each role has a number of products that are created by using the competencies. Products are the outcomes or results of what a person does with the competencies as he or she performs a role.

In four later chapters (5, 6, 7, and 8), 11 key roles are filled out and given form and substance. They are arranged in familiar categories or groupings, although each grouping is formed on a different basis. For example, four categories are presented: (1) analytical, (2) developmental, (3) mediational, and (4) instrumental. The analytical group consists of roles that involve similar methods, the developmental group consists of roles that involve creative processes, the mediational group consists of roles that serve as intermediaries between parties, and the instrumental group consists of roles seeking to bring about change.

Figure 4.7 portrays the roles and the categories and indicates that the *analytical* roles are needs analyst, researcher, and evaluator. The *developmental* roles are program designer and materials developer. The *mediational* roles are program administrator, HRD manager, and individual career development advisor. The *instrumental* roles are instructor/facilitator, organization change agent, and marketer. These role clusters are listed in the circle of the HRD roles model.

HRD roles are studied, in this book, in small clusters, so that the elements common to two or more roles can be treated together. Several roles may share key competencies, although they may produce slightly different products. On the other hand, other roles may form a sequence of activities that culminate in

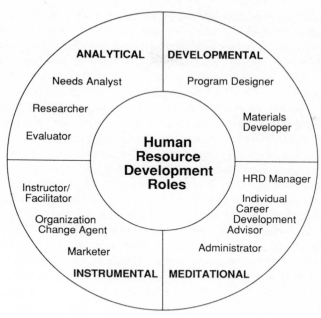

FIGURE 4.7
Human Resource Development Roles

a single product. Some of the roles are complementary while others are supplementary. The clusters were created, also, to help the reader recall all 11 roles more easily.

Jobs and positions in organizations frequently involve combinations of roles that appear somewhat different from the way in which they are clustered here. Practitioners, on occasion, may perform only one role, say, the program designer or HRD manager. Sometimes an HRD specialist, on the other hand, is asked to perform several roles, such as that of materials developer, program administrator, needs analyst, and marketer, all of which appear in different clusters. In an small HRD department, professionals may be required to do just about everything, but in a very large department, they may have only one critical specialty to perform.

HRD practitioners perform the roles, use the competencies described, and create the products identified, although they may do them in combinations that are considerably different from the manner in which they are clustered here. Nevertheless, performing each HRD role with skill is important in being considered an HRD professional.

First, HRD staff must be able to perform the key HRD roles of needs analyst, program designer, materials developer, and instructor/facilitator. Although the ability to perform other roles effectively makes a person valuable as an employee, these four roles, and particularly the last three, represent the fundamental skills required of entry-level employees.

In general, human resource development departments tend to be organized according to program areas, with staff members performing HRD roles to bring about changes with program employees. A major midwestern financial institution, for example, offers employees development opportunities in four program areas: management development, sales development, professional development, and skills development. Management development courses and activities are available for four types of employees: supervisors, section managers and assistant managers, division managers, and general managers. Employment interviewing is available for supervisors, but managerial interviewing is offered for section and assistant managers, whereas an organizational climate survey activity is provided for general managers. Staffing in the management development area means that a new employee must be able to design courses of the type mentioned above, among many others, produce materials to support the courses, and, especially, instruct and facilitate the work of employees in the courses and activities.

The analytical cluster of roles—needs analyst, researcher, and evaluator—include important skills for contributing to the HRD department. The mediational cluster of roles—administrator, manager, and career development advisor—are helpful in providing relevant competencies, as well, but the developmental and instrumental role clusters tend to take priority in staffing decisions, regardless of the program area.

Naturally, in the case of the high-tech company discussed earlier, the work of a training coordinator might draw upon the skills and competencies represented in the mediational role cluster, since more of a coordinator's work tends to involve facilitating relationships, maintaining records, and helping employees plan their career development opportunities, rather than designing programs, developing materials, or instructing employees.

The combinations of roles that constitute a particular organizational position are difficult to predict; nevertheless, most employees, over time, tend to draw upon or use skills associated with all four role clusters. Thus, preference in hiring HRD employees is likely to be given to those individuals who can perform well in a fairly large number of role-related competencies.

In organizations with an HRD staff of ten or more, some specialization tends to occur. In those instances, staff selections are made more often in terms of education and experience in one role, such as program designer or materials developer and media skills. The most common competency sought in new staff is that of making presentations in front of an audience, even though less time is usually spent on the job giving presentations, lectures, and conducting courses. When a class is to be met, the instructor role becomes critical.

A profile of HRD departments in some medium to large companies located in the northeastern part of the United States provides some insights into qualifications of staff members (Everard, 1987). Most departments averaged five employees: a manager, three training specialists, and a secretary. Most training courses were taught within the organization by HRD staff. Most of the companies had several general-purpose classrooms with well-equipped facilities, and technical units had computer labs. Most HRD departments had a training resource library containing both professionally produced and locally produced media programs for the individual use of employees. Most managers were concerned about the internal marketing of training activities. Most departments used personal contact with managers; forms of publicity such as newsletters, posters, and memos; and bulletins about training services. Staff members, including the manager of HRD, design and develop courses, instruct employees, and evaluate the results.

The department tends to respond to expressed needs and too often has little time to forecast organizational needs, conduct needs analyses, and evaluate the effectiveness of programs in influencing behavior change and having an impact on the organization.

❦ Staffing Implications

Everard's study tends to support the general staffing suggestions just offered, but also implies that some general competencies in the areas of interpersonal communication and technical writing may be very helpful. The report also highlights the central place of marketing skills, which tend to include working with media products (preparation of newsletters, bulletins, and video materials), in hiring staff. Of special importance, especially for managers, but of general significance to training staff, was the need to be familiar with standard budgeting procedures. A course in accounting or finance, or some experience with the preparation of budgets, seems like a plus in selecting HRD staff.

HRD departments typically have responsibility for several auxiliary activities, such as reviewing, selecting, and working with vendors of training programs; maintaining and managing video studios and associated media equipment; acquiring and administering library materials for use by employees; and providing after-hours education, educational reimbursement, and special career enhancement programs. Often, the corporate internship program is also handled by the human resource development staff.

SUMMARY

This chapter has described how HRD is structured in various-sized organizations to achieve the best results in providing development for human resources. The HRD function was described as a key part of the policy and strategy decisions that are made by management; thus, HRD should be situated close to the decision makers in the line organization charts. The responsibilities for operating an effective HRD department were presented and a list of the physical resources needed to provide the HRD services through training were outlined.

REFERENCES

AMERICAN SOCIETY FOR TRAINING AND DEVELOPMENT. *Serving the New Corporation.* Alexandria, VA: ASTD, 1986.

CAMP, RICHARD R., P. NICK BLANCHARD, AND GREGORY E. HUSZCZO. *Toward a More Organizationally Effective Training Strategy & Practice.* Englewood Cliffs, NJ: Prentice Hall, a Reston Book, 1986.

EURICH, NELL. *Corporate Classrooms: The Learning Business.* Princeton, NJ: The Carnegie Foundation for the Advancement of Teaching, 1985.

EVERARD, KENNETH E. "A Study of Organizational Training Departments in the Mid-Atlantic Region." Unpublished paper presented at the HRD Professor's Network of the American Society for Training and Development, Atlanta, Georgia, 1987.

GELBACH, DEBORAH L. "Designing the Training Room of Your Dreams." *Training/HRD* (December 1982), pp. 16–21.

HELLRIEGEL, DON, AND JOHN W. SLOCUM, JR. *Management: Contingency Approaches,* 2nd ed. Reading, MA: Addison-Wesley, 1978.

MURRAY, THOMAS J. "What Price Management Education?" *Dun's Review* (March 1979), pp. 104–106.

ROBBINS, STEPHEN P. *Organization Theory: Structure, Design, and Applications,* 2nd ed. Englewood Cliffs, NJ: Prentice Hall, 1987.

STEPHAN, ERIC, GORDON E. MILLS, R. WAYNE PACE, AND LENNY RALPHS. "HRD in the *Fortune* 500: A Survey." *Training and Development Journal,* 42 (January 1988), pp. 26–33.

CHAPTER 5

❦ ❦

Analytical Roles

INTRODUCTION

Henry Ford, founder of Ford Motor Company, had difficulty with the operation of the headlights on one of his vehicle models during the early phases of development. The lights worked when the car was moving, but when it stopped, the lights went out. The source of power for the lights was a generator that was connected to the wheels, and as long as the wheels turned, energy for the lights was ample.

After several fruitless efforts to solve the problem, Ford hired Charles Steinmetz, the foremost mechanical engineer of the time, to figure out what might be done to keep the lights on. Steinmetz's solution to the problem was a prototype of what later became the modern-day automobile battery. When Ford wrote Steinmetz to ask how much he wanted for his work, he replied with the following itemized bill.

Labor and materials	$ 100.00
Knowing what to do	$ 9,900.00
Total	$10,000.00

Steinmetz's itemized bill illustrates the value of "knowing what to do." This same value is placed on the men and women who perform the analytical roles in the human resource field; their work tells us "what to do" to solve many of the problems that occur in organizations.

The analytical roles of HRD are needs analyst, researcher, and evaluator. While the activities of each role are distinct and unique, they share the common goal of measuring and making judgments about things and people in the workplace. Critical thinking is a skill that is central to carrying out effectively the three roles in the analytical cluster.

The focus of each role is different. The needs analyst attempts to discover what is preventing organization members from performing to their full capacity. A researcher seeks to determine why things and people function the way they do. An evaluator looks at how effectively things and people operate.

The three roles are, nevertheless, bound by the common themes of measurement and judgment. The needs analyst measures the perceptions of organization members, the researcher measures actions and reactions, and the evaluator measures the quality of activities. The needs analyst makes judgments about the existence of personal "concerns" or problems, the researcher makes judgments about data, and the evaluator makes judgments about the quality of activities. Although all three roles are involved with gathering information about events and making judgments about those events, each engages in the process at different times and at different levels of sophistication. In this chapter, we shall attempt to make the distinctions among these three approaches clearer.

❧ *Value*

The HRD analytical roles provide the foundation for making decisions that solve problems in new, creative, and innovative ways. Without data about barriers to quality performance, or data about how and why people and things operate, or data about how well people and things are functioning, our decisions would lack the information to make them sound and reasonable.

❧ *Chapter Organization*

This chapter is arranged so that the discussion of needs analyst occurs first, researcher second, and evaluator third. For each role, definitions are provided, methods and techniques are described, and the results or products of their work are identified.

❧ *Learning Objectives*

After studying this chapter, you should be able to:

1. Define the three roles—needs analyst, researcher, and evaluator—included in the analytical cluster.

2. Identify and describe the methods and procedures associated with each role.
3. Illustrate the types of projects each role seeks to complete in a typical work setting.

NEEDS ANALYST ROLE

A needs analyst gathers information from organization members about organization tasks, the organizational system, and other productivity-related options in order to determine whether problems exist. A problem in an organization is simply the difference between the way things are being done and the most cost-effective way that things could be done. If problems do exist, the needs analyst's goal is to discover what is keeping employees from doing things in the most productive way. There are, essentially, three steps in the needs analysis process: recognizing, documenting, and defining a problem or concern.

❧ *Recognizing a Concern*

A concern is recognized by sensing some shift in regular activities in an organization. A slight reduction in production levels, increases in defective parts, increases in accidents, more absences, more complaints, or an increase in breakdowns represent concerns (Mills, Pace, and Peterson, 1989, p. 14).

To recognize these changes accurately requires a great deal of sensitivity to others and how they are accustomed to functioning. Sometimes a concern surfaces in the way in which people react to one another, such as behaving a little more coolly than usual or with more sarcasm than is typical. Concerns are sometimes revealed by the way in which employees treat equipment—banging it a little too hard—or in the way they talk about supervisors and other managers—more negative and snide comments than usual—or in the tone of voice and the lack of socialization and small-talk in the hallways. For some reason, either an unproductive situation exists or a change has taken place, and the role of the needs analyst is to recognize the condition or change and, if possible, to determine why it exists.

THE THREE ANALYTICAL ROLES

- **Needs analyst**
- **Researcher**
- **Evaluator**

To explain why a problem exists or a change has occurred may be more difficult than just recognizing the change. The cause of most negative changes, especially those involving people, can usually be found in attitudes of hostility, condescension, and apathy toward someone or something in the organization. A high degree of sensitivity and insight are often needed to detect subtle changes and their causes.

ℰ *Documenting a Concern*

After recognizing a concern, the needs analyst gathers information to verify the existence of the problem or concern. Although the analyst may feel that changes have taken place, it is important that changes be documented with "hard" data. Few managers want to act on a "hunch" that lacks supporting evidence. Documenting a concern involves securing information that points clearly toward a presumed shift in production or difference in interpersonal interactions as sensed in the first stage. The information needs to be specific, unwavering, and directly relevant to the problem area expressed in the concern.

Getting information about a concern may be approached from different points of view, each of which provides a different perspective on the concern and the existence of an authentic problem. If more than one approach can be used, the concern can be documented with more authority than using just one approach.

Several general methods are available for use by a needs analyst. Each method has a set of appropriate instruments and procedures that produce direct and efficient data about the concern. With some understanding of what is available, a needs analyst may then select appropriate instruments and procedures for documenting concerns in the most efficient manner.

ℰ *Five Approaches to Documenting Concerns*

A number of methods and procedures for securing information and documenting concerns are available; however, they are usually classified according to the five types of information derived from them: (1) historical information, (2) information about how a job is done, (3) information about how well organization members do their jobs, (4) information about employee perceptions of their jobs, and (5) information about the organizational system itself. Let's explore each of these methods and procedures.

Historical Information.   Every organization has a history, an understanding of which may help a needs analyst recognize when changes are occurring and why a particular change, such as a downturn in productivity, has occurred.

Historical information is gathered from records or files of an organization. Records may be written documents, pictures, drawings, tape recordings, or just scraps of paper; each contains clues about the concern.

Some records are not immediately available for analysis, such as personal correspondence, financial records, and even information about complaints and grievances. In most cases, however, the needs analyst can obtain this information by showing how the information directly relates to documenting the concern. For example, if the problem were based in labor relations, then files that reveal shifts in labor policy, practices, and directions need to be searched to verify the changes. Performance evaluations are usually key indicators of changes in the quality of employee activities; hence, annual performance review files may be very helpful in documenting certain kinds of concerns.

Job/Task Information.   A job usually includes a number of specific duties that are carried out through the completion of several tasks by the worker. A task is the smallest unit of behavior studied by the analyst and describes the specific sequence of events necessary to complete a unit of work. A task analysis reveals the steps required for a person to perform a job in the most efficient way. With information about how a job may be done, it is possible to discover differences between how a job should be done and how it is actually being done.

Two methods are usually used to complete a task analysis. The first studies top performers doing each of the tasks and records the events that represent the best way of doing the job. The second method uses subject matter experts or SME's who are usually very well informed about the way in which the task should be done. These experts write down and describe the events necessary to perform the task in the best way possible.

Performance Information.   While a task analysis describes what it takes to complete a task in the most efficient manner, performance analysis assesses how well employees actually perform a task. Performance analysis looks at the employee doing the job, rather than just at the job itself. Performance analysis uses observations made by a third-party observer. As observations are made of an employee's behavior, they are recorded and compared either against other employees or against some performance standard.

The comparison of the amount and quality of an employee's work to other workers may be accomplished in a number of different ways. If employees are compared against others, according to what they do and how well they do it, a straight ranking procedure may be used which simply lists employees from most effective to least effective on such standards as number of usable units produced, cost per unit produced, or number of hours worked without an accident. A second method, paired comparison, rates each employee against every other employee in the group being compared. A third approach, that of a forced distribution, requires the analyst to place employees in categories representing the top, middle, and low levels of performance. A certain percentage of the group of employees is placed in each category, giving a distribution regardless of how well the total group is performing.

When employee performance is compared to absolute performance standards rather than other employees, some form of scale is used. Statements representing worker performance or behaviors are placed on a page and numerical scales are assigned to each statement. The analyst selects a number on the scale that represents the level of performance. For example, a typical scale might read:

"The employee performs work in a safe way"
very safe   1   2   3   4   5   6   7   very careless

The employee's work behavior is then compared to some absolute standard and given a rating. On a seven-point scale, the employee might be rated 5, which would be a somewhat unfavorable comparison to other employees who are rated 2. Each rating represents a judgment concerning how well the employee is doing in comparison to some standard represented on the scale.

Direct measures of performance, rather than observations and ratings, are often used to evaluate quantity and quality of work (Gilbert, 1978). Measures of quantity of products created are the most common indexes of performance used as direct measures. The number of units produced per hour worked, percentage of work completed on time, volume of sales, and workdays without an accident are examples of direct measures of performance.

Measuring performance in nonproduction settings, such as in school classrooms, is challenging. Direct measures of teacher performance might include number of students taught, size of syllabus prepared for each class, and number of papers read. Quite often, indirect measures are used to evaluate teacher performance, like number of students securing jobs or student scores on tests.

❦ Perceptual Information

Perceptual information is derived from reports given by employees about how they feel about their work. When employees tell you what they think is keeping them from making their strongest contribution to the organization, the needs analyst is getting perceptual information.

Securing perceptual data from employees is useful to the needs analyst because many concerns have their causes in employee perceptions rather than in their actual abilities to perform a job or the job itself. Some concerns are a function of how employees feel about their supervisors, how interesting they think the work is, how valuable they think they are to the organization, or how much opportunity they have to make progress in the organization. The climate of the organization, as reflected in employee feelings of animosity, unfavorable work conditions, stress-related events, and supervisor attitudes, may be indicators of problems in the organization.

A needs analyst may get reports about employee perceptions by interviewing them face to face or over the telephone, or by interviewing them in groups. Group interviews may be an efficient way to gather data because as many as 10 or 12 employees may be surveyed at one time. Interviewing skills, whether employees are interviewed individually or in groups, are critical to getting useful perceptual information.

Perceptual information may also be secured in written form through the use of questionnaires. An excellent questionnaire can get information about employee perceptions more quickly and more extensively than interviews because upwards of hundreds of employees can complete a questionnaire simultaneously. The responses can be tabulated and classified more quickly than interviews can be analyzed, and questionnaire data can be subjected to statistical analysis in which more comparisons can be made than are possible with interview data. On the other hand, interview data may be richer in meaning and nuance. Interview and questionnaire information complement each other.

❦ Systems Information

Sometimes pertinent information about a concern may come from examining the operation of the organizational system itself, as well as from the task, performance, or perceptions of individuals. The working system is reflected most clearly in the way in which information and interpersonal interactions are communicated among members of the organization. An analysis of the organizational communication system, for example, focuses on people in positions getting and giving information, initiating and responding to one another, in order to give the organization life. A systems approach to analysis looks at the organization as a whole and complements other types of analyses that focus on individual performance and perceptions by examining problems that arise as the organization functions. Problems may have their major causes in the system rather than in the person.

Because a system is global in design and intent, it is analyzed from two different perspectives: a functional and an interpretive one. A functional analysis focuses on the processes used to achieve organizational goals and to implement managerial purposes and uses methods that measure and quantify the way in which the organization achieves both its internal and external goals.

MacKenzie (1969) identified three continuous processes in organizations—planning, problem solving, and communicating—that affect the manner in which organizations operate and accomplish their goals. A functional analysis attempts to determine how well one or more of those processes is working.

Such a comprehensive system for analyzing communication processes in organizations is described in Mills, Pace, and Peterson (1989, pp. 183–191). An organizational communication profile instrument was devised to measure eight key communication variables: organizational satisfaction, communication climate, information accessibility, information load, message fidelity, information dispersion, media quality, and organizational culture. The OCP is a written questionnaire that is relatively easy to administer and interpret, gives information about the overall functioning of the organization, and helps to confirm strengths and identify weaknesses.

The second perspective, an interpretive approach to systems analysis, relies heavily on the analyst as the "instrument," whereas a functional approach usually employs a formal questionnaire, such as the OCP described earlier. In interpretive analysis, the search is for symbolic behavior that has organizational significance. The best interpretive analyses focus on discovering the symbolic behavior that drives organized activity. Interpretive analyses require the analyst to recognize "taken-for-granted" behavior and its significance in the organization. What may appear to be mundane interaction may reveal significant organizational processes and assumptions.

Talk is the primary data of interpretive analysis. Through talk, cultures and organizations are brought to life—organizational reality is brought into being. While functional analysis uses numerical data, interpretive analysis relies on information found in organizational messages.

At least three types of messages have been the focus of interpretive analysis: accounts, stories, and metaphors. Accounts are explanations that people give for their behavior. An account is a statement used by people when their actions are challenged. People usually give accounts when they are asked to justify their actions. For example, the answer given to "Why is your report late?" becomes the basis for the analysis. The reasons offered help the analyst understand what is considered acceptable in the culture of the organization for not performing on time.

Stories are verbal recreations of events or incidents. Organization members use stories to make sense out of what happens to them in the organization. Thus, stories are used in analysis to reveal what kind of sensemaking is occurring in organizations. Stories told by employees, for example, may describe what it is like to get approval for a new idea they have or how to make improvements in their work. Such stories offer insights into the way the organization responds to suggestions from the work force. Stories often embody the practices, aspirations, and climate of the organization.

Metaphors are comparisons of unlike or dissimilar features. Organizations may be characterized as garbage cans or zoos or machines. Metaphors explain how organization members are thinking about their lives and what happens to them. For example, an employee may say that the organization is like riding an elevator. It has a lot of ups and downs, and someone is always pushing your buttons. Sometimes you get the shaft, but what really bothers you are the jerks. Metaphors are recorded from the daily talk of organization members in, preferably, naturally occurring interaction.

Sources of problems in an organization may be revealed by means of both functional and interpretive analyses. Each has its own philosophy and methods, but they tend to complement one another, providing a richness of data and a depth of understanding of the sources and causes of organizational concerns that transcend the analysis of individuals. Coupled with individual analyses of tasks, performance, and perceptions, functional and interpretive forms of analysis have much to contribute to understanding organizations and why they are both efficient and inefficient. A single perspective or approach is usually inadequate for properly defining and documenting critical concerns in organizations.

❦ *Defining a Problem*

Once a concern has been documented, the next step is to determine the magnitude of the problem. A problem, as was suggested earlier, is the difference between what you want and what you have. If the concern represents a sizable gap between what the organization wants and what it has, then plans to close the gap and somehow manage the problem go into effect (see subsequent chapters on developmental and instrumental roles).

The sources of problems are usually found in differences in (1) performance—individual gaps in knowledge, attitudes, and skills, (2) management—gaps in the way in which people are managed, and (3) organization—gaps in organization structure, authority, and task design (Mills, Pace, and Peterson, 1989). Performance gaps are narrowed by providing training and development, management gaps are narrowed by providing new ways of managing, and organizational gaps are reduced by making structural and job changes.

The work of a needs analyst focuses on using his or her critical abilities to identify and document the source and causes of problems or potential problems in the organization. The philosophy, methods, instruments, and procedures involved in analysis represent some of the most fundamental and essential forms of knowledge and skills available to the HRD professional.

RESEARCHER ROLE

In contrast to the work of a needs analyst, whose main goal is to identify and document the existence of potential and real problems in an organization, the work of a researcher is, primarily, to find general explanations of natural events. Rather than try to explain every unique behavior of people as they try to solve problems, the research seeks to find information that explains all kinds of problem-solving behaviors. Such a general explanation would be called a theory of problem solving.

In the field of human resource development, needs analysts attempt to identify and document problems of individuals in the workplace, whereas researchers attempt to find general explanations of factors that contribute to an understanding of how to develop the human resources of an organization. HRD researchers are like other social scientists in that they seek to understand what happens when certain activities occur, but they go beyond the pure social psychologists, at least as described by Milgram (1977), who says that "as a social psychologist, I look at the world not to master it in any practical sense, but to understand it and to communicate that understanding to others" (p. 1). In contrast, the HRD researcher seeks to understand and to master the technology and practices of human resource development in a very practical way. The HRD researcher wants to discover theories that provide the most accurate explanations for what happens in a situation and to decide which methods and technologies are most effective in bringing about the kinds of changes sought by practitioners. HRD research, therefore, is considered more applied than pure and is action research in the true sense; it is designed to discover what produces change in the most efficient way and what sustains change for the longest period of time.

To engage in empirical research is to pursue the systematic, controlled, and experimental testing of relations among events. The celebrated man in the street ("T. C. Mits"), in contrast, tends to use conceptual schemes and theories in a loose fashion and ordinarily makes little effort to control extraneous sources of contamination that might confuse or obscure clear explanations of what is actually happening. As Kerlinger (1964) observed, T. C. Mits often "seizes . . . on the fortuitous occurrence of two phenomena and immediately links them indissolubly as cause and effect" (p. 5) whereas the researcher consciously and systematically pursues events to see how they are linked, suspending judgment until the relations have been tested. If propositions or questions cannot be tested independently and in public, they do not come under the mantle of research. They may be important and meaningful, but they are not amenable to research methods.

Milgram (1977) has observed that "although experiments may be objective, they are rarely entirely neutral" (p. 1). In HRD, as in other behavioral sciences, the researcher is studying activities of which he or she is frequently a part. Each investigation has a point of view or paradigm that colors the manner in which it is carried out. HRD researchers tend to design their investigations on the assumption that human activities are law governed rather than rule governed.

A law-governed philosophy operates on the assumption that general laws can be derived to explain consequences, whereas a rule-governed philosophy assumes that behavior is a result of agreements made between people that can only be explained by understanding what the agreements are and how they came about.

Many of the outcomes of the HRD researcher may appear to overlap with those of the needs analyst and evaluator, and the methods used by HRD researchers are similar to those found in allied behavioral and social sciences, education, communication, and management sciences. Nevertheless, each research design in HRD should take into account those practices and theories somewhat unique to HRD.

The remainder of this section will focus on specific activities and products that are part of the HRD research process:

1. Creating and defining concepts, theories, and models of development and change
2. Testing practices and relationships among elements to determine authentic causal factors
3. Developing research designs
4. Writing reports of completed research
5. Writing articles for publication

Rather than discuss each of these activities individually, we shall place them in the context of a general model of research based on a research game.

❦ The "If-Then" Game of Research

Scientific research is like playing a board game such as Monopoly. To win, one must proceed through a series of starts, stops, and returns until the goals of the game are achieved. Incorrect decisions and moves may lead to losing points, but correct decisions and moves nearly always help to accomplish the objectives of the game. Effective research means progressing systematically toward the end of the game, realizing that mistakes may create barriers to winning or, at least, require different avenues and approaches to complete the game successfully (Pace, Peterson, and Boren, 1975).

The "If-Then" Game (Figure 5.1, on pages 80 and 81) was created to show the steps in the research process. To complete the game, the researcher must progress sequentially through each of the sections of the board: I. The Question; II. Literature Search; III. Research Design; and IV. Data Collection and Outcomes. Begin the game in the upper left-hand corner where the words "Start Here" are located. The rules for each step in the game are as follows:

I. The Question.   1. *Thinking and Fooling Around.*   Although this may seem like a silly way to begin a game about research, many of our most provocative ideas come from interacting with others, eating apples, watching dust settle, and just plain daydreaming. Out of feelings of frustration about HRD methods and their effects may come the sense of a problem. If so, advance three spaces to step 4.

2. *Getting an Idea.*   Out of thinking and fooling around, questions may arise. As the questions about effectiveness begin to germinate, step 2 emerges. Many people lose the research game because they never get to this point. Sometimes they daydream, but they never really get a clear idea. In fact, step 1 is where many good ideas rest; they fail to move ahead, and the game is lost. Do not hold interesting ideas too long before moving to step 3.

3. *Question.*   Now, the ideas must be made specific and phrased as a question. Precise questions are phrased at this step. The questions are those that must be answered to more clearly understand what effects are produced and why they occurred. If the questions are still unclear, lose one turn and go back one space to step 2 and refine the idea.

4. *Statement.*   At this stage, the general questions must be translated into specific approaches, like stating a specific purpose for the research. That is, if the concern is about what impact different types of trainers have on trainee's reactions, the statement should indicate a particular direction, such as comparing the effects on trainees of trainers who come from technical areas with technical competence versus trainers who come from the training staff without technical knowledge but who have excellent presentational skills. After stating specifically what is to be studied, advance one space to step 5.

5. *Worthwhile.*   If the idea cannot be stated specifically enough, possibly the difficulty lies in not understanding its significance in the field. Review why the idea seems to stir research interests. If the idea still cannot be stated clearly, go back four spaces to step 1 (Thinking and Fooling Around) and begin the game over. If the idea seems to have value, but the question is still not specific, lose two spaces and return to step 3 (Question) to identify an alternative question that gets at the heart of the issue.

6. *Clarity.*   Once specific and worthwhile questions have been identified and phrased, advance to step 6 where the following questions are to be answered: Is the statement of the idea and its purpose clear? Is the question and the potential answer going to be a worthwhile contribution to HRD? If the first question is

"No," lose two turns and go back two spaces to step 4, and restate the question more clearly. If the second question is answered in the negative, go back one space and reevaluate the worth of the question. If both questions are answered positively, move forward one space and begin Part II of the game, Literature Search.

II. Literature Search. 7. *Read.* Go to the library and read as many sources as possible to find out if the idea and tentative question have been studied already and what is known about the HRD issue (see Appendix B for a list of HRD journals). If someone else has reported a study on the general area of the question, determine what the results reveal about the question and how the study was conducted to discover how the study is similar and different from other thinking on the issue. After a wide range of journals have been reviewed for relevant research and a record made of what has already been published on the general question, advance one space to step 8.

8. *Answer.* After reading widely, the question—Does the published research already provide a clear answer to the potential research question?—must be answered to determine whether someone else has already done the research and answered the question. If the research has been completed, *the other researchers win the game!* You lose! and return to the beginning. If, however, the question is not answered directly, proceed to step 9.

9. *Depth.* At this step, an in-depth and critical analysis of the available research is made to determine why no clear-cut answer to the question appears in the literature. Possibly, the precise question has not been raised or the procedures used were not handled well. On the other hand, the research results may provide conflicting answers. The published research must be analyzed to determine why the question was not answered adequately. If the critical analysis does not indicate why an answer does not exist, lose two turns, return to step 8, and go back to the library. You have probably missed something. If a reasonable answer is created, advance one space to step 10.

10. *Problem.* When the reasons for not having a clear answer to the research question surface, a more specific problem and a clearer question usually emerges. If a critical problem and research question do not become clear after an in-depth analysis of the journal articles, go back two spaces to step 7 and begin the literature search again. If a problem question becomes clear, progress to the third area of the game, Research Design. Often a more fundamental question becomes apparent following a detailed analysis of extant research (Leedy, 1974, pp. 46–57). Since fundamental questions are more exciting and productive than routine questions, consider this a breakthrough, award yourself four tokens, and advance immediately to Part III.

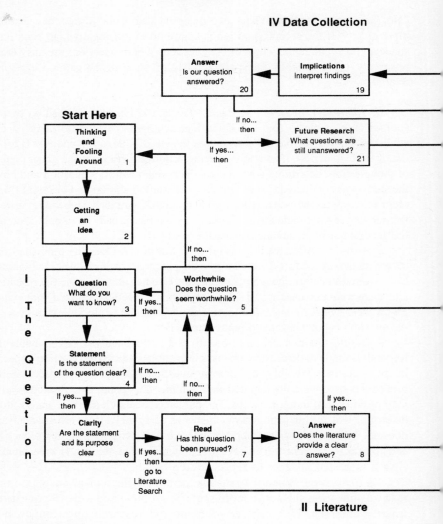

IV Data Collection

Answer
Is our question
answered?   20

Implications
Interpret findings   19

Start Here

**Thinking
and
Fooling
Around**   1

If no...
then

Future Research
What questions are
still unanswered?   21

If yes...
then

**Getting
an
Idea**   2

I

T
h
e

Question
What do you
want to know?   3

If no...
then

Worthwhile
Does the question
seem worthwhile?   5

If yes...
then

Q
u
e
s
t
i
o
n

Statement
Is the statement
of the question clear?   4

If no...
then

If no...
then

If yes...
then

Answer
Does the literature
provide a clear
answer?   8

If yes...
then

Clarity
Are the statement
and its purpose
clear   6

Read
Has this question
been pursued?   7

If yes...
then
go to
Literature
Search

II Literature

FIGURE 5.1
The If-Then Game

III. Research Design.   11. *Methods.*   The first task in research design is
to determine which methods seem best suited for studying the question (Agnew
and Pyke, 1969, p. 53). Although several ways of classifying research methods
are available (Isaac and Michael, 1971, pp. 13–15), four types of empirical
research approaches are the focus of step 11: correlational, causal-comparative,

and Outcome

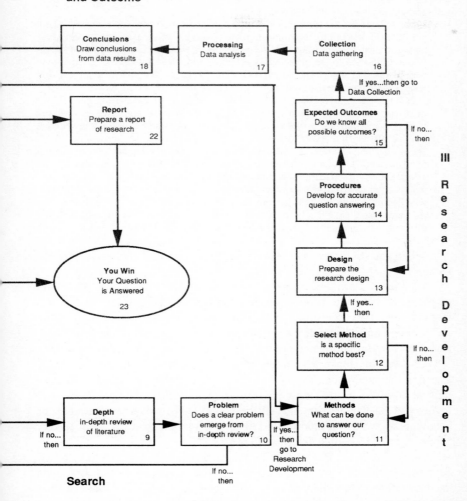

quasi-experimental, and true experimental. Other approaches to gathering data have been discussed under the role of needs analyst, and some alternative data-gathering methods will be described as part of the evaluator role, resulting in a fairly comprehensive survey of basic data-gathering methods often clustered under the category of research.

- *Correlational Method.* This method involves discovering the extent to which performance of one skill varies when one or more other factors vary. For example, correlations might indicate how trainer enthusiasm and trainee ratings vary. When enthusiasm goes up, do ratings go up?

- *Causal-Comparative Method.* This method involves discovering information about possible cause-and-effect relationships by observing some existing consequences and searching back through data for plausible causes. For example, a study comparing trainers who are rated highly effective with those rated less effective over several years, using data already in HRD department files, might lead to information about which characteristics of trainers produced the highest ratings.
- *Quasi-Experimental Method.* This method attempts to approximate the conditions of a true experiment, but in a field setting that does not allow for control and management of all relevant variables. Studies that control some variables in an actual training setting fit this category.
- *True Experimental Method.* This method follows data-gathering procedures existing in an authentic laboratory setting. One or more groups of subjects that are carefully selected are exposed to different training techniques under specified conditions. The results obtained from the experimental groups are compared with groups of subjects who had no contact with the training techniques to see if differences occurred. The data are treated statistically to determine what the probabilities are of getting the differences between the two groups by chance (Glass and Stanley, 1970).

When you have considered possible methods for use in the study, proceed to step 12.

12. *Method Selection.* Select the method that has the greatest likelihood of providing data and information that may answer the question. If the best method cannot be identified, go back one space to step 11 and review the methods of similar research to see if they might suggest an appropriate method. As soon as a relevant method has been selected, move one space to step 13.

13. *Design.* Make a tentative list of the procedures which must be followed to implement the method. The procedures include decisions about who will be involved in the study, how information will be secured from those involved, what factors can and will be controlled to isolate the variables or behaviors on which the study is focusing, and how the data will be analyzed. Move to step 14 when the list is complete.

14. *Procedures.* Begin to refine the tentative list by specifying who will be the subjects, how they will be tested, and where and under what conditions the data will be collected. Describe in great detail the step-by-step sequence that is to be used throughout the data-gathering stage. Develop the most complete and efficient set of procedures possible. Once completed, move one space to step 15.

15. *Expected Outcomes.* Prior to conducting the study, try to explain what the possible outcomes might be. How might the subjects respond to the procedures? What might the responses look like? Could the subjects react differently? How? What interpretations might be given to different types of data? Because experiments result in somewhat objective data, researchers must interpret the

data and make sense out of it (Nettler, 1970). The same data may be interpreted in different ways (Huck and Sandler, 1979). When the possible outcomes have been identified, move one space forward to the final area of the game, Data Collection and Outcomes.

IV. Data Collection and Outcomes. 16. *Collection.* This step involves carefully following the procedures described in earlier steps to make certain that the most reliable and valid data are obtained. When all the data are in the hands of the researcher, move one space to step 17.

17. *Processing.* This step involves tabulating the data, portraying it in tables, and applying appropriate statistical tests to determine the quality of the data. When finished, move ahead one space to step 18.

18. *Conclusions.* Study, analyze, and interpret the data to determine what can be concluded from the results obtained. Carefully write out the conclusions, then move one space to step 19.

19. *Implications.* This step involves thinking about and projecting the results and conclusions of the study into the future to speculate about the meaning of the results for HRD practices in real organizations. Consider what other questions have been raised by the study just completed. Move one space forward to step 20.

20. *Answer.* The study is now finished, but the issue remaining is whether the question has been answered. If the answer is "No," two choices remain: to return to step 11 and develop a new research design in hopes of conducting a more appropriate project or to return to step 1 and think and fool around some more. If the answer is "Yes," move to step 21 and discuss possible future research that might extend the results of the completed research.

21. *Future Research.* At this point, review unanswered questions, discuss where research should go from here, and outline possible research studies for the future. When completed, move one space ahead.

22. *Report.* The final step prior to winning the game is to report the results. For research to be understood and used, to help others avoid going over the same question, and to allow research to build systematically upon that which has gone before, it must be reported and distributed for others to read and study. Journals that report the results of HRD research are specific and varied. For example, the *Training and Development Journal, Training,* the *Personnel Administrator,* the *Journal of Management Development,* the *Journal of Applied Psychology, Personnel Psychology, Communication Education, Adult Education, Harvard Educational Review,* the *Journal of Industrial Teacher Education,* and the *Human Resource Development Quarterly* are all professional journals that report research about human resource development issues and variables. These are the types of journals that are also consulted as part of the literature

review step. HRD professionals should be familiar with appropriate and relevant journals for purposes of both keeping abreast of new developments in the field and reporting their own research.

The written report should follow a standard format, but include statements about the question being studied, the literature reviewed, the way the methods and procedures were developed, how the data were collected, the results obtained, and the conclusions and recommendations derived. The report should be submitted to an appropriate journal for publication. At that point, the game is over. If the steps of the game have been followed in a systematic fashion, an effective and meaningful research study will have been completed.

23. *You Win!*   Once the game is completed and the data made available for others to examine, the research begins to contribute to HRD theory. Practices, techniques, and basic methods of HRD need to be observed, described, and tested in order to determine what are the best ways to develop the HRD profession. The principles need to be based on solid research and justified by both theory and excellent studies. The primary purpose of research is to describe what has happened in order to formulate predictions about what will happen in the future. Research does not prescribe or stipulate what ought to happen. That is part of the decisions made by other roles in HRD.

ETHICAL CONSIDERATIONS IN RESEARCH

When research involves human beings, as it does in human resource development, a number of ethical considerations must be taken into account. Researchers do not have the right to abuse people who volunteer to serve as subjects. Thus, the following guidelines have been generally accepted for evaluating the appropriateness of methods and procedures when using human subjects.

- Human subjects should be given all reasonable protection for health and well-being.
- The purpose of the study, the procedures to be followed, and the possible risks involved must be explained to subjects.
- Explanations about the research must be understood and consent to participate must be obtained without duress or deception, although an explanation may be postponed if there are no risks to the subjects and when a full accounting of the purpose and procedures in advance might bias the results.
- Subjects' personal privacy and the confidentiality of information received from them must be protected.
- Subjects' time should not be invaded to the extent that the research creates conflicts with other obligations.
- Subjects should be able to request termination of participation in the study, and it should be honored promptly and without prejudice.

Appendix A includes a bibliography of articles on ethics in human resource development.

EVALUATOR ROLE

Evaluation is the process of determining the value, worth, or effect of something. HRD program evaluation involves deciding whether a particular development activity—a day's training or a week-long seminar—achieved the objectives set for it. Evaluation is important because it provides information about the outcomes or results of human resource development programs. Although *outcome* evaluation is the most common type conducted, it is possible, as well, to evaluate HRD activities at the needs, design, and process stages.

Research and evaluation share the fundamental notion of data gathering, including the use of some statistics to report the results. Evaluation, however, focuses on the program or unit being evaluated with the goal of improving the program, whereas research has longer-range goals and seeks to provide information about why something occurred. The focus of this section is on the unique features of evaluation.

Evaluations may be conducted for a variety of purposes and for different publics. For example, HRD staff may choose to evaluate a program to improve their own productivity, but the same evaluation may be conducted also for upper management to help them make decisions about the overall HRD function. Evaluation may be conducted for consumers for their use in selecting among competing products, or to help specialists choose between alternative ways of approaching a problem. Although the methods may be essentially the same, the purpose and user of the evaluation may significantly affect how the evaluation is conducted.

Evaluations of HRD activities may focus on five different areas: (1) the value of the training materials; (2) the effect of the trainer; (3) the impact of training on the trainee in terms of satisfaction, information learned, and skills

---

THE FIVE EVALUATION AREAS

- **Value of training materials**
- **Effect of the trainer**
- **Impact on the trainee**
- **Influence of the learning environment**
- **Impact on the organization**

acquired; (4) the influence of the learning environment; and (5) the impact of training on the organization (Smith, 1980; Pace, 1983).

¿ *Value of Training Materials*

The value of training materials is measured, in part, by how well they produce the training results desired. Evaluations of training materials occur early in the development process and continue throughout the design, production, marketing, and user phases of the life of training products. The formal process of developing materials for training is described in a later chapter and refers to two evaluation processes: formative evaluation (while the training materials are being developed) and summative evaluation (after the training materials have been used).

Formative evaluation begins when the needs analyst completes the front-end analysis. At this point, the objectives for training materials are evaluated to determine how directly they relate to the point of concern and what their potential is for closing the training gap. As information is gathered during the design process, the evaluator makes a second assessment about how well the content matches and fulfills the intent stated in the learning objectives. As formal production begins, the evaluator again checks the materials produced to determine if they complement and meet the requirements stated in the training objectives. During the field test, training materials are examined for how well the objectives are achieved and how easy it is for the instructor and student to use the materials.

Summative evaluation occurs as trainees use the materials; it answers the following questions: Can performance standards stated in the objectives actually be achieved? Is the content valid; that is, do the material presented and the testing instruments match one another? Do the questions asked represent the scope and relevance of what is being taught? Answers to those questions, and the assessments that occurred during the development phase, determine the value of the training materials.

¿ *The Effect of the Trainer*

A second key component in evaluating how well training works is the effectiveness of the trainer in presenting the materials to the trainees. The trainer is the key interface between the materials and the trainee, or, as some expressed the idea in a metaphor, this is where the rubber meets the road. The power and potential designed into the training materials are strongly influenced by how well they are presented. Trainers are evaluated by assessing their overall effectiveness, knowledge of the subject, presentation skills, and concern for participants' needs. The evaluator may observe the trainer in person, or video tape a training session, or use participant questionnaires to evaluate the trainer. Using a combination of methods is usually best because it increases the likelihood of getting a fair assessment.

✦ The Impact on the Trainee

Trainees are the key persons in the training and development process. The entire training effort is focused on helping them develop and improve by exposing them to instructional materials and methods. Three outcomes are typically measured to determine the impact of training on participants: (1) trainee satisfaction, (2) amount of information gained, and (3) new skills acquired.

Trainee Satisfaction. Satisfaction involves a variety of issues. For instance, did training meet the needs of trainees? How valuable, essential, useful, practical, and important were the materials to trainees? Was the training session presented well? How exciting, interesting, energizing, pleasant, and enlightening was the trainer? The evaluator uses observation, interviews, focus groups, and participant questionnaires to evaluate these issues.

Information Gained. The information to be acquired is usually specified in the standards of performance included in the objectives for the training session. Information can be of different types (Bloom, 1956), such as knowledge (recalling information), comprehension (interpreting information), application (applying information), analysis (breaking information into parts), synthesis (bring together elements of information to produce new learning), and evaluation (determining how well something has worked).

The evaluator creates instruments such as basic multiple-choice tests that show whether the trainees can recall the knowledge learned or use their intellectual abilities in applying, analyzing or synthesizing the information. Intellectual activities are measured by case studies, problem solving, games and simulations, or original research projects. One way, for example, to determine whether information has been gained is to do a content analysis of trainee conversations on the job, to see if what was taught has become part of the thinking and reasoning of the trainees.

Skills Acquired. The trainees' abilities to perform skills in a competent, creative, and intelligent manner are evaluated by observing them do something. Detailed checklists guide the observer to focus on key behaviors. Skill development usually represents the performance of a specific task in a specified sequence in a fixed amount of time (Mills, Pace, and Peterson, 1989). The evaluator assesses the abilities of trainees to perform skills during training and when they return to the work setting to perform them on the job. The focus of the final evaluation is on how well the transfer of training has occurred and what sustained improvements are found as the skills are applied on the job.

❦ *The Learning Environment*

The learning environment represents the physical facilities where training and development occur. Factors that influence the learning environment are lighting, temperature of the classroom, and the comfort of the chairs provided. The flexibility of facilities, such as being able to move chairs, use break-out rooms for small-group activity, use media support, and interact freely with other trainees, is also evaluated. The evaluator may also determine the feelings of both participants and trainers about the learning environment.

❦ *Impact on the Organization*

The benefits of human resource development are felt, ultimately, as organizations become more efficient and productive. Once training and development has taken place, the evaluator tracks the performance of those who were trained to determine whether increases in productivity have occurred. The evaluator should also continuously monitor the efficiency of all the units to find ways to help individuals perform and achieve at higher levels. The evaluator role is an important part of the HRD function and makes significant contributions to the organization by determining what is occurring and where improvements may be made.

SUMMARY

This chapter has described three roles that are part of the analytical cluster. The common thread that binds these roles together is the process of thinking analytically to understand human resource development issues. While all three roles use critical methods, the needs analyst looks primarily at factors related to specifying and documenting concerns and determining the causes and effects of gaps in the performances of organization members. The researcher engages in conceptualizing, theorizing, designing, and conducting research, the purpose of which is to provide explanations for why HRD practices are effective or ineffective. The evaluator monitors the value of training through formative, summative, and periodic assessments of training materials, processes, and consequences.

While these roles are described separately, they are often performed collectively, under the direction of the manager of the HRD function of an organization by one person or a number of people. These roles encompass the analytical, assessment, and evaluation skills used to monitor how well employees and the organization are doing toward accomplishing the goals of the organization.

REFERENCES

AGNEW, NEIL MCK., AND SANDRA W. PYKE. *The Science Game: An Introduction to Research in the Behavioral Sciences*. Englewood Cliffs, NJ: Prentice Hall, 1969.

BLOOM, BENJAMIN S., ET AL. *A Taxonomy of Educational Objectives Handbook I: The Cognitive Domain*. New York: Longman, 1956.

GILBERT, T. *Human Competence, Engineering Worthy Performance*. New York: McGraw-Hill, 1978.

GLASS, GENE V., AND JULIAN C. STANLEY. *Statistical Methods in Education and Psychology*. Englewood Cliffs, NJ: Prentice Hall, 1970.

GOLDHABER, G. "The ICA Communication Audit: Rationale and Development." Paper presented at the Academy of Management Convention, Kansas City, 1976.

HUCK, SCHUYLER W., AND HOWARD M. SANDLER. *Rival Hypotheses: Alternative Interpretations of Data Based Conclusions*. New York: Harper & Row, 1979.

ISAAC, STEPHEN, AND WILLIAM B. MICHAEL. *Handbook in Research Evaluation*. San Diego, CA: Robert K. Knapp, 1971.

JUECHTER, M. "Bringing Spirit Back to the Workplace." *Training and Development Journal, 42* (1988), pp. 35–39.

KERLINGER, FRED N. *Foundations of Behavioral Research*. New York: Holt, Rinehart and Winston, 1964.

LEEDY, PAUL D. *Practical Research: Planning and Design*. New York: Macmillan, 1974.

LUNDBERG, C. C. "On the Feasibility of Cultural Intervention in Organizations." In P. J. Frost et al., eds., *Organizational Culture*. Beverly Hills, CA: Sage, 1985.

MACKENZIE, A. "A Three-D Model of Management Processes." *Harvard Business Review, 47* (1969), pp. 80–87.

MILGRAM, STANLEY. *The Individual in a Social World: Essays and Experiments*. Reading, MA: Addison-Wesley, 1977.

MILLS, G., R. W. PACE, AND B. PETERSON. *Analysis in Human Resource Training and Organization Development*. Reading, MA: Addison-Wesley, 1989.

NETTLER, GWYNN. *Explanations*. New York: McGraw-Hill, 1970.

PACE, R. WAYNE. *Organizational Communication*. Englewood Cliffs, NJ: Prentice Hall, 1983.

PACE, R. WAYNE, AND BRENT PETERSON. *Organizational Communication Profile*. Provo, UT: Organizational Associates, 1985.

PACE, R. WAYNE, ROBERT R. BOREN, AND BRENT D. PETERSON. *Communication Behavior and Experiments: A Scientific Approach*. Belmont, CA: Wadsworth, 1975.

PACE, R. WAYNE, BRENT D. PETERSON, AND ROBERT R. BOREN. *Communication Experiments: A Manual for Conducting Experiments.* Belmont, CA: Wadsworth, 1975.

PACE, R. WAYNE, B. PETERSON, AND M. D. BURNETT. *Techniques for Effective Communication.* Reading, MA: Addison-Wesley, 1979.

ROETHLISBERGER, F. J. *The Exclusive Phenomena.* Cambridge, MA: Harvard University Press, 1977.

SMITH, G. D., AND L. E. STEADMAN. "The Value of Corporate History." *Harvard Business Review,* 59 (1981), 69–76.

SMITH, MARTIN E. "Evaluating Training Operations and Programs." *Training and Development Journal,* 35 (1980), p. 71.

CHAPTER 6

❦ ❦

Developmental Roles

INTRODUCTION

Bill looked at George and shook his head. "Only two hours and we can go home. This annual safety training is more than I can stand . . . it's the same old rot, year in and year out. If the labor contract said I didn't need to be here, I'd be gone. Why can't these trainers develop something that is interesting and really worthwhile?"

"Well, one thing, Bill, it does beat working in the warehouse . . . at least it is cool in here. I agree with you; however, if this weren't required, I'm not sure I would attend on my own."

"I think I would rather be there in the warehouse. At least I would feel I had accomplished something. Here, we get the same old straight lecture . . . there is never any media used to help make the points clear."

"Yeh, I know what you mean. Look, there are sure a lot of people who are trying to stay awake. It looks like we're not the only ones who feel this is a waste of time."

George and Bill's dialogue illustrates some of the problems of poorly developed training materials. Some topics may not be interesting, or the presentation of them may not be captivating, but properly designed instruction can overcome criticisms that training is boring and ineffective.

Those who are charged with the responsibility of making the training both interesting and beneficial are program designers and materials developers. Their developmental roles focus on how to solve the problems, narrow the gaps, and reduce the deficiencies identified and documented by the analytical roles. They study available training and development resources, combine them into unique configurations, and emerge with exciting and clever ways for helping employees acquire information, develop skills, and strengthen attitudes.

❦ *Value*

Although those who perform the program design and materials development roles generally work behind the scenes, they provide essential foundations and tools for facilitating change in people. If the foundation is weak, the entire program is weak; if the design is effective, the entire program is likely to be effective. Nothing can be more critical to the field of human resource development than to have practitioners who can design and develop the plans and materials for use in implementing change activities. The best laid plans underlie the best programs.

❦ *Chapter Organization*

This chapter describes the process of creating plans and materials for use in human resource training and development programs. The chapter focuses on the program designer role first and the materials developer role second, since design should precede development.

❦ *Learning Objectives*

After studying this chapter, you should be able to:

1. Define and characterize the work of the program designer and materials developer roles.
2. Describe the steps in a model of training design.
3. Prepare an agenda that incorporates the primary elements and procedures involved in the design of a training program.
4. Prepare an outline of the process of producing a media product for use in a training program.

THE TWO DEVELOPMENTAL ROLES

-   **Program designer**
-   **Materials developer**

PROGRAM DESIGNER ROLE

The primary task of the program designer is to prepare the plans for a training session. The program designer is involved in writing objectives, selecting the materials to be used to accomplish the objectives, sequencing activities, deciding how outcomes are to be evaluated, and determining how the skills taught are to be transferred to and reinforced in the workplace.

The program designer, in addition, devises an overall training strategy, creates daily training schedules, and establishes time blocks for completion of activities. There are six preliminary but essential concepts to understand in order to create a plan: (1) design, (2) strategy, (3) program, (4) training session, (5) training sequence, and (6) time blocks and periods.

❦ Design

For a program designer, design is the process used to create a plan that is used to produce changes through training. These designed plans include all the activities and instructions to be used in conducting the training session. Design occurs in all intentional activities and encompasses both micro or small (e.g., time blocks, specific activities) and macro or large (e.g., strategies) elements. (See Figure 6.1.)

❦ Strategy

The overarching concept that guides the program designer's plan or product for achieving objectives is called a strategy. A strategy provides the training

FIGURE 6.1
Elements of Design

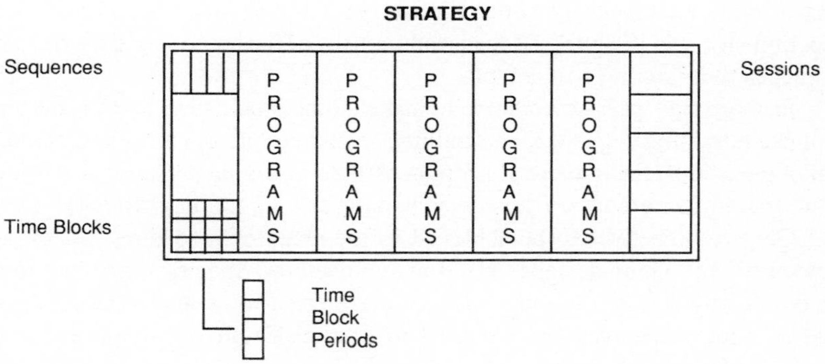

rationale for the series of programs set up to improve productivity and the quality of work occurring in the organization. Designers are concerned about the overall strategy an organization takes to develop its employees, since much of their time is devoted to implementing the strategy through the creation of programs.

❦ Program

The term "program" refers to a unit of time involving one or more days that are tied together by a common theme. A program may be a one-day or a multiple-week activity. Some examples or common themes that represent a program use generic titles such as Supervisory Skills Development, Management Development, Sales Training, Technical Skills Development, or Personal Skills Development.

❦ Training Session

A training session consists of those activities organized to accomplish a single terminal objective within the program, which usually means a day or two of training.

❦ Training Sequence

A training sequence consists of those activities associated with the accomplishment of one intermediate objective within the training session, which may encompass one or more time blocks.

❦ Time Blocks and Periods

A time block is the amount of time that occurs between breaks; a training day is usually divided into 60- or 75-minute time blocks with 10- or 15-minute breaks between blocks of time. Blocks are divided into time periods that accomplish a specific goal. Time periods consist of the amount of time devoted to each activity during a time block.

In short, time periods combine to make a time block, time blocks combine to make a training sequence, and training sequences are developed to create a training session. One or more sessions constitute a training program, and one or more training programs are developed to carry out the training strategy.

General objectives to be achieved as the result of a training session are stated by the program designer as *terminal* objectives. Specific objectives to be accomplished during a training session are referred to as *intermediate* objectives. Training manuals are prepared to provide detailed guidelines for an instructor or facilitator to follow in conducting the training session. Procedures for designing a training session generally follow the stages in a model such as Carnarius's (1981) which fits the realities of management training and matches most theories of design. The model lists seven steps a program designer uses to create a training session.

1. Identify and outline the content of the session.
2. List possible activities to be incorporated into the session.
3. Write objectives for the session.
4. Select activities and match them with the objectives.
5. Sequence the activities (exercises, lectures, analysis, practice).
6. Check the agenda to make certain that everything follows logically or naturally from preceding activities.
7. Prepare and develop materials.

Identify and Outline Content. The program designer's first task is to define what the content for the training session should be. The content is a subdivision of the common theme included in the training program. For instance, a program designed to develop the complete manager may have sessions on managing people, developing vision, preparing strategies, implementing change in the organization, evaluating performance, and action planning. Content in any given training session is usually identified through consultation between the human resource development staff and the line managers. Their decision on what should be included is based on practical experience, theory, and an analysis.

Most content issues, however, usually involve a hierarchy of learning; this means that some prerequisite concepts must be learned by the trainees in order to achieve the performance standards included in the session's objective. To complete the identification of content,

- Include the prerequisite information to be learned.
- Describe the skills to be developed.
- List what ought to go into the session.
- Develop a topical outline with two or three levels of information to show the substance of the content.

List Possible Activities. The next step the program designer takes in designing the training session is to identify a number of activities that might be used to achieve the tentative objectives set for the training session. This effort consists of identifying activities such as experiences, instruments, simulations, role plays, questionnaires, inventories, and puzzles and then preparing any other materials and instructions necessary to conduct each activity.

Most people who design training programs maintain a file of activities that can be used in training. This collection is organized into large files and boxes of materials that can be used during this stage in the design process. One of the most extensive and useful published collections of activities is that of University Associates, a publishing company located in LaJolla, California. Since about 1972 they have been publishing annual handbooks of structured experiences that include instruments, lecturettes, instructions, and other aids for use in management and leadership training and development, as well as personal growth.

In 1988 University Associates published a *Reference Guide to Handbooks and Annuals* (Volumes I–X including the years 1972–1988) that classifies, describes, and indexes over 400 activities. The materials themselves are published in a single 8½ × 11-inch format and distributed in a box for immediate and convenient use. They are divided into six categories:

1. *Personal activities* that focus on the expansion of personal insight, awareness, and development of interpersonal skills.
2. *Communication activities* that emphasize verbal and nonverbal skills in interpersonal and intragroup relationships.
3. *Group characteristics activities* that examine how individuals affect group functioning.
4. *Group task behavior activities* that focus on how groups organize and function to accomplish objectives.
5. *Organizations activities* that help individuals and groups function within an organizational context.
6. *Facilitating learning activities* that create a climate of responsiveness and encourage skill development.

Ninety paper-and-pencil instruments are included and classified as personal, interpersonal, management/leadership, organization, and group behavior. Although the "kit" of activities published by University Associates is a valuable collection, it is not the only one. Other companies also publish activities and related materials. Consult a library or training and development professionals in your local community for additional sources.

Write Objectives.   The program designer next takes the content outline and the lists of activities gathered during steps 1 and 2 and prepares the written objectives. In most instances, precise, measurable objectives are written to guide the training session. Such objectives are written to help learners master three types of experiences:

1. Those dealing with what *knowledge* trainees are to acquire during the training session.
2. Those dealing with what *attitudes* trainees are to develop during the training session.

3. Those dealing with what *skills* trainees are to perform during and after the training session.

Objectives state what the trainees or participants are going to do to demonstrate that they have learned the knowledge, developed the attitudes, and acquired the skills during the training session. A clear statement of an objective specifies

*   The *audience* (A) who is to achieve the objective.
*   The *behavior* (B) to be achieved by the trainee.
*   The *conditions* (C) that apply when the trainees demonstrate they have mastered the task.
*   The *degree* (D) of excellence that is required to show that the training effect has been achieved. (Chisholm and Ely, 1976)

In writing clear statements, the program designer specifies the A, B, C, and D's (audience, behavior, conditions, and degree) in each objective. *Audience* describes the participant or trainee. *Behaviors* are represented by verbs that indicate the precise actions to be performed. These action verbs reflect the three types of learning experiences suggested. For example, knowledge to be learned is revealed by verbs such as list, label, write, name, illustrate, identify, classify, compare, formulate, theorize, judge, weigh, and rate. Skills to be acquired are indicated by verbs such as demonstrate, develop, eliminate, decrease, obtain, use, determine, predict, paraphrase, support. Where attitudes are to be developed, verbs such as acknowledge, perceive, accept, test, comply, approve, influence, return, make commitment, and defend are used. *Conditions* specifies where the behavior is to be demonstrated and what equipment or materials the trainee may use, such as "while driving a truck," "by consulting a book of instructions," or "without notes." This part of the statement frequently reveals conditions through the preposition "while" or "by" and a verb ending in "ing" to represent the action of displaying the behavior, such as "while climbing." The *degree* of the statement specifies the level of performance that is expected of all trainees. This standard indicates specifically how many items or behaviors must be listed or demonstrated to be acceptable and what levels of performance fall below the standard. Here is an example of an objective, including these statements:

Audience: At the end of the instruction, the *trainee* will be able to:
Behavior: *list* the four key statements to include in a properly stated behavioral objective
Condition: *by writing* from memory
Degree: all *four* stated in the book.

To accomplish this objective, for example, trainees must demonstrate that they know the four steps by writing them down; the restrictions imposed require that the trainees accomplish the objective without written aids, while the standard requires that all four elements of a good objective must be stated.

Select Activities and Match with Objectives.   The intermediate objectives indicate what is to be accomplished during the session. All the activities work in harmony with each other to produce the outcomes listed in the session objectives. At this time in the design process, the program designer selects training activities that seem most likely to accomplish the objectives. The designer should have as many relevant activities as possible to select from so that the most powerful activities can be used in the session. Matching activities with objectives is refined in the next stage because sequencing requires putting things in order to achieve the greatest impact.

Sequence the Session.   The basic unit of design is the training sequence. Management and leadership training sessions are ordered or sequenced according to the stages in the experiential model of training. Although the development of a training sequence is governed to a large extent by the overall strategy, the design of the sequence may be strengthened by adhering to four principles of activity alternation (Lynton and Pareek, 1967):

Principle 1: Alternate Stimulation with Reflection.   Training sequences are something like great dramas; they provide tension but allow for relaxation. Continuous activity should not be regarded as the primary goal of design. Trainees need time to reflect on the activity and to make sense out of what is happening.

Principle 2: Alternate Personal Involvement with Safe Distance.   Training sequences need to be balanced between intense personal experience and opportunities to offer detached, analytical, and conceptual comments. Too much intense interaction may produce stress rather than learning, so it is important to alternate intensity with detachment.

Principle 3: Alternate Talking About Something with Practicing It.   Training sequences need to provide practice opportunities until improvement in the skill tapers off. Then time needs to be devoted to thinking and talking about those items of training that still present problems in order to prepare for the next practice session.

Principle 4: Alternate Individual Tasks with Group Processes.   Training sequences ought to have a balance between individual events and group events, in which the group activities provide stimulation and the individual activities allow participants to push themselves along as individuals.

Program designers seek to build training sequences that meet these requirements. Experience and research (*ASTD Competencies and Standards Project,* 1988) indicate that, to function well in this role, individuals have a critical need to know about theories of human learning and change, about organizational behavior, and about the methods and techniques of training and development. Program designers need special skills in the creation of models of performance, preparation of objectives, and writing for technical and instructional purposes. They also need to be able to use computers and to think creatively.

The theoretical foundation most frequently used by the program designer is experiential theory which includes a training sequence strategy consisting of four basic activities: the experience, explanatory information, an analysis, and a practice or rehearsal period. For best results, it is important that activities be placed in the order of the experiential sequence. An exercise that allows trainees to "feel" a problem and that acquaints them with the training issue occurs first; following the experience, theoretical information that explains why the problem occurred is presented. Third, the experience is analyzed using the theoretical information to show how it affects the trainees directly; finally, trainees practice and develop specific skills.

Each training session has a specified amount of time in which to prepare trainees to achieve each objective. Thus, a training day is divided into time blocks and time periods, and all the activities (experiences, information, analysis, and practice) are adjusted to fit the time blocks and time periods. Nevertheless, the activities are placed in the order of the experiential sequence: (1) supervise an experience that demonstrates a problem, (2) present theoretical information that explains why the problem occurred, (3) analyze the experience using the theory, and (4) practice a skill that helps solve the problem created during the experience.

Although the amount of time devoted to each activity usually varies from objective to objective, the order is quite constant, except for the practice period. Since the acquisition of a skill may depend on learning several elements before practice or rehearsal can proceed, the actual amount of time devoted to the accomplishment of a skill objective may vary considerably.

A training day is usually divided into 60- and 75-minute blocks of time. An exercise or experience may require 15 minutes, the presentation of information 5 minutes, and the processing or analysis of the experience 10 minutes. If a second segment were designed so that an additional 30 minutes were involved, two preparatory segments could be completed in the first time block. If a skill could be practiced following the two preparatory segments of time, the practice or rehearsal period could occur during the next 60- or 75-minute time block, with a break between.

The entire day is designed so that trainees proceed through the experiential sequence from experience to analysis as many times as necessary to prepare them to practice or rehearse required skills. Specific procedures have been developed for the conduct of practice sessions and for using video feedback to assure that skills are acquired and transferred back to the job. Most practice and video feedback activities can be accomplished in 60- and 75-minute time blocks, although the complexity of the skills being practiced affects the length of the practice session. Two or more 60-minute time blocks are often used for practice and video feedback.

Check the Agenda.   Once the sequence of events for the session has been determined, an agenda is created to formalize time blocks and to add the information that describes what will occur during each minute of the session. In developing the agenda, objectives are stated, the activities are listed, instructions are included, and specific times are assigned.

The program designer checks the agenda by laying out the entire training session according to small time periods. Each of the 60- and 75-minute blocks clearly shows the amount of time devoted to each of the training activities. The goal to be achieved by the trainer during each 5-, 10-, 15-, or 30-minute time period is stated. Even though a time period may consist of only a few minutes, a clearly stated goal allows the agenda to be evaluated in terms of how well the activities are sequenced and how well the entire day holds together.

As the program designer prepares the trainer's manual, all of the information for each small time period is placed on a separate page; hence, just as often as possible, each page in the trainer's manual is self-contained. With a detailed picture of what is to occur during every time period, it is possible to check the agenda for consistency, flow, relevance of activities to accomplish objectives, and the quality of the entire sequence.

A sample agenda is shown in Figure 6.2, on pages 102 and 103.

Prepare and Develop Materials.   As soon as the agenda has been checked and the training session appears ready for presentation, the next task is the creation of training materials. The trainer's guide, lecturettes and other ways of presenting information, instruments and items for supervising exercises, handouts, and audio, visual, and video materials must be prepared. The role of materials developer includes the competencies to complete this step in the overall design process. Even though the actual work of developing media products is shifted to the materials developer, the program designer retains ultimate control over the entire process.

In contrast to the program designer, who primarily uses an experiential theory base, the HRD materials developer uses primarily behavioral theory. Behavioral theory is grounded in the work of Skinner (1953) and relies greatly on using the learning environment to reinforce and support the desired change.

To implement behavioral theory, trainers generally do the following:

*   Induce trainees to engage in some behavior.
*   Positively reinforce them for performing the behavior.
*   Assist trainees in matching the new behavior with the positive consequences.
*   Help trainees to reinforce the new behavior in a variety of new situations.

Sequencing activities using this theory differ from those employed with the experiential theory. Trainees change by responding to pressures they feel from the environment; in this sense, the trainer manages the sequence of activities to achieve specific results. If something hurts, trainees avoid it; if something feels good, they tend to adopt it. Situations are created so that the pressures to which a person responds leads them in the direction of the planned change. A behavioral approach assumes that new behaviors are determined by the consequences that result from what a person does now. To produce change, it is necessary to provide situations that reinforce people for performing the behaviors you want. This reinforced behavior tends to eradicate old behaviors and properly institute new ones.

As can be seen, the theory of change used by the program designer influences the design of the training session. On the whole, the experiential model guides the overall development of the session, while the behavioral model is best used in the creation of specific media products that may be part of a training activity.

HRD MATERIALS DEVELOPER ROLE

HRD materials developer is the second major role associated with the developmental role cluster. This HRD specialist's primary task is producing materials, such as videotapes, films, audiotapes, graphics, computer software, and combinations of print and nonprint media, to help employees learn how to do their work more effectively. Although a materials developer may be considered by some as only a production person, such a view is not entirely accurate since the full cycle of design, production, and evaluation is involved in creating finished products.

❦ *Materials Design Process*

Design, as described, is the process of planning for change. To achieve change, several tasks are completed by the materials developer during the design stage, including establishing the need for the media products, writing objectives for the products, and selecting the appropriate format for the media products. Let's look at each of these activities as they relate to the design process.

Time Block: 9:30 A.M.–10:15 A.M.
  Objective: At the end of this time block, participants will recognize an "unknown" customer need by writing the name of a need portrayed in a role-playing situation. The need identified will correspond with the need listed in the manual as the one portrayed in the role play.

Time Period: 9:30 A.M.–9:35 A.M.
  Goal: To experience recognizing an unknown customer need.
  Instructions: 1. Show video vignette of customer waiting in line for a rather long period of time.
  2. Ask each trainee to write down a one-sentence statement of what the customer might need.
  3. Have each trainee pair off with another trainee and compare statements.
  4. Call participants up and post statement from the manual: "Need: To avoid being late for next appointment."

Time Period: 9:35 A.M.–9:50 A.M.
  Goal: To explain what happens when an unknown customer need is not recognized.
  Instructions: 1. Present short lecturette on topic of consequences of failures to recognize unknown customer needs.
  2. Outline:
      A. Customers bring their business to a company in order to satisfy a need.
        (1) To a bank to feel more secure by leaving money in a safe place or by getting money to ensure their safety in not losing something.
        (2) To a grocery store to relieve hunger or to socialize.
        (3) To a video rental store to find entertainment and relaxation.
      B. Customers, on the other hand, also sacrifice satisfaction of needs to do business with a company.
        (1) They may be inconvenienced and uncomfortable.
        (2) They could be taking care of other business.
        (3) They could be saving money by shopping elsewhere.

Time Period: 9:50 A.M.–10:00 A.M.
  Goal: To help trainees to identify needs that are not recognized (are unknown) in their own businesses.
  Instructions: 1. Divide participants into groups of six on the basis of similarity of business.
  2. Ask participants to reflect on the video vignette shown earlier and identity other possible unknown needs in the situation.
  3. Ask participants to make a list of situations that involve customers in their business in which the customers would have both an obvious and an unknown need. Identify and describe both types of needs.
  4. Call up participants and have each group make a short report about what they discovered.

FIGURE 6.2
Sample Agenda

Time Period: 10:00 A.M.–10:15 A.M.

Goal: To practice recognizing unknown or unstated needs in service settings.

Instructions: 1. Prepare trainees: Explain that they will be going through a series of incidents involving customers who have unstated needs. Their task will be to recognize quickly and name the unstated needs. Have them arrange paper and pencil for use in exercise.

2. Set the pattern: The skill of recognizing and articulating unstated needs involves three steps.
   A. Step 1: Focus on the situation and the customer.
   B. Step 2: Notice inconsistencies between what is ideal and what is happening.
   C. Step 3: Declare the inconsistency an unstated need and give it a name.

3. Demonstrate skill: Show video vignette of a woman with three small children approaching an employee seated behind a desk.
   A. Illustrate how to focus on the customer.
   B. Illustrate how to notice inconsistencies.
   C. Illustrate how to name the unstated need.

4. Form a habit (rehearsal period):
   A. Pair trainees and designate one the recognizer and the other the observer.
   B. Instruct the recognizer to watch the vignette to be shown and overtly go through the three steps in recognizing an unstated need.
   C. Instruct the observer to watch the recognizer and record on the checklist whether and how well he or she completed each step.
   D. Explain that the recognizer and the observer will compare their reactions to the vignette and what was happening as soon as the recognizer has identified and named the unstated need.
   E. Show the vignette.
   F. Have the recognizer and the observer confer about how well the steps were completed.
   G. Have recognizer and observer switch roles.
   H. Show the next vignette.
   I. Have new recognizer and observers confer.
   J. Follow the same process for two more vignettes.

5. Check on progress:
   A. Explain that three final vignettes will be shown and that each trainee will be expected to recognize the unstated need by completing a response form.
   B. The response forms will be scored for accuracy.
   C. Show vignettes and have trainees complete response forms.
   D. Display the unstated needs as identified in the manual and have the trainees score their own response forms; have trainees record their score and turn the forms in to the trainer.
   E. Entertain questions and answers, and make preparation for transition to the next time block.
   F. Summarize the objective and the steps in the skill.

Need for Materials. In most cases, the need for materials is defined by the program designer and given to the materials developer. The need is determined by studying the session plan and agenda to decide what types of materials would be helpful in producing the changes called for in the objectives. When this information is not provided by the program designer, however, the materials developer conducts a materials needs analysis that suggests how media materials might be used to improve employee performance. From this assessment, the materials are identified, a plan is developed, and the objectives are written to specify how such materials will be developed.

Write Objectives. The materials developer writes objectives for the materials that are to be produced. Objectives specify short-term enabling goals that are narrow and specific and relate directly to the materials to be created. The materials developer writes objectives that contain the four specific "A, B, C, D" elements noted previously, namely, audience, behavior, conditions, and degree. In a like manner, objectives are written in three specific areas that involve learning information (knowledge), acquiring skills, and developing attitudes (Edwards, 1977; Schmidt, Lutterodt, and Grafinger, 1985). An example of each may be helpful.

Information: At the conclusion of instruction, the trainee will be able to clarify the difference between a television close-up shot and medium shot by drawing the cropping lines of each shot on a stick figure person and place the cropping line within one-fourth inch of the standard.

Trainees demonstrate that they know the difference between the two television shots by drawing the cropping lines on the stick figure in the correct places; the tolerance given to receive credit is one-fourth inch. A multiple-choice test could have been used to determine whether the objective had been achieved, but in this objective, a drawing was used to see if learning had occurred.

Skills: At the conclusion of instruction, the trainee will be able to decrease the error rate in assembling a unit by refining the arm, wrist, and hand motion while doing the task until it is accurately performed 20 times in a row.

The physical skill involved in doing a task is measured in this objective by observing how well the task is performed. Focus is placed on the correct use of arm, wrist, and hand motion and being able to do the task accurately 20 times in a row. The test instrument becomes a checklist of the appropriate behaviors that should be displayed as the trainee repeats the task a number of times.

> *Attitude:* At the conclusion of instruction, the trainee will be able to communicate supportive information about the policy of operating equipment safely by instructing five colleagues on proper operating procedures. Acceptance of the policy will be shown by the trainees scoring at least 4 on a Likert scale of agreement with the policy.

The attitude toward the safety policy is measured by a self-report about how strongly the trainees agree with the safety policy of operating the equipment. Affective responses associated with attitudes are usually measured by self-report methods such as scales because feelings and emotions cannot be measured directly.

As noted in these examples, the objectives include a clear statement of the audience, the behavior to be shaped, and the conditions under which behaviors are performed; in addition, the objectives state the standards of acceptable behavior the trainees were to perform. In these examples, a variety of methods are used to determine whether the trainees achieve the objectives.

Selection of the Proper Format. With the objectives formally and clearly stated, the next step is to decide which format will be used to produce the training materials. Although objectives do not indicate the format to be used in presenting information, they do define what behavior is to be shaped. Thus, the selection of the medium comes after the objectives are clearly stated.

The materials developer considers five criteria when making the decision about which medium or a combination of media to use:

1. The size of the audience.
2. The characteristics of the learning outcomes.
3. The media attributes.
4. The ease of use of materials by instructors and trainees.
5. The budget allocated.

Definitions of each of these criteria are provided to show their importance to the media selection process.

Size of Audience. Sizes of audiences are measured by the number of participants involved, ranging from a single individual learning independently, to a small group of less than 20, to large groups in excess of thousands of people.

The choice is made on how well the individual materials can display information to the training audience.

Characteristics of Learning. The objectives, as stated, might require participants to perform different tasks such as learning factual information, making visual identifications, recalling principles, concepts, rules, or procedures, performing skills, or changing attitudes. Here again, each medium has some special strengths and weaknesses to help realize these goals.

Characteristics of Medium. Each medium is judged by its ability to display motion; to show color; to provide cues that are three dimensional; to demonstrate visual, print, or audio capabilities; to provide feedback to participants; and to be easy for trainer and participants to handle (Kemp, 1971; Sredl and Rothwell, 1987). The learning outcomes are reviewed in conjunction with these display attributes when the selection is made.

Ease of Use. Not all training approaches are user friendly. Some users are frightened by new technologies such as a computer, video equipment, or teleconferencing. If the medium is not user-friendly to both trainer and trainee, then the medium becomes a liability to the training process.

Costs. The final consideration is how costly the product is to produce; in short, can it be done within budget? Staying within budget limits is essential since a preferred medium may be rejected because of excessive production costs. Time is another cost that is subtle. Not all training materials can be developed and brought on line at the same rate. For example, it usually takes more time to produce a quality videotape than to create overhead transparencies.

To demonstrate how the materials developer uses these criteria to weigh the value of each medium, let's look at both an information and a skills objective and consider the selection process.

Objective 1: The first-line supervisor will be able to identify passive, aggressive, and assertive behaviors by correctly labeling the appropriate behavior displayed in three situations.

Objective 2: The first-line supervisor will be able to display passive, aggressive, and assertive behaviors by role playing three situations and achieve a mean score of seven on the observation form used to evaluate assertive behavior.

The selection process begins by studying the learning outcomes that are included in the objectives and identifying the behaviors that are to be shaped during the instruction. For the trainee to succeed in the first objective, he or she must (1) receive information that describes the characteristics of the three types of behavior, (2) be shown examples of the three interaction behaviors so that they can be properly classified, and (3) understand the consequences of the interaction style on others.

For the second objective to be achieved, the trainee must perform and display the three types of interaction behaviors. To properly do this, he or she must (4) identify nonverbal and verbal behaviors of each style, and (5) convincingly imitate them in a role-play situation. With the learning outcomes clearly stated, the material developer begins the selection process according to the five criteria just noted.

Group Size. The group includes 15 first-line supervisors; most media formats work well with groups this small.

Characteristics of Objectives. The objectives call for the first-line supervisors to learn factual information (outcomes 1 and 3), classify behavior (outcomes 2 and 4), and demonstrate a skill (outcome 5). Media formats that are well suited to achieve these objectives may include

• Written materials and overheads which are effective methods to present factual information.
• Video and film which are effective methods for presenting visual information so that the consequences of using them are understood and the skill of classifying the behavior can be shown.
• Role playing which is also an effective way to learn and practice skills.

Characteristics of Medium. To develop interpersonal behaviors, visual, aural, motion, and print materials are needed. These characteristics are found in both video and film which make them effective tools for showing "models" of behavior. The trainees can see examples and nonexamples of the desired behavior, they can see the consequences of acceptable and unacceptable behavior, and they can classify the consequences as the tape or film is viewed. Print materials in the form of handouts, diagrams, and overhead projections may also be used.

Ease of Use and Costs. The cost of producing video and film is higher than producing other materials, which means that care should be taken to arrange for a proper budget. If a proper budget cannot be obtained, alternative formats might include having the instructor model the three types of behavior in the training session; this is acceptable as long as consistency in demonstrating the behaviors can be maintained. To establish consistency, a single camera might be used to video tape the instructor role-playing training models; while the videotaped role play may be less costly than a professional production, it may not be as dramatic and realistic. In making this decision, the factor of time needs to be considered. If the time between production and when it is needed for use is short, then producing a professional model may not be possible. Consequently, the budget and time line determines which production format will be used to make modeling materials; can one afford a professional production, a videotape role play of the instructor, or a live role play by the instructor each time the visual material is displayed? Overheads or written material are relatively inexpensive and production schedules should be able to meet most budgets and time lines.

In summary, media materials are designed by planning what needs to be done, by writing proper objectives, and by making good judgments about the media format. The design phase determines what materials can be produced to achieve short-term media objectives.

❦ *Production Phase*

Producing training materials may be as simple as taking the plans prepared by the designer and making a few simple overhead transparencies or as complex as planning and producing detailed computer-based training materials. As the complexity of the production increases, more planning is required.

Three steps make up this phase, namely, visualization, scheduling, and completion. A basic plan for completing complex productions should include

1. Listing the set of events that need to be displayed.
2. Visualizing each event by sketching on 3 × 5 cards how the information might look when displayed for the learner (Kemp and Dayton, 1985).
3. Writing script material or information that explains the content on each card.
4. Noting on each frame of information the proper colors and, if applicable, sound effects or music that need to be used. Decisions are made by reviewing each frame and thinking whether any other graphic or support materials might increase the effectiveness of what is displayed.
5. Reviewing the sequence of events again to determine whether each concept is covered adequately and that the order of events flows smoothly from one incident to the next.

When the visualization step is completed, the second step, *scheduling* for the production, begins. Scheduling is accomplished by completing four tasks: (1) hiring personnel or specialists to do specific tasks, (2) purchasing the materials required to produce the product, (3) arranging for the facilities required, and (4) securing the equipment needed. Let's look at some of the material developer's considerations during this step.

Personnel.   Although a trainer can prepare some of the training materials on his or her own, usually a team of professionals is needed. Their services are generally used on an "as-needed" basis and for a fixed fee. Scheduling outside people often requires building in more lead time in order to prepare materials on schedule. It may take several months to arrange for a video production crew, actors, and equipment to complete the project.

Materials. Many of the items needed for production are inexpensive, such as transparencies, art supplies, and clip art, and are usually kept on hand for use as needed. Other specialty items are purchased as demand occurs. Materials developers maintain lists of vendors, suppliers, and places where production materials can be purchased so they can be acquired rapidly.

Facilities and Equipment. Facilities and equipment needed are not always available at the workplace. Labs, production facilities, or extended technologies are examples of capital outlays that are less expensive to lease than to own. In terms of planning, scheduling leased equipment increases the time required to complete materials production.

Once these resources are identified and scheduled, a time line is established for product completion. The paragraphs that follow illustrate the activities that might take place during the production stage of creating the overhead transparencies to use in presenting the concept of passive, aggressive, and assertive behavior.

Plan:	List behaviors that represent passive, aggressive, and assertive behavior.
Visualize:	List each action to be taken under the appropriate heading on a 3 × 5 card, using color graphics as shown in the three boxes that follow.

Passive Behavior

- **Let others control you.**
- **Retreat from situations.**
- **Feel victimized.**
- **Always feel apologetic.**
- **Pity yourself.**
- **Feel like crying.**
- **Often feel humiliated.**

(Blue background with yellow letters)

Each card contains the information to be placed on the overhead. The colors are described at the bottom. Graphics are added to the written text to show what will be displayed. The card not only lists the ideas, but it gives some sense of how to lay out the information when the product is completed.

AGGRESSIVE BEHAVIOR

- **Enjoy controlling others.**
- **Have dominating personality.**
- **Consider yourself superior to others.**
- **Act pushy, inconsiderate, and rude.**
- **Engage in punishing and being hostile to others.**

(Red background with black letters)

ASSERTIVE BEHAVIOR

- **Be in control of yourself.**
- **Be confident and relaxed.**
- **Be considerate of others.**
- **Be open and flexible to situations and others.**
- **Listen to others and work through solutions.**

(Yellow background with black letters)

Personnel:	List and hire any personnel that may be needed to produce the overhead transparency.
Materials:	Secure three types of color acetates, three transparency mounts, tape, and a file folder in which to store the finished transparencies.
Facilities:	Identify where the production work can be done, such as an office or graphics studio.
Equipment:	Locate computer and graphic packages and a heat-sensitive copy machine to make transparencies.

The materials developer can prepare this material in a relatively short time using equipment in a regular training department. More complex productions could not be done in this manner because they require additional scheduling of equipment, facilities, personnel, and talent.

EVALUATION

The final phase is materials evaluation. The value or utility of the materials produced are tested either in training sessions or in the marketplace. In many cases, media experts are used to evaluate the design and the resulting products. Content experts may also offer suggestions on potential improvements. In most cases, however, the materials prove their worth by whether or not trainees are able to show that they have mastered the objectives.

OTHER SKILLS

The skills of the HRD materials developer include taking ideas prepared by the program designer and turning them into instructional materials that can be used in actual training sessions. In addition, audio-visual and computer competence have emerged as some of the important skills related to this role. Increasingly, the visualization of materials is required in order to create effective training materials. The move is toward products that require the use of the computer as the delivery system in conjunction with interactive video.

The materials developer must have a good foundation in the basics of print media, since the development of nearly all materials starts with print copy. The creation of trainer guides, job aids, posters, and other support materials begins with a knowledge of such skills.

Using almost a sixth sense, the materials developer must purchase, maintain, and repair most of the equipment used in the delivery of training. Identifying and acquiring appropriate computer software is also one of the tasks of a materials developer. Much is expected of someone who takes a design prepared by another person and translates the words and ideas into audio and visual materials. For this reason, competent materials developers are much in demand in the human resource development marketplace.

SUMMARY

This chapter has described two of the major HRD roles, namely, those of program designer and HRD materials developer. They are grouped as a developmental roles cluster. The program designer plans the training program, creates the objectives and content of the training session, and evaluates its logical flow and internal consistency. The materials developer, on the other hand, plans the media that are best suited to supporting the training program, creates the products, and evaluates their potential impact on the training session.

The program designer provides the blueprint for what training should occur to achieve the desired outcomes, and the materials developer prepares relevant support materials. Together, they are a key part of the HRD function within an organization.

REFERENCES

AMERICAN SOCIETY OF TRAINING AND DEVELOPMENT, *ASTD Competency and Standards Project*. Alexandria, VA: ASTD, 1988.

CARNARIUS, STAN. "A New Approach to Designing Training Programs." *Training and Development Journal*, 35 (1981), pp. 40–44.

CHISHOLM, MARGARET, AND DONALD P. ELY. *Media Personnel in Education: A Competency Approach*. Englewood Cliffs, NJ: Prentice Hall, 1976.

EDWARDS, C. H. *A Systematic Approach to Instructional Design*. Champaign, IL: Stripes, 1977.

KEMP, JERROLD. "Which Medium?" *Audio Visual Instruction*, 21 (1971), pp. 32–36.

KEMP, JERROLD, AND DEANE K. DAYTON. *Planning & Producing Instructional Media*, 5th ed. New York: Harper & Row, 1985.

KOLB, DAVID A., I. RUBIN, AND J. MCINTYRE. *Organizational Psychology: A Book of Readings*, 2nd ed. Englewood Cliffs, NJ: Prentice Hall, 1974.

MILLS, GORDON E., AND R. WAYNE PACE. "Providing Practice for Skill Development." *Training and Development Journal*, 42 (1988), pp. 36–38.

LYNTON, ROLF P., AND UDAI PAREEK. *Training for Development*. Homewood, IL: Richard D. Irwin, 1967.

PFEIFFER, J. W., AND J. E. JONES. *Reference Guides to Handbooks and Annual*. San Diego, CA: University Associates, 1988.

SCHMIDT, R., S. A. LUTTERODT, AND D. J. GRAFINGER. *Classifying Learning Objectives*. Columbia, MD: G. P. Courseware, 1985.

SKINNER, B. F. *Science and Human Behavior*. New York: Macmillan, 1953.

SREDL, HENRY, AND WILLIAM J. ROTHWELL. *Professional Training Roles and Competencies*. Amherst, MA: HRD Press, 1987.

CHAPTER 7

❦ ❦

Instrumental Roles

INTRODUCTION

In Aesop's fable of the Lion and the Mouse, the King of the Jungle spares the tiny Mouse's life on the promise that he will return the kindness sometime in the future. The Lion is later trapped by hunters, and the Mouse gnaws away the rope that binds the King of Beasts, freeing the Lion and paying the debt. The skills of the tiny Mouse were perfectly suited to completing the task at hand, loosening the bond that held the mighty Lion captive. In short, the Mouse was able to produce a unique change in circumstances that benefited the Lion greatly.

In a similar sense, those who are involved in carrying out the cluster of instrumental roles produce change using specialized skills. The instructor/facilitator supervises learning activities to bring about positive changes in individuals. The organization change agent seeks to facilitate adjustments among interdependent work groups, such as task groups, departments, divisions, or regional centers, in order to help them operate more effectively. The marketer, on the other hand, seeks to influence individuals who might use the products or services of the HRD function. Each role differs in perspective and serves a different audience, but each one is committed in a similar way to improving an aspect of the organization. Their skills, like those of the tiny Mouse of the fable, are nicely suited to produce changes that enable the organization to benefit from them.

Three HRD roles share the common goal of being instrumental in that they each attempt to produce change in a special way and with a special group: other individuals (instructor/facilitator role), the organization (organization change agent role), and the marketplace (marketer role). The instructor attempts to affect the way in which individuals think, feel, and behave; the organization change agent attempts to influence the way in which change occurs in the larger system or organization; and the marketer attempts to influence the way in which programs are made available to other members of the organization, and on occasion to people outside the organization.

THE THREE INSTRUMENTAL ROLES

- **Instructor/facilitator**
- **Organization change agent**
- **Marketer**

❦ *Value*

The instrumental roles cluster represents some of the most visible activities in the profession of HRD. The instructor occupies an outfront position, facilitating the learning process in training programs by influencing individuals, the change agent seeks to facilitate changes that might affect everyone in the system, and the marketer by frequent exposure and regular contact with potential clients in the organization and with many outside the organization, seeks to encourage clients to purchase and use appropriate training materials. A clear sense of the meaning and methods of the instrumental role cluster provides a look at some of the most critical and sensitive roles performed by HRD specialists. Many career decisions are made on how well a person executes the skills and competencies associated with these roles.

❦ *Chapter Organization*

In this chapter, the process of change—the underlying theory common to the instrumental roles—is explained, the roles in the instrumental cluster are defined and characterized, their basic competencies and skills are identified, and some key products associated with the roles are described.

❦ *Learning Objectives*

After studying this chapter, you should be able to:

1. List, define, and describe the attributes of the three roles included in the instrumental role cluster.
2. Recognize, organize according to role, and explain most of the key competencies and skills of the three roles of the instrumental cluster.
3. Identify, describe, and explain products that result from performing roles that are part of the instrumental cluster.

CHANGE: THE GOAL OF INSTRUMENTAL ROLES

The impelling concept of *change* is common to the roles of the instrumental cluster. The idea of change is widely accepted as meaning some movement from one state to another. Schein (1969) describes three stages in the change process (see Figure 7.1). For change to occur smoothly, it is important to define the initial state from which change is to occur, since it may not be possible to determine whether change has occurred if we do not know where we started.

In change situations, also, an intermediate state always occurs—some position between the original starting state and the terminal ending state. The intermediate state may be unsettling because it usually involves feelings of instability and inconsistency in the person, the organization, or the marketplace. People seem to experience high levels of emotional stress and a sense that conflict exists. They seem to lose control, but they want control over their lives, which often results in a great deal of energy expenditure that lacks direction.

Since change is basic to all of the roles in the instrumental cluster, the methods and mechanisms for creating motivation to change (unfreezing), developing new responses (changing), and stabilizing and integrating the new responses (refreezing) are part of each of the roles. Although the three instrumental roles may use different ways to produce change, the change process itself underlies and explains what happens as the roles are performed.

FIGURE 7.1
The Process of Change

Stage 1 Unfreezing (creating motivation to change)	Stage 2 Changing (developing new responses)	Stage 3 Refreezing (stabilizing and integrating changes)

The instructor/facilitator role seeks to bring about change in organization members, the organization change agent role seeks to bring about change in the structure and environment of the organization, and the marketer role seeks to bring about change in the decisions of clients, whether inside the organization or outside the organization. Instructors need to unfreeze, change, and refreeze the minds and behavior of trainees, whereas the organization change agent and the marketer must unfreeze, change, and refreeze organization systems and clients.

Ries and Trout (1986) add an interesting dimension to the idea of change with what they call "positioning." They explain that positioning has to do with any activity that involves "influencing the minds of other people" (p. 2). Instructing, changing organizational behavior, and marketing services and products all involve influencing the minds of others. Positioning, the authors argue, is important in a society in which "overcommunication" is occurring. When overcommunication takes places, "the mind, as a defense against the volume of today's communications, screens and rejects much of the information offered it" (p. 6). To overcome the assault of information on the mind, instructors, organization change agents, and marketers must position their ideas in the minds of their clients. Let us look at how these three roles function.

INSTRUCTOR/FACILITATOR ROLE

The instructor/facilitator positions ideas and seeks to help trainees to learn and behave in ways that make them more productive. The instructor/facilitator brings about change by presenting information, directing learning experiences, and managing group discussions and processes.

At least five different philosophies of change (Pace and Faules, 1989) affect an instructor's decisions about the change process and what methods to use.

Rational theory (Coombs, Avila, and Purkey 1976; Ellis and Harper, 1975) suggests that people behave as a result of what they believe. To achieve change, the instructor engages trainees in a dialogue that challenges beliefs that keep them from changing or inculcates beliefs that facilitate appropriate changes.

Behavioral theory (Bandura, 1969) is based on the premise that trainees learn from the consequences of their actions. The instructor/facilitator demonstrates and provides models of the behavior to be acquired and reinforces those specific behaviors during the training session.

Achievement theory (McClelland, 1953) brings about change by focusing on the aspirations of trainees. Achievement theory assumes that people want to be successful. Individuals who have the strongest disposition toward doing things better also have the highest probability of making changes in their lives.

Thus, the instructor/facilitator helps trainees to focus persistently on goals they would like to achieve.

Role/positional theory (Hill, 1983) is based on the premise that a person's behavior is largely determined by the roles he or she enacts in organizations and society. Behavior is shaped by the demands, expectations, and rules of others and what actions are acceptable under certain circumstances. The instructor/facilitator creates situations that allow and encourage trainees to discover what expectations are hindering changes in their behavior. As a result, trainees decide to make appropriate changes in their behaviors.

Experiential theory (Kolb, 1974) is based on the premise that people are more likely to believe their own experience than those of other people. People change their behavior by examining their current beliefs in light of their reactions to situations in which they feel some significant emotional response. By analyzing what is happening to them, trainees develop a personal explanation for their reactions and make a conscious effort to try alternative ways of behaving in other settings.

Of these five theories, experiential methods are used quite frequently, and they can be used to illustrate behaviors and activities in which the instructor/facilitator engages to bring about change. Using the experiential perspective, four types of activities can be identified and described: supervising experiences, presenting information, facilitating analysis, and directing practice.

THE FOUR EXPERIENTIAL ACTIVITIES

- **Supervising experiences**
- **Presenting information**
- **Facilitating analysis**
- **Directing practice**

❧ *Supervising Experiences*

The most common type of activity involved in experiential training is called a "structured experience." An experience is some type of event that reveals a problem and creates an emotional response on the part of participants. Experiences are "structured" when they are constructed in advance and set in motion by a facilitator. The structured experience has a boundary that separates the experience itself from the discussion or analysis of the experience. Structured experiences may involve solving puzzles, creating things and designs, completing inventories, interacting with people, and completing action assignments, among many other things.

An experience is an encounter with some aspect of reality that evokes an emotional response. Taking a field trip to a new and exotic site may evoke an emotional response in a person, as might participating in a trust walk in which a person is blindfolded and led through a maze of unpredictable events, or hiking in the mountains. All those activities meet the conditions of an experience.

For purposes of bringing about behavior change in human resource development, experiential learning implies imposing a degree of structure on the process to allow participants to generalize and recognize patterns and skills. The phrase *structured experience* has been coined to refer to this special type of experience.

Middleman and Goldberg (1972) describe a structured experience as a closed system deliberately constructed and set in motion by the facilitator. The experience might consist of simple or complex activities in which participants actually do something. It might take the form of role playing or making an object. It could involve completing a questionnaire or inventory. Some structured experiences have participants solve puzzles, analyze problems, create designs, engage in activities like brainstorming, and participate in simulations.

Pace (1977) identified 36 different exercises for teaching concepts in organizational communication, all of which have been used in training sessions over the years.

One of the most common sources of structured experiences is the Pfeiffer and Jones handbooks for human relations training and for group facilitators. The *Reference Guide* (Pfeiffer, 1988) indicates that the contents of 27 books of exercises are classified in this edition. The structured experiences are classified according to six categories: *personal,* including self-disclosure, feelings, values, life and career planning; *communication,* including oral and nonverbal awareness, trust, listening, interviewing, and assertion; *group characteristics,* including process, power, styles, motivation, leadership, stereotyping; *task behavior,* including problem solving, generating alternatives, feedback, competition, collaboration, conflict, and consensus; *organizations,* including diagnosis, team building, decision making, and consultation skills; and *facilitating learning,* including getting acquainted, forming subgroups, expectations, blocks to learning, building trust, openness, energizers, evaluating group process, facilitator skills, and closure.

Casse (1981) has prepared a unique manual for international/intercultural trainers that includes 17 workshops with exercises and materials to prepare individuals for crossing cultures. The entire book illustrates the use of structured experiences in experiential learning.

Each structured experience should include a statement of the goals of the exercise, the materials necessary to supervise it, the physical setting and group size for which it is best suited, the process or step-by-step procedures and amount of time required to complete the exercise, and copies of worksheets, questionnaires, scales, or tests used in the exercise (Grove, 1976).

Figure 7.2, on pages 120 through 122, illustrates how a structured experience is designed and supervised. The next step in the experiential process is the presentation of explanatory information or theory that helps participants to understand *why* problems in communication occurred.

❦ *Presenting Information*

Instructors/facilitators frequently present or arrange for the presentation of information. If they present the information themselves, the process is usually accomplished by means of a lecture or experiential lecturette. A lecture is a formal presentation of theory that explains why, for example, the problem surfaced in the experiment, whereas an experiential lecturette combines pictorial, visual elements and involves participants in the learning process. Information may also be presented by means of essays, programmed materials, cases, diagrams, charts, pictures, slides, and videotapes and motion pictures.

This stage in the model of experiential training is designed to provide the theory and explanations to help understand what happened during the experience and to lay the foundation for analyzing the exercise. There are usually three aspects of a presentation that are important in human resource development:

1. The form or method in which the presentation is made
2. The style of the presenter
3. The supporting equipment and materials used

❦ *Form or Method*

Three general categories of form or method are usually used: (1) oral methods, (2) written methods, and (3) audio-visual methods.

Oral Methods. The most common method for making short oral presentations of theory, ten minutes or less, is the *lecture*. It is possible to illustrate the three aspects of presenting information using the lecture form as an example.

Form. The lecture uses a one-person talking-to-an-audience format. The trainer talks relatively continuously, except for some involvement of the audience or trainees in the presentation through reactions, answering questions, or asking questions, with the information becoming available to the trainees following some structure or system.

Goal: To demonstrate that the critical act of communication is assigning meaning or significance to people, objects, and events.

Group Size: Minimum of five individuals, with one to serve as communicator and the others to serve as communicatees.

Time Required: About 45 minutes.

Materials/Equipment Needed: 1. A master five-piece puzzle, each piece of it a different color, prepared by reproducing the figures shown here, on acetate, cardboard, masonite, plywood, or whatever material you have available

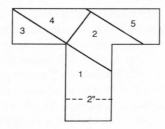
FRACTURED "T" PUZZLE

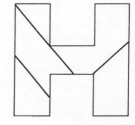
FRACTURED "H" PUZZLE

2. Copies of the master puzzle for audience members (at least one copy for each six persons), with pieces having a different color combination from that of the master set
3. A 2' × 3' cardboard screen
4. A small table on which to put the puzzle and screen
5. A chair for the communicator
6. Student desks or tables and chairs for the communicatees

Physical Setting: The communicator is seated at the table, behind the screen, with the completed puzzle in front of him or her; the communicatees are seated at student desks or tables with scrambled pieces of the puzzle in front of them.

Procedure: 1. Facilitator explains to the group that he or she would like to conduct an exercise that demonstrates a major characteristic of communication.

FIGURE 7.2
The Fractured Puzzle Exercise

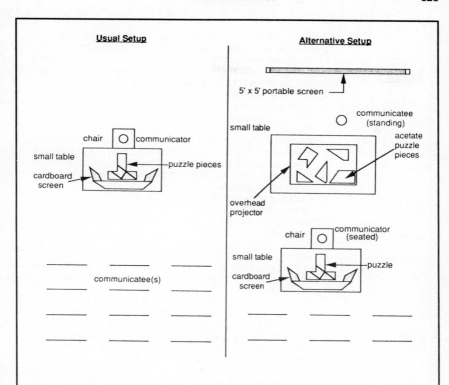

2. Explain that to perform the demonstration, it will be necessary to select a person whom others consider to be a reasonably effective communicator.
3. Have the person selected, or who volunteers, take a seat at the front of the room at the table on which the small cardboard screen has been placed between the volunteer and the group. The communicator and the group should be able to hear each other but they should not be able to see each another.
4. Distribute copies of the puzzle to communicatees, either singly or in groups, depending upon the number of puzzles available. If in groups, one person is assigned to work with the pieces while the others observe quietly. The five pieces of the puzzle should be gently tossed onto the table in front of the individual, with instructions to remove the rubber band holding them together and wait for instructions.

5. The volunteer communicator is given the five pieces of another, master, set, identical in size and shape, but having a different color combination. The communicator's set should be assembled behind the screen out of view of the group, but in front of the communicator, by the trainer.

6. Explain the nature of the problem to the communicator and communicatees: Communicatees are to play the role of machine operators who have been given the parts of a new machine, but with no instructions on how to assemble it. The communicator is to play the role of a manager whose job it is to explain to the operators how to assemble the machine. The manager has an assembled machine in front of him or her, made of pieces which are the same size and shape as those which the operators have.

7. Explain that the manager may say anything he or she wishes to the operators, but they may *not* talk back to him, ask questions, or make any audible sounds during his or her explanation.

8. As the manager gives instructions, simply monitor the operators for violations of the *no talking or audible reacting* rules and for examples of misinterpretations of what the manager says on the part of operators as they attempt to assemble machines.

9. Allow the manager to complete his or her instructions on how to assemble the machine, which may take 15 minutes or less. As soon as the manager has completed giving instructions, ask everyone to "freeze" (not to move puzzle pieces any further) while the manager walks around and observes the results of his or her instructions. Ask the manager to look for information (called feedback) about the results of his or her instructions and anything that might be useful in modifying his or her instructions.

10. Interview the manager for a few minutes about what he or she observed. Attempt to draw out and highlight some of the sources of misinterpretation that occurred, such as assuming that all the pieces were the same color, using unfamiliar or complex terminology, giving instructions too rapidly, or neglecting to explain the ultimate objective of his or her instructions—to assemble the shape that looks like the shape of his or her puzzle (a block T or F or H). Relate, whenever possible, the reactions and behavior of the operators to the main idea that assigning meaning is the key feature of communication.

The structure can usually be portrayed in the form of an outline of the main and supporting ideas. By following an outline somewhat carefully, the trainer increases the likelihood that the trainees will make sense out of the flow of ideas. The outline also helps to ensure that the presenter will not exceed the time allocated in the design for the lecture.

Style. For the period of the presentation, it is important that the presenter exhibit five characteristics of effective, forceful presentational style: (1) presence, (2) urgency, (3) consistency, (4) directness, and (5) animation.

(1) Presence is revealed through controlled confidence. This implies that you should maintain a "bold front" even in the face of unavoidable, spontaneous, and inconsequential "errors." Move ahead unfazed an occasional shortcoming surfaces. Show confidence in spite of your fear and trembling; it is much more apparent to you than it is to your audience.

(2) Urgency represents a quiet intensity that indicates a genuine enthusiasm for the ideas and information being presented. Your manner must reveal that the theory is important to both you and the trainees in understanding what is happening. To find the most acceptable level of enthusiasm, exaggerate beyond what you think seems to express the appropriate degree of urgency. You may find that you have still not externalized your enthusiasm adequately.

(3) Consistency means that your vocal tones and your physical movements and actions are complementary with the meaning of the words you are using. Where events are gigantic, your voice must sound enormous and your movements should indicate a size comparable to the events. If the idea is serious, let your voice and movements portray the seriousness.

(4) Directness is accomplished by making eye contact as you talk with each member of the training session, one at a time and in a positive manner. When you speak to someone, orient your body toward them; do not talk over your shoulder to someone, but face each person directly. Take each member of the audience into account throughout the presentation, not at the same time, but in an orderly fashion.

(5) Animation represents giving emphasis to ideas. This is accomplished by behaving in a physically active way by gesturing and punctuating points with your entire body. Dramatize your meanings with bodily action to give nonverbal support to your words. Be alert, however, to avoid painful and unpleasant extremes in force, loudness, and explosiveness. Maintain a range in both your vocal sounds and your physical actions.

Supporting Materials and Equipment. There are two common types of supporting materials and equipment: (1) the flip chart with newsprint and (2) the overhead projector with transparencies.

(1) The flip chart with newsprint is the most reliable unit of support a presenter can have. It can be taken most places. It operates without electricity and bulbs. Materials can be portrayed on it so that they can be seen from all parts of the room. It can be used with spontaneity or with advanced planning.

A disadvantage of the flip chart is that once you write on a sheet of newsprint, it must be flipped over the back of the stand, out of sight of the trainees. This disadvantage can be overcome by posting the used sheets on the walls of the training room. This might be time consuming, but usually worth it, and there is usually only a limited amount of wall space. You might use several flip charts, however, which could provide a writing area as large as most chalkboards.

In using a flip chart and newsprint effectively, it is important to plan the development of each sheet. The information on the sheets should develop in a logical manner and one that parallels the lecture. Make certain that the colors of felt pens are easily seen in the room. Avoid cluttering the materials on each sheet, but use diagrams and sketches for simplicity and quick grasp of ideas, and because they give trainees something to do with their minds during the presentation.

The flip chart should be placed so that the audience can see it easily. This may take some rearrangement in rooms of unusual shapes and sizes, but make certain that the charts can be seen easily from the furthest chair. Usually, angle the flip chart approximately 20 degrees toward yourself and at a 45-degree angle to the audience, off to one side. The overhead projector is located at an angle on the other side of the room.

(2) The overhead projector with transparencies is the second most popular unit of equipment and materials used by trainers. Transparencies used on an overhead projector have several advantages. They have a very high visual impact, since all types of pictures, sketches, models, diagrams, and charts can be translated on to transparencies. Since transparencies must be made ahead of time, they give structure and order to the presentation as well as visual impact.

Most important for the trainer during the training process itself is that he or she maintains control over what trainees will see and when they will see it. Elements of suspense and surprise can be built into the presentation. Problems can be presented for analysis; then the answers can be shown. There is also a cost saving in the use of transparencies. Puzzles, instructions, inventories, and other elements of exercises can be displayed for trainees without making copies for everyone.

The most common disadvantage of the overhead projector and transparencies is that the information cannot be kept in front of the trainees for the whole session. Unlike a sheet of newsprint, a transparency cannot be posted on the wall for trainees to study later. Thus, transparencies must have minimal information on them and maximum illustrative value. That is one reason why cartoons are shown on transparencies; the cartoon develops and makes its point and does not need to be studied later.

In making transparencies, use one transparency for each idea. Use print that is about one-fourth inch high; do not use ordinary typed copy. Use about four words per line and about six lines per transparency.

Other Presentational Forms.   If you expand the presentation to include more than one person and go beyond the lecture, other forms for presenting information orally are possible. They include the dialogue or interview, the colloquy or panel, and the symposium.

Written Methods. The most common way to present information in a training session in written form is through the *short essay*. In its most frequently used form, the short essay consists essentially of a one or two page explanation of a theoretical or philosophical point. The short essay is instructional or informational in intent and is written directly and systematically. The main ideas are highlighted in headings and the paragraphs are relatively short.

Beyond the short essay, occasionally articles and books are assigned as readings in a training session, but they are usually prereadings to be completed before attending the training session. From time to time, programmed materials are used in training, but the tendency is to use computer programs for independent study and practice rather than to use them in a classroom setting.

Audio-Visual Methods. Often, sometimes too often, information is presented in training sessions by means of sound filmstrips, slide tapes, motion pictures, and videotapes. A speaker is filmed and the tape is shown to the trainees. Some exciting speakers can have their messages distributed to large numbers of people using contemporary videotapes, videodisks, and motion pictures.

The design and development of mediated materials for presentation and demonstration are discussed in Chapter 6 and other sources, which should be consulted for details. For purposes of design of a training session, the critical question to answer concerns the relative cost and effectiveness of having a live presenter versus a presenter available on film or video.

❦ Facilitating Analysis

To set the stage for analysis of the experience and to get the most out of the process, participants should be encouraged to

1. Get involved in the exercise and participate with enthusiasm in the activities.
2. Think consciously about the relevance of the exercise to the theory and information presented for use in the analysis phase.
3. Think about and make notes about what kinds of generalizations might be developed from the exercise and what specific skills might be identified that could be practiced.

The third activity in the experiential training process is designed to assist trainees to relate the theory and information to what happened during the exercise. Analysis is a discovery activity in which participants recognize a potential difference between how they responded and other, possibly more effective ways of handling the situation. If the exercise produced the appropriately intense emotional reaction to what happened, then participants will be prepared to engage in analysis. They will want to discover why things happened and what they can do about them.

From a trainer's point of view, two aspects of analysis must be designed: the form in which the analysis will occur and the questions that comprise and facilitate the process.

Forms of Analysis. Analysis is usually conducted either privately and individually or publicly and in groups.

Individual. Individual analysis takes place by having participants write private entries in a private journal. The journal is maintained throughout the training session, with interpretive comments written at an appropriate time after both the exercise and the information have been experienced. Journal entries should describe what the exercise means in terms of the theory and the objectives of the session.

Group. Group analysis occurs in about four different formats: (1) buzz groups, (2) Phillips 66, (3) fishbowls, and (4) ring responses.

(1) With buzz groups, participants are divided into small groups of three individuals. A system for creating the groups should be written into the design. It can be done by counting off according to the number of groups needed; with a session of 24 trainees, eight groups of 3 individuals would be needed. Thus, have trainees count to eight; then, all of the one's constitute a group, all of the two's, all of the three's, and so forth. The analysis of the exercise takes place in the small group, after which a member of the group may report to the larger group.

(2) With Phillips 66, participants are divided into groups of six individuals who are given six minutes (6–6) to discuss the exercise. Because of the slightly larger size, 66 groups often select a leader and a recorder who keeps a list of the key points of analysis and reports to the larger group.

(3) With the fishbowl format, participants are arranged in a double circle— half inside and half outside: the inner group analyzes the exercise while the outer group listens; then the groups change places. A member of the outer group who would like to comment must tap the shoulder of a member of the inner group and change places with the inner person while the comment is made; after making the comment, the individuals return to their respective positions in the inner and outer groups.

(4) With the ring response, participants are divided into small groups of three or four; analysis of the exercise is lead by the facilitator working with one of the small groups. As the analysis warms up, the facilitator enlarges the group

involved in the analysis by incorporating members of another group in the process. Eventually, the facilitator may involve all members of the training session or return the analysis to the small groups.

Following small-group analysis, the trainer usually assembles (calls up) the entire group and facilitates a large group analysis designed to formulate workable generalizations and identify specific skills. The next step in the experiential process is to have participants engage in the practice of the skills identified.

This is a period of time devoted to having participants share what they saw and how they felt during the experience in light of the explanatory theory. The facilitator's task is to help participants make available to other members of the session what happened to them at both the intellectual and the emotional levels of experience. The instructor/facilitator must encourage individuals to report what happened to them, make a record of the reactions, and engage everyone in analyzing what happened. Skill in facilitating group interaction is particularly important at this stage. Part of this stage is, also, to help participants relate what was gained in the training session to life back on the job. One major outcome of this stage is the identification and description of specific skills that may be useful and even critical to improved job performance in their own work.

❦ *Directing Practice*

The final activity in the experiential process is designed to help trainees apply what has been learned, specifically the knowledge gained, attitudes developed, and skills acquired, to the work environment. The main goal of the instructor/facilitator is to help everyone become comfortable with the changes that have occurred—to refreeze. This is accomplished in part by directed practice sessions that help trainees to form habits and to set skills related to a particular job. In addition, feedback periods involving the replay of video recordings of participants performing the skills can be extremely helpful in fixing skills so that they do transfer back to the workplace. Procedures for conducting video feedback and practice sessions should be planned and executed carefully (Mills and Pace, 1988).

The fourth stage in the experiential training process is to direct participants in the process of practicing or rehearsing skills. The main purpose is to prepare employees to use the skills on the job. Although the practice session occurs in the training setting, it is designed to prepare individuals to transfer the skills to their work.

Research by Mills and Pace (1988) indicates that skills practice is essential to the acquisition of even simple behaviors.

Four standard steps have been identified through which an effective practice session proceeds (Mills and Pace, 1988):

Prepare the trainees for practice.   Trainees need to feel that the skill or skills can be acquired with some reasonable degree of effort and that the trainer is interested in helping the trainees to develop skills that will make them more effective. This step involves motivating trainees to want to learn the skill by relating it to the real work setting. Put the trainees at ease, mention the name of the skill, comment on the purpose of the skill, and relate the skill to the trainees' past experience. Each of these elements must be designed into the training manual.

Set the pattern or sequence.   For simple skills, steps in completing the skill should be presented in some sequence. Explain and demonstrate the pattern or sequence for doing the skill one step at a time. Focus on the main steps and key points. Avoid giving too much information at one time. Use simple, direct language. Demonstrate how the skill is to be performed. Highlight those behaviors that are essential to executing the skill well. Set a high standard. As the trainees watch, you will be serving as a behavior model. The performance you give not only demonstrates how to do the skill but it also represents how to do it well.

When the skills are more complex, the evidence (Jeffery, 1976; MacKay, 1981) suggests that mental traces or patterns must be established prior to learning meaningful motor skills. That is, mental rehearsal must precede the motor development of skills. With communication skills, especially, some well-established ways of behaving have already been formed. Learning, in those cases, is as much an *unlearning* process as it is a direct learning one. For individuals to display key actions effectively and overcome "old" behaviors, it is essential that the rehearsal of motor, physical skills be preceded by visualization and mental rehearsal.

Begin to form a habit.   During this step, the habit of behaving as directed is developed. Habits are formed by performing the skill, by doing it over and over. This is often called physical rehearsal. As trainees perform the skill and repeat it in rehearsal, the trainer corrects errors and omissions as the trainees make them. Rather than criticize trainees, the trainer should show them how to perform the skill more accurately. A correction, in this context, is actually more training and is usually accepted more eagerly than when it is thought of as criticism. The best way to make changes is to have the trainees identify them and make adjustments. Have trainees tell you how and why the skill is done a particular way. If the trainees are unable to identify what needs to be corrected, then make a suggestion in the form of additional instructions. Avoid correcting too frequently. Exercise restraint in correcting during actual rehearsal.

Check how well the skill has been acquired.   Allow trainees to perform the skill without your help. Encourage them to ask questions about performing the skill. No matter how simple the question appears, respond to it with instructions that are serious and respectful. Check the trainees' performances as they do them alone but gradually taper off as their abilities to perform the skill increase. Finally, if trainees are doing well, tell them.

Some of the skills and competencies of an instructor/facilitator are also employed by the organization change agent and the marketer, but each has a unique mission within the cluster of instrumental roles.

ORGANIZATION CHANGE AGENT ROLE

The focal point of activity for the organization change agent is the system itself. This role combines elements of organizational development (OD) with basic individual behavior change. Hellriegel, Slocum, and Woodman (1986) point out that organizational change represents an attempt to improve the functioning of groups, departments, and the entire organization, as well as to change the behavioral patterns of individuals within the organization. They explain that "an organization may not be able to change its adaptation strategy for reacting to its relevant environment unless its members behave differently in their relationships with one another and to their jobs" (p. 577). The organizational change agent provides the expertise, competencies, and skills to achieve the goals of improving group, department, and system functioning.

Organizational change agents tend to use methods of change that affect three elements of organizations: interpersonal relations and processes, tasks and technology, and organizational structure. The methods bear on affecting relations, technology, and structure rather than individual knowledge, attitudes, and skills. The organizational change agent role incorporates into the HRD function relational, technological, and structural change skills that complement the competencies of other roles (e.g., instructor/facilitator) that focus more on individual change.

**ORGANIZATION CHANGE AGENT FACILITATES
SYSTEM CHANGES BY:**

Affecting	*Rather Than*
Relationships	**Knowledge**
Technology	**Attitudes**
Structure	**Skills**

❦ *Interpersonal Relations and Processes*

Three general approaches, with wide variations in application, that seek to affect interpersonal relations and processes in an organization are survey feedback, team building, and third-party interventions. Each of these approaches has unique features and may contribute in different ways to changes in interpersonal relations in an organization.

Survey Feedback.   This method involves gathering questionnaire or interview data and reporting the results back to relevant groups in the organization. The groups of employees are helped to understand the data, and then they are guided to develop action plans to resolve problems revealed by the data (Nadler, 1977). Some specific techniques related to this method were covered previously in Chapter 5.

Team Building.   This method involves a process in which complete working groups—all those people who report to a common superordinate, whose work connects them with each other, and who must have at least a minimal degree of coordination, common planning, shared goals, and shared decision making in order for them to get work done—analyze how they work together (Dyer, 1977). Team building usually begins with a block of time, one to three days, devoted to helping the working group look at how it is currently functioning. The initial meeting should be held away from the work site, primarily to ensure that team members are available to give their full time and attention to the task.

A team-building program tends to follow a problem-solving cycle. Someone feels that a problem exists, data are gathered to describe the problem, identify causes, and prioritize problem-related issues that can be dealt with during team-building meetings. During this analysis period, underlying factors such as work rules or job assignments are identified. Out of the analysis, an agenda is created.

During the early team-building phases, the consultant (a person who comes

---

THREE APPROACHES TO INTERPERSONAL RELATIONS AND PROCESSES

- **Survey feedback (passive)**
- **Team building (active)**
- **Third-party interventions (consultative)**

from outside the work group to facilitate the analysis) plays a more active role in analysis and solution identification. As the final phase nears its end, the manager assumes the more customary role of group leader and the consultant becomes more a group observer and facilitator. The manager takes the issues identified earlier and treats them as problems to be solved, while the consultant supports the manager's efforts by helping the group look at the way it functions in solving the problems. If the group gets bogged down or ram-rodded into making decisions to which group members are not committed, the consultant intervenes and directs the group to examine what has happened. In this way, the consultant helps group members learn to handle their own problems.

Third-Party Interventions. Third-party intervention is a method designed primarily to reduce interpersonal conflict through the use of a mediator. The third person attempts to foster a climate of neutrality and objectivity during the training exercise. Frost and Wilmot (1978) identify three competencies needed by third-party consultants: sufficient analytical ability to understand the processes of conflict, a communication style appropriate to the interventionist role, and tactical skills and choices that facilitate the management of the conflict (pp. 151–152). Nevertheless, they caution that when a third party gets involved, group relations are either strengthened or weakened, but are not likely to remain the same.

Nearly all strategies used in conflict management are based on a philosophy of *integrative decision making* (Filley, 1975; Pace, 1983; Walton, 1969; Frost and Wilmot, 1978). The philosophy of IDM is to handle conflict by reaching consensus. The consensus development process is pursued by resolving differences in thinking, feeling, and behaving and incorporating the points of view of all parties into the decision or plans. Cooperative effort is facilitated by finding, isolating, and clarifying areas of agreement and disagreement among group members, and thus systematically narrowing the area of difference and enlarging the area of acceptability (Pace, Peterson, and Burnett, 1979).

❦ Tasks and Technology

Rather than focusing on interpersonal relations, some methods are used to initiate changes in the way in which work is done. These are referred to as technological methods, those that seek to bring about changes in jobs and work life. The most common methods of change focusing on technology are quality-of-work-life projects (QWL) and sociotechnical systems design (STS).

Quality-of-Work-Life Projects. QWL projects and programs attracted widespread attention during the 1980s because of the strong interest in influencing the environment in which work occurs. QWL projects tend to focus on real work-life issues such as security, participation in decisions, safety and health, meaningful work, and protection from arbitrary or unfair treatment. A distinctive characteristic of QWL projects is their concern about the impact of the work environment on individuals and their effectiveness in organizations.

QWL projects are usually initiated by the creation of a steering committee and a consultant to help the committee function. The steering committee agrees on the mission and focus of the QWL project, the support and other resources needed, and the ways in which the procedures are to be implemented throughout the organization. The entire process should, of course, avoid infringing on the collective bargaining domain and contract. Joint facilitators representing management and the union are selected to coordinate the work on a day-to-day basis and to report to the steering committee.

Sociotechnical Systems Design.   The rationale underlying a sociotechnical systems design is to help organization members perform a technical function in a complex environment. This rationale is based on the premise that the quality of work life may be enhanced by designing technical systems that recognize the social needs of workers. The consequence of an STS design are changes in both the technological and the social system of an organization. The objective of STS is to identify and design the best possible working conditions, taking into account the technology, the people, and the demands of the organization.

Sociotechnical systems design examines highly interdependent clusters of tasks and creates natural work groups that include individuals who are doing the tasks. Autonomy and self-management are the basis, then, for identifying reciprocal and/or sequential interdependent jobs within each of the work groups.

The social system is of major concern, also, since the human side of the organization influences how both individuals and groups perform their jobs. The social system consists of all the individual and group influences that comprise the culture of the work groups and the larger organization, as well as the styles of leadership and management that pervade interpersonal relationships.

In the sociotechnical systems design approach to organizational change, worker's role, skills, and abilities and organization goals influence the relationship between the technical and the social system. For example, an autonomous work team may have a goal of assembling 100 heating units per day. As long as the technology they are using permits them to do so, they are free to structure the work processes any way they want to as long as they meet the organizational goal of producing 100 heating units per day.

The technological demands, nevertheless, are likely to influence how work can be done and how a group can organize. For example, the process of assembling small heater units may require a great deal of direct labor by individuals in the group, whereas the operation of an automated steel mill may involve mostly watching dials and maintaining equipment. The way in which the work is done, therefore, does have an important and serious impact on decisions.

Other issues such as the physical work setting (light, noise, temperature, neatness), the complexity of the production process (manufacturing computer chips versus creating a hamburger), nature of the raw materials, and time pressures and schedules must be taken into account when making organizational changes following the model of sociotechnical systems design.

❦ *Organization Structure*

Although sociotechnical systems design changes often include structural changes, some methods are more directly oriented to implementing structural changes in organizations. Matrix restructuring is a structural change strategy that illustrates how organization change agents bring about structural changes in organizations.

The traditional and probably the most widely used structural system is called the *bureaucracy*. The elements of a bureaucratic organization may be recognized in most medium and large companies and government agencies. Nearly all alternative ways of organizing represent some variation on the bureaucratic idea. Hence, the goal of organization change agents, when looking at structural changes, is to adjust the prevailing bureaucratic structure so as to improve the chance of achieving the goals and objectives of those involved in the organization.

Bureaucratic organizational structures tend to have ten basic characteristics (Pace, 1983):

1. *Positions.* The building block of the organization is the concept of "position." Role theorists provide a simple definition of position: individuals in social locations who behave with reference to expectations (Deasy, 1969, p. 8).

STRUCTURAL CHARACTERISTICS

Positions	Impersonality
Hierarchical Order	Discipline
Official Duties	Technical Qualifications
Authority	Security
Rules and Regulations	Separate Personal and Work Lives

Organizational positions are usually given titles such as supervisor, machinist, lecturer, analyst, trainer, manager, and nurse.

2. *Hierarchial Order.* Organization structure comes into existence when the positions are arranged in an order that provides for each lower position to be under the supervision and control of a higher one. Hierarchical orders usually take the general shape of a pyramid.

3. *Official Duties.* The broad purpose of the organization is pursued by setting objectives, dividing the work related thereto into tasks, and distributing these among the positions as official duties. The definitions of duties and responsibilities are inherent in the position. Job descriptions are a method of ensuring that the tasks are well defined and able to be performed by a person appointed to the position.

4. *Authority.* Authorization to perform the duties is vested in the position; thus, the only time that a person may carry out the duties is when he or she legitimately occupies a position. Authority is legitimized by a belief in the supremacy of the law. In such a system, obedience is owed to a set of principles, not to a person. This characteristic includes the obligation to follow directives originating from a position that is superior to one's own, regardless of who occupies the higher position.

5. *Rules and Regulations.* A formally established system of general but definite policies, rules, and regulations governs the thinking and actions of people in the positions. The rules and regulations ensure uniformity and stability of decisions emanating from positions.

6. *Employment Based on Technical Qualifications.* Individuals are selected to fill positions on the basis of technical qualifications rather than political, family, or other connections.

7. *Impersonality.* Procedures in the organization are formal and impersonal; that is, the rules and regulations apply to everyone who falls within the categories defined by the policies. Officials are expected to assume an impersonal orientation in their contacts with other members of the organization as well as with its clients. Impersonal procedures help to prevent the feelings of officials from distorting their judgments in carrying out their duties.

8. *Discipline.* An attitude of and procedures for making certain that occupants of positions carry out their duties in an efficient and impersonal manner are part of the organization. Those who apply regulations with capriciousness or are not pursuing organizational objectives consistent with the plan find that sanctions are applied to them.

9. *Security.* Although employment in the bureaucracy is based on technical competence, advancements are based on both performance and seniority. After a trial period, officials gain tenure in positions and are protected against

arbitrary dismissal. Employment in the organization constitutes a lifelong career, providing security in the position.

10. *Separate Personal and Organizational Lives.* Organization members are not to allow their personal lives to interfere with their positional duties. Family members of organization employees, for example, are not to make contact with employees during working hours. Organization members are not to engage in personal activities on company time.

A major assumption of bureaucratic structure is that violations of these ten principles lead to inefficiency and irrational decision making. Those who tinker with the bureaucracy are subject to undermining an ideal system.

As do many theorists and practitioners, Robbins (1987) argues that "despite the criticism directed at bureaucracy, you cannot ignore the obvious. Bureaucracies are everywhere! The vast majority of large organizations are predominantly bureaucratic in structure, and for all but a few, bureaucracy represents the most efficient way for them to organize" (p. 243).

The challenge of organization change agents has been to discover ways to help clients bring their activities and structure into line with the principles of bureaucracy. Their task is to find out where the current structure has deviated from the principles and make recommendations for how the organization can reclaim the order of the bureaucratic model.

Some organizations have missions that are difficult to implement within the guidelines of a pure bureaucracy. In those instances, organization change agents seek to refine the operations of the bureaucratic system to allow greater adaptability; to reduce conflict, frustration, and boredom; to increase planning and coordination; to accentuate innovation; and to make modifications that accommodate new technological realities (Schein and Greiner, 1977).

Matrix restructuring, when carried on successfully, may be able, as well, to lead to the modification of the bureaucracy so as to allow specialists from certain functional departments to work on one or more interdepartmental teams. The matrix structure lends more flexibility to the bureaucratic system and facilitates innovative and complex activities (Robbins, 1987, pp. 248–255). Organization change agents find that both temporary and permanent matrix structures can be implemented in organizations.

Temporary Matrix Structures. The structure of the HRD function in an organization may appear much like a traditional bureaucracy, but it allows for the creation of project teams or units. To each project is assigned one or more persons from each of the functional areas. A project manager takes responsibility for leading the group in completing its assignment. At the end of the project, each person returns to his or her initial functional area. Figure 7.3 portrays an organization chart showing how the matrix idea is implemented. For the most part, temporary matrix structures are made up of individuals assigned from functional areas to the project. Employees in the matrix, however, have two bosses: their functional manager and their project director.

Permanent Matrix Structure.   In some organizations, such as advertising agencies, hospitals, construction companies, and consulting firms, the type of projects are relatively permanent. The development and management of a new product may take years, or the manufacture of a component for some large industrial machinery may go on for a dozen years. Individuals from each of the functional units may be assigned somewhat permanently to the project. In other organizations, particularly those faced by rapidly changing market conditions and needs for higher levels of cooperation among functional lines and projects, the matrix structure is appealing.

The role of organization change agent, then, is one that requires skills in many areas ranging from interpersonal relations to organizational restructuring.

FIGURE 7.3
Matrix Organization Chart

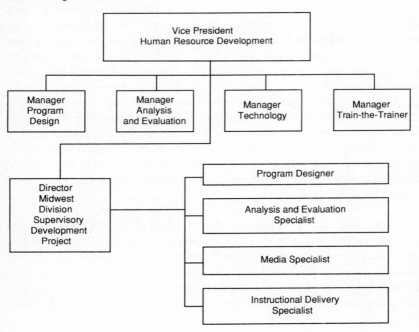

The methods are often detailed and rigorous. This role performs many exciting functions and affects the lives of people. Preparation for the role of organization change agent should be taken seriously.

MARKETER ROLE

The design of training and development programs and the preparation of effective media materials is of little value if the products fail to reach the client or user. Positioning HRD products and opening minds to accept HRD programs is one of the key activities of the marketer role. The marketer is also expected to improve the image of human resource development, both within the organization and among potential external users.

As with the organization change agent, the role of marketer has many fascinating areas of application. The general goals and direction are similar, but the clients and target audiences differ from both the instructor/facilitator and the organization change agent.

The task of marketing HRD products is particularly challenging given the present acceptance level of HRD among line managers. Stephan et al. (1988) discovered in a recent study that among *Fortune* 500 companies, HRD ranked fifth in importance behind operations/manufacturing, marketing/sales, engineering/R&D, and finance. While the relative position of HRD may move up in the future, particularly as more well-trained HRD practitioners move from universities into the marketplace, it is nonetheless critical for the marketer to demonstrate the regular benefits of the HRD function and how it can become a greater resource in policy formation, planning, and implementing change programs.

Five vital functions are performed by those taking the role of marketer, namely, (1) market research, (2) product development assistance, (3) distribution, (4) pricing, and (5) promotion (Kotler, 1976).

MARKETER FUNCTIONS

- **Market Research**
- **Product Identification**
- **Distribution**
- **Pricing**
- **Promotion**

❦ Market Research

The purpose of HRD market research is to identify probable users of human resource development products and services. Within an organization, this means identifying the departments where a training need exists and convincing the powers-that-be to schedule training. Central to the marketing role is developing profiles of those likely to respond to training activities. Internally, cultivating and educating managers in this regard is probably the most important dimension of market research.

Along with marketing the desirability of training programs, market research can be used to indicate where HRD practitioners can be of service in career and personnel development. Management education and development programs for employees, for example, are often advertised and, occasionally, offered without cost to attract participants. Skills in designing, producing, and distributing both print and electronic media products are central to the marketer role.

❦ Product Development Assistance

The second important aspect of the marketer role is making decisions about what HRD programs should be produced and offered for both internal and external markets. To do this, a marketer must be a key member of the HRD system. Although not directly involved in the mechanics of design and materials production, the marketer must understand these functions well enough to explain how the products are produced and what impact they may have. The marketer is instrumental in getting clients to accept HRD programs, so the marketer must be able to represent the products accurately and persuasively.

❦ Distribution

Distribution is that part of the marketer's role where products are actually put into the hands of interested users. Internally, this means creating a system where those who seek training can have easy access to it. Marketing involves an effort to facilitate smooth relationships between design and manufacturing so that production levels are maintained to meet training needs. Marketers must provide information about programs so as to notify employees of the benefits they can derive by participating in personal and professional development programs.

Externally, a marketer may develop an entire plan for advertising available goods and services to solicit clients. Many training vendors, for example, mail a steady stream of brochures and handbills to individuals and organizations advertising the products they have to offer. Part of this aspect of the marketer role may also involve setting up warehouses, distribution centers, and accounting processes.

❦ *Pricing*

In some organizations, the human resource development function is considered a *profit center*. This means that other departments in the organization reimburse it for materials and services. In other instances, the HRD department is considered a *service center* and is budgeted by the organization. In both cases, HRD products and services are priced. Production and distribution costs are calculated, and a fair price is set.

Pricing is a complicated process in which prices may be set on several different bases: costs, rate of return, intensity of demand, and competition. In any case, where competition exists, the company must meet price changes. When a competitor cuts the prices of its products and services, a department or firm has the option of lowering its prices to avoid losing its market share, or the option of maintaining its prices and reducing its market share. Between these two extremes, the department might consider a partial price reduction to limit the market share loss. Most companies calculate tentative prices for its products and services according to costs and then modify the prices by individual demand and competitive factors.

❦ *Promotion*

The core of the instrumental roles cluster is represented in the concept of promotion. Modern marketing, both inside and outside the organization, requires having a strategy for developing attention-getting messages and getting them to appropriate publics. Sales campaigns and programs to enhance the image of the company and its products are important.

Effective promotion requires having an *integrated marketing communications concept (IMCC)*. The IMCC views the relationship between the client or user as a "courtship." Four metaphors of instrumental communication serve as the basis of marketing decisions: the rhetorical model, the propagandistic model, the negotiation model, and the communication model.

The communication model ties together the elements of marketing in such a way as to provide guidance in how to arrange effective messages and media for an intended audience. This model indicates that the "function of marketing communication is to build product awareness and to support favorable attitudes after purchase" (Kotler, 1976, p. 327). Important aspects of this process are assessing the audience's currently held image of the company and its products,

---

THE PROMOTION MIX IS MADE OF FOUR COMPONENTS:

- *Advertising:* **Paid presentations, in nonpersonal forms, of ideas, products, or services**
- *Personal Selling:* **Oral interviews with one or more potential clients about ideas, products, or services**
- *Publicity:* **Unpaid favorable presentations about ideas, products, or services**
- *Sales Promotion:* **Displays, shows, exhibitions, demonstrations, and other marketing activities other than personal selling**

---

and understanding the personal influence process in which nonpersonal media create awareness and personal influence closes the sale.

Designing the marketing plan and putting together contracts and agreements for those interested in HRD products and services are activities that must take into account the life cycle of products, how they can be promoted, and when they are to be revised, improved, and replaced with new product lines. Designing the sales approach, establishing sales goals, developing a sales force, and keeping track of actual and potential markets are important parts of the marketing effort.

Managing the marketing plan is more of an administrative act than it is a creative act. The success of a marketing plan depends not only on its design but also on the efforts of people in manufacturing and production, warehousing, distribution, sales, accounting, and management. In effect, creating a marketing plan, coordinating its activities, deploying the sales force, delivering the product on time to the client, servicing accounts, and revising the product all combine to constitute a major effort. Marketing is truly a central role in the instrumental cluster.

SUMMARY

The instrumental role cluster involves HRD professionals who are charged with the responsibility of producing change in the organization. The role of the instructor/facilitator is to motivate the trainee to desire to change, adopt new behaviors, and integrate those new behaviors into the workplace to improve the organization. The organization change agent is also engaged in producing change, specifically in the organization using methods that make it more effective. The organization change agent develops the plans for programs to produce positive change, obtains the commitment from management to implement them in the organization, and integrates the program into the existing system. The implementation process includes motivating those involved to use the new program, helping them use the new techniques successfully, and stabilizing the integration activities while the program is adopted. The marketer role helps the client or user understand the benefits of the programs, materials produced, and the HRD function within the organization. The marketer also works with external audiences to sell them on the values of human resource development and the contribution HRD makes to the organization.

In any of these roles, the process of influencing change, within or outside the organization, uses the change model of unfreezing (motivation to change), changing (new responses are displayed), and refreezing (stabilizing and integrating the change into the system). The outcomes for each of the roles, while different in focus, are centered on making improvements and developing people and programs to make the organization more efficient.

REFERENCES

BANDURA, ALBERT. *Principles of Behavior Modification.* New York: Holt, Rinehart and Winston, 1969.

CASSE, PIERRE. *Training for the Cross-Cultural Mind,* 2nd ed. Washington, D.C.: Society for Intercultural Education, Training and Research, 1981.

COOMBS, ARTHUR W. *The Professional Education of Teachers.* Boston: Allyn & Bacon, 1965.

COOMBS, ARTHUR W., DONALD L. AVILA, AND WILLIAM W. PURKEY. *Helping Relationships: Basic Concepts for the Helping Professions.* Boston: Allyn & Bacon, 1971.

DEASY, LEILA CALHOUN. *Persons and Positions.* Washington, D.C.: Catholic University Press, 1969.

DYER, WILLIAM G. *Teambuilding: Issues and Alternatives.* Reading, MA: Addison-Wesley, 1977.

ELLIS, ALBERT, AND ROBERT A. HARPER. *A New Guide to Rational Living.* North Hollywood, CA: Wilshire Book Company, 1975.

FILLEY, ALAN C. *Interpersonal Conflict Resolution.* Glenview, IL: Scott, Foresman, 1975.

FROST, JOYCE HOCKER, AND WILLIAM W. WILMOT. *Interpersonal Conflict.* Dubuque, IA: Wm. C. Brown, 1978.

GROVE, THEODORE. *Experiences in Interpersonal Communication.* Englewood Cliffs, NJ: Prentice Hall, 1976.

HELLRIEGEL, DON, JOHN W. SLOCUM, AND RICHARD W. WOODMAN. *Organizational Behavior,* 4th ed. St. Paul, MN: West, 1986.

HILL, RICHARD L. *Role Negotiation.* Plymouth, MI: Human Synergistics, 1983.

JEFFERY, R. W. "The Influence of Symbolic and Motor Rehearsal on Observational Learning." *Journal of Experimental Research in Personality,* 1967 (10), pp. 116–127.

KOLB, DAVID A. "On Management and the Learning Process." In David A. Kolb, Irwin M. Rubin, and James M. McIntyre, eds., *Organizational Psychology: A Book of Readings,* 2nd ed. Englewood Cliffs, NJ: Prentice Hall, 1974.

KOTLER, PHILIP. *Marketing Management: Analysis, Planning, and Control.* Englewood Cliffs, NJ: Prentice Hall, 1976.

MCCLELLAND, D. C. *The Achievement Motive.* New York: Appleton-Century-Crofts, 1953.

MACKAY, D. G. "The Problem of Rehearsal or Mental Practice." *Journal of Motor Behavior,* 1981 (13), pp. 274–285.

MIDDLEMAN, RUTH R., AND GALE GOLDBERG. "The Concept of Structure in Experiential Learning." *The 1972 Annual Handbook for Group Facilitators.* Iowa City, IA: University Associates, 1972, pp. 203–210.

MILLS, GORDON E., AND R. WAYNE PACE. "Providing Practice for Skill Development." *Training and Development Journal,* 45 (May 1988), pp. 26–38.

NADLER, DAVID A. *Feedback and Organization Development: Using Data-Based Methods.* Reading, MA: Addison-Wesley, 1977.

PACE, R. WAYNE. "An Experiential Approach to Teaching Organizational Communication." *The Journal of Business Communication,* 14 (Summer 1977), pp. 37–47.

————. *Organizational Communication: Foundations for Human Resource Development.* Englewood Cliffs, NJ: Prentice Hall, 1983.

PACE, R. WAYNE, AND DON F. FAULES. *Organizational Communication,* 2nd ed. Englewood Cliffs, NJ: Prentice Hall, 1989.

PACE, R. WAYNE, BRENT D. PETERSON, AND M. DALLAS BURNETT. *Techniques for Effective Communication.* Reading, MA: Addison-Wesley, 1979.

PFEIFFER, J. WILLIAM. *Reference Guide to Handbooks and Annuals.* San Diego, CA: University Associates, 1988.

RIES, AL, AND JACK TROUT. *Positioning: The Battle for Your Mind,* rev. ed. New York: Warner Books, 1986.

ROBBINS, STEPHEN P. *Organization Theory: Structure, Design, and Applications,* 2nd ed. Englewood Cliffs, NJ: Prentice Hall, 1987.

SCHEIN, EDGAR. "The Mechanisms of Change." In Warren G. Bennis, Edgar H. Schein, Fred I. Steele, and David E. Berlew, eds., *Interpersonal Dynamics: Essays and Readings on Human Interaction,* pp. 362–378. Homewood, IL: Dorsey Press, 1964.

SCHEIN, V. E., AND L. E. GREINER. "Can Organization Development Be Fine Tuned to Bureaucracies?" *Organizational Dynamics* (1977), pp. 48–61.

STEPHAN, ERIC, GORDON E. MILLS, R. WAYNE PACE, AND LENNY RALPHS. "HRD in the *Fortune* 500." *Training and Development Journal,* 42 (January 1988), pp. 26–32.

WALTON, RICHARD E. *Interpersonal Peacemaking: Confrontations and Third Party Consultation.* Reading, MA: Addison-Wesley, 1969.

CHAPTER 8

ೆ ೆ

Mediational Roles

INTRODUCTION

The 1967 and 1973 wars between Arab states and Israel were the focus of many grievances and hostilities between these Mideast neighbors. In 1977, President Anwar el-Sadat of Egypt and Prime Minister Menachem Begin of Israel began discussions, with meetings in Israel and Egypt, on ways to end the disputes that had long confronted their nations. In 1978, U.S. President Jimmy Carter extended an invitation to Sadat and Begin to come to the United States and discuss ways and methods in which the differences between them could be resolved. The outcome of the meetings resulted in a major agreement called the Camp David Accords.

In the plan, Israel agreed to complete withdrawal from the Sinai, to the restoration of self-government for the peoples of the Gaza Strip and West Bank, and to the writing of a peace treaty. This accord was later formalized into a 1979 treaty between these two nations. During the Camp David meetings, Carter played a mediational role which helped bring together a plan for peace; while not a major player, his integrative efforts helped the two nations plan and work together to achieve a common goal of peace.

In today's world of business, human resource development personnel play a similar mediational role in helping to bring together the organization's strate-

gic business plan. While not a major player, they provide integrative functions
that help two or more groups of people to plan and work together to achieve
organizational goals.

There are three HRD roles that contribute to the achievement of this
integration: (1) the manager of HRD, (2) the individual career development
advisor, and (3) the program administrator. Thus, activities unique to these roles
include coordination on what is done within the HRD department, between it
and other departments, as well as within the organization itself. Roles in this
cluster represent activities that occupy an intermediate position and carry on
integrative activities between organizational units.

THE THREE MEDIATIONAL ROLES

- **HRD manager**
- **Individual career development advisor**
- **Program administrator**

Rather than acting as "major players," as many of the other roles do,
these roles attempt to effect a resolution between those who do act directly.
For example, the role of HRD manager mediates between the HRD function
of the organization on one hand, and organization executives and selected
key individuals on the other; the role of individual career development
advisor mediates between an employee and his or her eventual career
direction; conversely, the role of program administrator mediates between
programs and trainees.

While the mediational philosophy dominates these three roles, managing
is a second characteristic that is crucial to their success. As managers, they
integrate resources and tasks, provide direction, take charge, provide policies,
and administer programs.

❦ *Value*

Mediational roles involve working with others. Managers, administrators,
and advisors require special interpersonal and problem-solving skills and competencies, as well as the ability to motivate, lead, and communicate in difficult
situations. The ability to perform these roles contributes greatly to accomplishing goals in the field of HRD.

❦ Chapter Organization

This chapter describes and characterizes each of the mediational roles—HRD manager, individual career development advisor, and program administrator. Each section includes descriptions of the key behaviors involved in performing the roles.

❦ Learning Objectives

After studying this chapter, you should be able to:

1. Explain the rationale for grouping these roles into a mediational cluster.
2. Describe, characterize, and explain the role of HRD manager, individual career development advisor, and program administrator, and identify key behaviors involved in performing each role.

HRD MANAGER ROLE

A manager is a person who integrates resources and tasks to achieve organizational and personal goals (Szilagyi, 1988, p. 5). Although the job of a manager is complex, management scholars describe the role by listing several functions. Mackenzie's (1969) model, which is similar to the managerial processes described by Hellriegel and Slocum (1978), Szilagyi (1988), and Terry and Franklin (1982), provides a substantive framework for describing how a manager of human resource development uses planning, organizing, staffing, directing, and controlling in his or her work. As Rose (1964) notes in treating similar materials, "it is difficult to clearly discuss a single function because in practice all functions are interwoven" (p. 51). In order to explain the total process in understandable terms, nevertheless, this section deals with the functions in sequence as shown in Figure 8.1, on the following page.

❦ Planning

The first function of an HRD manager is that of determining a course of action. Planning usually involves seven steps of its own. Before preparing a plan of action to direct the resources and tasks, Otto and Glaser (1970) explain, an HRD manager must first analyze the organization in which he or she is located and determine the contribution the HRD function is making to the organization's mission. This step is often called forecasting.

Forecasting. Forecasting is the process of analyzing the total organiza-

1. Planning
     Forecasting
     Formulating Objectives
     Developing Strategies
     Establishing program priorities
     Budgeting
     Setting procedures
     Stating policies
2. Organizing
     Creating an organization structure
     Delineating relationships
     Writing position descriptions
     Establishing position qualifications
3. Staffing
     Selecting personnel
     Orienting employees
     Training people
     Developing organization members
4. Directing
     Delegating
     Motivating
     Coordinating
     Managing differences
     Facilitating change
5. Controlling
     Establishing reporting systems
     Developing performance standards
     Measuring results
     Taking corrective action
     Rewarding good performance

FIGURE 8.1
Five Managerial Functions

tion and each of its parts to determine what the human resource development function can contribute to its overall mission. This is accomplished by visiting several locations and talking with as many staff and hourly workers, supervisors, managers, department heads, executives, and CEOs, as possible. The HRD manager becomes immersed in the spirit and intent of the company by reading reports, booklets, and house organs.

Forecasting is done in several stages. First, lists are made of the types of available training and development activities that are in use. The HRD manager records the purpose, number of people involved, number of hours and days devoted to each activity, where they were presented, the training methods used, the estimated costs per trainee, and the estimated effectiveness, according to organization members, for each activity.

Second, present and potential problems that the human resource development function might help alleviate are defined. This may involve the development of a comprehensive analysis plan, including task, needs, performance, and systems methods. Out of this analysis should come a set of long-range objectives that indicate the major areas of emphasis, often called programs.

Third, the HRD manager assesses the capabilities of the present HRD staff, equipment, and space to implement the goals and strengthen employees. Realistic assessments are then stated about how well each of the resources can contribute to accomplishing the tentative goals. The assessment may show that it is desirable to request more resources or to limit the scope of the plan.

Writing Objectives. The second step, that of writing objectives, describes the possible work load for the HRD function, including major programs and other activities. The stated objectives project what will be done in the future and specify formal courses and workshops, counseling, on-the-job training, contract programs, and personal development activities. Attendance at ASTD national and regional conferences and expositions as well as other professional development activities are included. Objectives are written by the HRD manager that enable others to know whether or not they are achieved and include measures of how many, how often, and where activities are to occur.

Developing Strategies. Strategies represent the methods or ways by which objectives are achieved. A strategy involves the adoption of a course of action and the allocation of necessary resources to carry out the actions. Although strategies may evolve as a result of some important decisions, the manager specifies plans in advance so that a systematic approach can be taken to goal accomplishment.

In preparing the strategy, the HRD manager may take one of the four

---

THE SEVEN STEPS IN PLANNING

- **Forecasting**
- **Writing objectives**
- **Developing strategies**
- **Establishing program priorities**
- **Budgeting**
- **Setting procedures**
- **Developing policies**

business strategies identified by Miles and Snow (1978): defender, prospector, analyzer, and reactor. Each of these approaches to strategy development positions the HRD function differently.

The *defender* approach positions the HRD function somewhat narrowly in order to aggressively prevent competitors from encroaching upon its domain. An HRD function that uses this strategy specializes in providing excellent management development, for example, but ignores trends toward career development and organization development. Functions that are successful defenders are able to maintain small segments within the field that competitors find difficult to penetrate.

The *prospector* approach finds its strength in new products and new markets, making innovation of greater importance than profitability. An HRD function that uses this strategy develops and adopts new training and development activities quickly, markets the products and services, then moves on to newer activities. A prospector strategy depends on locating new potential opportunities.

The *analyzer* approach makes the most of both innovation and domain. The analyzer strategy involves moving into new products and services after competitors have demonstrated their value; they take the successful ideas of others and imitate them. A successful analyzer strategy means following competitors with superior products and services.

The *reactor* approach is used when the other three strategies are mishandled or performed poorly. The result is a tendency not to have a specific strategy and for the company or function to languish in inconsistent and unstable decisions. A reactor strategy attempts to maintain whatever approach is being used, making the function or company unable to respond to change or positioning it to respond to change reluctantly. A reactor strategy may appear similar to a defender's strategy, but without a clear product or service domain to be protected.

Establishing Program Priorities. The choice of a strategy affects program priorities quite directly. Some HRD functions carve out a specialty and are known for providing personnel development programs that are superior in a limited number of areas. Other HRD departments keep abreast of the newest developments and are known far and wide as innovators. Still, other HRD functions pick and choose from the best of the current offerings. And, of course, some HRD departments seem to react to the urgencies of their company rather than to have a clear strategy in mind.

The best overall strategy for a given HRD department should be carefully chosen. Priorities should be established for decisions to be made. What programs should be implemented by the HRD function? Such a decision comes directly from the strategy chosen.

Budgeting. The most defensible way of creating a budget, according to Otto and Glaser (1970), is around programs. Instead of presenting top management with a budget, offer them programs. If they agree with the strategy and the programs that follow from it, they are more likely to provide the funds. The budget is an effort to cost out the forecast for each program. If the price is too high, some programs may need to be cut or held for implementation later.

For each program, in addition to fixed costs such as staff salaries, support personnel, office space, and operating supplies, the following costs may be incurred:

1. Staff preparation time
2. Lost production time (average salary per day of training)
3. Course design and development, including reproduction costs and extra copies for file and distribution
4. Promotional costs such as marketing brochures and advertising
5. Production of media materials, such as videotapes, audiotapes, slides, illustrations, photographs, and overhead transparencies
6. Location costs involving conference room rental, meals and refreshments, travel, and housing

The budget should also include funds to manage the budget, especially for accounting help, word processing, and computer time. Some of the most difficult parts of managing an HRD function is building and managing the budget and keeping costs within budget.

Setting Procedures. The most common way to standardize ways of carrying out activities is through the development of formal procedures. Clear explanatory statements that specify how routine tasks are to be performed provide staff members with step-by-step procedures for completing assignments. Managers should have a file of standard operating procedures. These procedures should be reviewed regularly and updated.

Developing Policies. Policies are general statements that guide the thinking of organization members. Policies give direction to and provide guidelines for making decisions. They encourage more uniform treatment of problems and people. A policy specifies a course of action to be taken under certain circumstances. Policies are discretionary in that they are phrased as suggestions. Policies should avoid dictating how a person is to behave, but they should offer guidance in making decisions.

HRD policies represent a set of goals and objectives that the organization wishes to achieve with regard to the development of its employees. One company indicates in its policy statement that the HRD function is responsible for providing assistance and monitoring for all plant training programs by

- Assessing training needs
- Coordinating training program development
- Conducting training or arranging for instructor/facilitators to conduct classes
- Participating in an advisory capacity on human resource issues for all in-house programs where implementation is coordinated by other areas
- Monitoring employee participation in external seminars to track costs and determine trends in training requirements
- Maintaining a library of training materials, seminar/course catalogs, video/film catalogs, and various other training tools
- Publishing a training catalog of courses to be offered

The policy statement of the company also includes a brief note about primary training program areas, notably, management, technical, skills, and personal development.

The training offered should be consistent with both plant and company human resource development philosophy. A set of policies that reflect the mission and goals of the organization contributes to maintaining a coherent and consistent training approach.

❦ *Organizing*

Once planning has been completed, the next step is to organize the resources to carry out the plans. Organizing consists of arranging and relating the resources for the efficient accomplishment of objectives. Details of structuring the HRD function were discussed in an earlier chapter, so only a short review of four closely related steps is presented here.

Establishing Structure. The human resource development function or department has a structure of its own, usually with a manager or director, assistants, specialists, and support personnel. Staff members are responsible for development activities in the company in major program areas such as technical

---

THE FOUR STEPS IN ORGANIZING

- **Establishing structure**
- **Delineating relationships**
- **Creating position descriptions**
- **Establishing qualifications**

training, secretarial/clerical training, sales training, management training, and organization development.

Delineating Relationships. Reporting and authority relationships are usually portrayed in an organization chart showing the main positions in the HRD function and who reports to whom. Lines connecting the boxes indicate the chain of command and who has authority over whom.

Creating Position Descriptions. In a formal organization, the authority and duties are assigned to positions. Thus, a major organizing activity is writing position descriptions. Clear descriptions give the person occupying the position a basis for performing duties and carrying out assignments in the most efficient manner.

Establishing Qualifications. Although the specific educational background desirable for careers in human resource training and development may not be uniform across industries, a bachelor's or master's degree in human resource development from an accredited college or university definitely provides the best preparation. Nevertheless, each position may require some special preparation, such as talent and experience in using media equipment or in designing technical training manuals. The manager is responsible for making certain that the duties for each position are described accurately.

❧ Staffing

Staffing consists of selecting the most competent people to fill the positions in the organization. The manager attempts to match the preparation, experience, and abilities of applicants with the demands of the position as expressed in the position description. Because the definition of competence changes as the level of position changes, finding the best match is often a difficult task. Rose (1964), for example, estimates that first-level supervisors use their technical abilities 50 percent of the time, but top-level managers use technical abilities only 15

THE FOUR STEPS IN STAFFING

- **Selecting employees**
- **Orienting**
- **Training**
- **Developing**

---

percent of the time. On the other hand, first-level supervisors use conceptual abilities only 10 percent of the time and top-level managers use conceptual abilities 60 percent of the time.

Selecting Employees.   In an HRD program, entry-level employees should probably be chosen on the basis of their technical qualifications in performing HRD roles, as well as their human relations abilities. As they are promoted into higher-level management positions, the types of abilities used changes. Thus, HRD employees ought to have a professional development program of their own that enhances their conceptual abilities.

Otto and Glaser (1970) report that research on *The Predictive Index,* a self-report instrument using lists of adjectives, indicates that trainers are people who have a strong interest in other people, who cooperate rather than compete, who are usually unselfish and friendly, who are capable of following detailed instructions, who are patient and enjoy communicating with others, and who are generally service oriented in their ambitions. Those may be the general, human relations competencies and abilities that characterize professionals in human resource development.

Orienting.   Orienting is the task of familiarizing new employees with the organization, department, and job. An effective orientation includes an introduction to the facilities, workstation, colleagues, and the larger organization.

Training.   Like other employees, the human resource development specialist should have a program for professional and personal development. A career development plan takes into account what Charland (1981) calls the "career cycle." He suggests that *novice, expert,* and *mentor* are three essential stages in a career cycle. The novice is the young adult who is new to the responsibilities, roles, and skills of the profession; the expert is the person who is more or less adept at the skills of the profession, and the mentor is the mature advisor and guide for others. The stages may not necessarily be age-bound in that most of us are functioning as novices in some areas, as experts in others, and as mentors in still others. Training is generally provided to help the novice become an expert and the expert become a mentor.

Developing.   The concept of development is closely tied to that of training, but development is concerned more with preparing employees to make maximum use of their skills and abilities, to achieve satisfaction in their work, and to become top performers in the future. Development is also linked to career paths in an organization. A novice, for example, may enter the work force with a bachelor's degree in human resource development and work as a training specialist for a few years, then get a master's degree in instructional science or business administration as an expert, and work as a manager of merchandising, but move into a career counseling position and eventually become corporate director of training and development as a mentor.

✾ *Directing*

Directing is the function focused on bringing about purposeful action to accomplish objectives. Five activities are involved in directing: delegating, motivating, coordinating, managing differences, and managing change.

Delegating. Delegating involves communicating the objectives, policies, and plans of the organization to employees and making clear what employees' duties and responsibilities are, as well as how employees will be held accountable for completing assignments. To carry out delegation, a supervisor or manager assigns duties, responsibilities, and authority to an employee. If the assignment is accepted, the manager has a delegate or representative. After delegation has occurred, the supervisor is primarily responsible for seeing that the delegate completes the tasks.

Motivating. Motivating involves getting employees to take the desired action, to carry out assignments that they have accepted. Motivating usually involves two sets of activities: (1) keeping employees focused on the goal to be achieved or the task to be accomplished and (2) helping them care about accomplishing the goal. Goal clarity provides something toward which effort can be directed, while caring provides the emotional incentive to expend the energy necessary to accomplish the goal.

Coordinating. Coordinating consists of relating the efforts of various individuals in the most effective combinations to accomplish a goal. Coordinating is concerned with bringing all elements and aspects of a situation into some

---

THE FIVE ACTIVITIES INVOLVED IN DIRECTING

- Delegating
- Motivating
- Coordinating
- Managing differences
- Managing change

type of harmonious union. The HRD manager coordinates the workers, materials, and plans within the HRD unit and with those of other units, as well as with units outside the organization. Coordinating in HRD may involve working with supervisors to select the most appropriate programs; serving as liaison between trainers and top management; assisting staff members with daily training schedules; arranging for special demonstrations; providing information about sources of exercises, films, and other tools; acting as a clearinghouse for new ideas; and participating in meetings.

Managing Differences.   The management of almost any function requires dealing with differences in ideas, preferences, cultures, and actions. Employees should be encouraged to be creative and think independently to minimize tendencies toward conformity and "groupthink." In doing so, however, differences tend to surface, creating conflicts that may interfere with goal accomplishment and affect productivity negatively. Managers have the responsibility to resolve conflict that is counterproductive, but without squelching the motivating and creative outcomes fostered by differences and the resulting tension in the organization.

Managing Change.   Employees should be stimulated to be creative in their work. Stability exists and employees make better adjustments in those organizations in which employees have learned how to deal with one another, how to do their work, and what to expect next. When change occurs or is introduced, employees may be required to adjust to new circumstances. Change is managed well when adjustments are made with a degree of ease, and the organization returns to a state of balance. The manager takes responsibility for recommending change, and for helping employees adjust to it.

❧ Controlling

The controlling function has five sets of activities that help accomplish the program activities that have been prepared.

Establishing Reporting Systems.   Control is executed through a system of reports on activities. The HRD function, for example, keeps records of financial transactions, training activities and achievements, effectiveness of training facilitators and instructors, and indicators of the impact of HRD on the organization. Reports may be either informal descriptions to complex statistical summaries. To maintain control over the system, a manager needs information about what is happening. Every manager and employee must balance the issue of cost against the value of information reported. Managers must make impor-

---

THE FIVE ACTIVITIES INVOLVED IN CONTROLLING

- **Establishing reporting systems**
- **Developing performance standards**
- **Measuring results**
- **Taking corrective action**
- **Rewarding good performance**

---

tant decisions about how frequently information is needed, what kinds of information to get, and from what sources to get it.

Developing Performance Standards. Performance standards are set and used to achieve quality performance. To determine whether a job has been done in an acceptable manner, a manager must have in mind what the end result should look like. Standards indicate when a task has been completed in a satisfactory way. As a general rule, standards of satisfactory performance should be stated in terms of quantity and quality so that agreement can be reached on what is meant by the standard. Managers and employees should work together in developing appropriate performance standards for use in controlling activities, outputs, and results.

Measuring Results. Determining whether the work has progressed as expected is one of the most difficult tasks of a manager. Some objectives, such as "do a good job," are just not very amenable to measurement. To measure something means that the activity can be translated into some quantity or unit to which a number can be assigned. Thus, we usually look for the number of training sessions conducted and the number of employees involved in training courses as measures of the results of the HRD function.

The quality of an activity is usually measured in terms of a scale. For example, on a scale of 1 to 10 where 1 is poor and 10 is excellent, is the quality of a training activity a 2 or a 9? Judgments of the quality of something can usually be translated into numbers on a scale. Control over the quantity and quality of HRD activities is achieved by measuring the results.

Taking Corrective Action. Every manager must be flexible and willing to make adjustments in the plans or changes in personnel in order to achieve the goals and objectives stated in the performance standards. When performance drops below standards during periods of measurement, a manager reviews what is happening and takes steps to bring activities into line with the standards, or changes the standards. Changes are often identified during counseling interviews that follow performance evaluations.

Rewarding Good Performance. When performances meet and exceed expectations, some form of reward is appropriate. Rewards take many forms, but a common classification is extrinsic and intrinsic. Money and better working conditions are examples of extrinsic rewards since they are external to the individual. Intrinsic rewards, on the other hand, come from internal feelings, such as satisfaction from completing a difficult task, or the feeling of intellectual achievement that comes from solving a problem. Effective managers are sensitive to providing both types of rewards—praise and financial gain—to help ensure progress toward the accomplishment of program goals and objectives.

In sum, the work of a manager is complex and comprehensive. Mackenzie's (1969) model of the management process was used as the framework in which the human resource development manager's function was analyzed. Five sequential functions and 25 sets of activities of managers were discussed in terms of how they apply to the role of HRD manager.

INDIVIDUAL CAREER DEVELOPMENT ADVISOR ROLE

Some managers have expressed reservations about trying to plan a career for others (Jelinek, 1979, pp. 10–16). Employees, in turn, consider themselves as either "planners" or "wingers," depending on whether they have laid down some formal career goals of their own or have simply gone with the flow of events and operated with maximum flexibility in career choices. A career development advisor probably has little to offer to wingers, since they tend not to allow plans to influence their choices.

Planners, on the other hand, seek to have direction in their lives and can use the assistance of a career development advisor.

A basic assumption underlying career counseling/advising is that all aspects of a person's life are interrelated; that is, the career itself, attitudes, and

---

TWO ASPECTS OF CAREER DEVELOPMENT ADVISING

- **Distinguishing between planners (structure) and wingers (flexibility)**
- **Understanding the link between professional and personal planning**

competencies have an impact upon a person's philosophy of life, interpersonal relationships, self-concept, and social development. The overarching goal of career advising is the development of employees so that they are able to function intellectually, personally, socially, and professionally. In career advising, the ultimate focus is upon professional or vocational dimensions, but such advising can embrace all aspects of a person's life.

Assisting a person to select a career direction helps the recipient to relieve tension, achieve insight, acquire a sense of competence, and attain a degree of success, in effect, cope more adequately with many aspects of his or her life. Thus, at the heart of the work of an individual career development advisor is the satisfaction that improvements have been made in the employee's general place in society in both professional and personal areas.

Understanding the close relationship between career development and general adjustment is critical to performing as an effective career advisor. As one learns to cope with career problems, an overall improvement in self-esteem and general adjustment to life occurs. The better adjusted worker is also a better adjusted person. This, then, is the work of the individual career development advisor, to help people find their way in the world of work.

Crites (1981) formulated a model of comprehensive career counseling that consisted of three stages—diagnosis, process, and outcomes—and used three basic methods—interviews, test interpretation, and occupational information. In understanding the role of individual career development advisor, a brief look at the stages and methods may be helpful.

❦ *Diagnosis*

The decision to use diagnosis depends on the individual to be advised and his or her understanding of career progress. Two basic questions motivate the

---

CAREER DEVELOPMENT ADVISING

Diagnosis *(Answers to Questions)*	*Counseling* *Process* *(Methods Used)*	*Outcomes* *(Results of Advising)*
What?	**Interviews**	**Career choices**
Why?	**Test interpretations**	**Decision making**
Why?	**Occupational information**	**Personal development**

diagnosis: "What is the employee's problem?" and "Why does the employee experience the problem?" The diagnostic approach depends on which question is to be answered. A *differential* diagnostic approach attempts to determine what the employee's career decision problem is, whereas a *dynamic* diagnostic approach seeks to identify why the employee has the problem. The former approach tries to define the problem and the latter searches for the causes of the problem (Crites, 1981, pp. 169–182).

In diagnosis, a distinction is made between the "content" of a career choice and the "process" of making a career choice. Content refers to which career the employee chooses to enter, whereas process refers to how the decision was made to enter the career.

Career decisions are usually based on perceived interests and perceived ability or aptitude to prepare for and perform skills required of potential positions. A variety of instruments have been created to assist a person and/or an advisor to determine, or at least make some predictions, about a person's interests and aptitudes prior to plunging into a career choice. Nevertheless, using the results of tests and inventories alone is probably not a good idea because of the complexity of a person's experience. When combined with educated judgments and reasonable hunches, information from tests and inventories may add valuable data and increase the likelihood of making a good decision (Isaacson, 1985, pp. 150–151).

❦ *Counseling Process*

The second stage in career advising is the counseling process. Diagnosis leads into the process of career advising. A sequence of activities similar to the steps in traditional problem solving occurs, ranging from problem background, problem statement, and problem resolution. The dynamics of the process are facilitated through the three basic techniques: interview, test interpretation, and use of occupational information (Crites, 1981, pp. 169–192).

The basic method of career advising is the *interview*. On occasion, only one interview may be involved, but more likely the process will involve a series of interviews. As a rule, however, the process follows a somewhat predictable pattern, with an opening interview in which the advisor finds out about the advisee, a second interview in which the diagnostic test results are reviewed and interpreted, and a third interview in which occupational information is discussed.

The first interview usually has three major purposes: (1) establishing a climate in which the other interviews can continue, (2) determining for sure that the advisee has a career development problem, and (3) laying out the plan for counseling and related activities, possibly including taking diagnostic tests, as discussed earlier. Topics that are often discussed include the advisee's view of himself or herself; the advisee's abilities, achievements, aptitudes, interests, and values; the advisee's view of the future; the advisee's health and physical status; and the advisee's family and educational background. Finally, work experience, significant others, and important experiences and events in the advisee's life may be reviewed. Although not all topics may be included in every interview, the data gathered at this point lays the foundation for the next interview (Isaacson, 1985, pp. 99–120).

The second interview usually follows the administration of relevant tests and focuses on the presentation and *interpretation* of the results. This interview attempts to provide a more complete and accurate understanding of the advisee for the advisee. The advisor tries to adopt an instructional mode on the assumption that the advisee is probably not very familiar with tests and measurements. The goal is to help the advisee learn enough about the testing process to understand the results.

The third interview is designed to provide *occupational information* that allows the advisee to begin to see alternatives and ways of finding potential career opportunities. Occupational information can be made available in three ways: (1) the advisor can simply present it directly to the advisee, (2) the advisor can direct the advisee to information and ways to locate relevant data, or (3) a computerized occupational information system might be used (Crites, 1981, pp. 190–191).

☙ *Outcomes*

The primary outcome of career advising is to assist the advisee to make an occupational and/or career choice. Indirectly, however, the process contributes to a second outcome, that of assisting the advisee to cope with decision ambiguity and acquire skills in decision making. Finally, the third goal of career advising, as was discussed earlier, is to enhance the general adjustment of the advisee and strengthen the advisee's personal development.

The role of individual career development advisor has important goals to accomplish and many well-established methods with which to approach the task.

PROGRAM ADMINISTRATOR ROLE

The final mediational role in this cluster is the administrator of human resource development programs. The program administrator coordinates support services for the delivery of training programs by (1) determining needs, (2) planning to meet the needs, (3) implementing the plan, and (4) evaluating the results. The administrator is responsible essentially for following the training process from beginning to ending.

❦ *Administrative Process*

Determining Needs. From the administrator's point of view, the identification of training needs is the HRD manager's responsibility, or that of an HRD needs analyst, as discussed in an earlier chapter. The needs analysis process should include a review of the entire organization so as to ensure that all needs that are or could thwart the accomplishment of the organization's mission are discovered.

Managers, supervisors, and employees should be involved in this process and encouraged to discuss such basic issues as changes in the mission; technology; procedures; and equipment, work procedures, and skills needed by employees to do the work. In addition, a periodic review of employee performance (with checks of work samples to determine to what extent employee performance meets stated performance requirements), adequacy of records and reports, and career development plans are assessed. Out of these analyses comes the definition of *what* should be included in the training process.

Planning to Meet Needs. As soon as training and development needs have been documented, administrative procedures move to the second step, planning to meet the needs. The administrator usually has or prepares a catalog of useful organization resources and plans. The resulting administrative planning attempts to respond to three questions: Where? When? and By whom?

Where? A determination must be made about whether the training is to be given at the worksite by regular HRD staff, in a classroom, or off-the-job at another location. Such a decision depends upon budget and available facilities. At the same time, every effort should be made to carry on the training in those locations that help the trainees realize the greatest amount of skill transfer.

THE FOUR STEPS IN THE ADMINISTRATIVE PROCESS

- **Determining needs (what)**
- **Planning to meet needs (what to do)**
- **Implementing the plan (doing it)**
- **Evaluating the results (how was it?)**

When? A major administrative requirement is that training must take into account work load, leaves, and availability of both the employee and the training staff. In most cases, timing is critical, making the work of the administrator subject to a multitude of external demands. A schedule of courses, programs, staff, facilities, equipment, and other logistics must be maintained.

By Whom? The HRD staff is usually scheduled to conduct most routine training. Special requests and demands for expertise in unusual areas often make it desirable to contract for training consultants to conduct courses. In most cases, contract training must be approved and authorized on the grounds that organization training is (1) not available, (2) more expensive than vendor training, or (3) lower quality than vendor training. At times, regular employees and supervisors can be used, provided that their work loads and schedules permit time to prepare for and conduct the training. The administrator should maintain a list of qualified employees and consultants who can be called upon to handle training courses.

Implementing the Plan. The third stage in implementing the training process involves actually providing the training and development activities. If the course selected for presentation is part of the regular offerings of the HRD function and the staff are prepared to proceed, the work of the administrator centers on handling the logistics of scheduling facilities, equipment, staff and participants; arranging for materials and teaching aids, food, and refreshments; creating promotional materials and directional signs; and making travel arrangements. Records of those enrolled and who complete the program must be maintained. Procedures for registering participants must be prepared. Finally, room setup for tables, chairs, and placement of equipment must be completed.

On the other hand, if the course is new and must be designed, program/course designers must be involved and their efforts coordinated. The program designer role is described in another chapter and involves quite different skills and competencies, although the administrator may need to work closely with designers in order to have a program ready for presentation on schedule.

Evaluating the Results. Although evaluation is a separate role, the administrator has responsibility for making arrangements for evaluation to occur. Evaluation during the training session may be easier to facilitate than attempting to evaluate a participant's progress back on the job. Managers and supervisors must understand the evaluation process and place in improving productivity and be involved in worksite evaluation.

❦ *Training Resources*

The program administrator is a combination of a scheduler, legman, time coordinator for diverse interests, and coordinator of trainees, resources, and facilities at the right time and the right place. Success in coordinating these diverse interests in order to administer training and development projects depends in great measure on the effective use of other resources in the organization. Three major resources are available and should be used as needed: (1) training committees, (2) training coordinators from line departments, and (3) audio-visual and library services.

Training Committees. A useful way to help administer training and development plans is to establish one or more training committees. Members of a committee consist of managers of the major units within the organization. Committee members should have the authority to speak for their units on training matters.

The purpose of a training committee is to assist the chief operations officer in planning, coordinating, and evaluating training programs and to advise the chief operating officer (COO) on fiscal year and long-range training programs. The committee also serves as a point of contact through which the HRD function can provide more realistic and effective assistance on training and development matters to all levels of management in the organization.

Training committee responsibilities may include some of the following:

1. Assist management in planning the approach for an annual training needs survey using various methods recommended by the manager of HRD and that meet the limitations of the organizational budget.
2. Assist in the determination of overall organizational training needs, funding requirements, and the most cost-effective means of accomplishing the training and development goals.
3. Promote an understanding and acceptance of training and development policies and programs among employees, supervisors, and managers.
4. Assist the manager of HRD in the preparation, coordination, and evaluation of the fiscal year training plan, and in solving training problems that cross organizational lines.

THE THREE MAJOR TRAINING RESOURCES

- **Training committees**
- **Training coordinators**
- **Audio-visual and library services**

---

5. Assist the HRD function in preparing an annual report indicating the degree to which training and development activities were accomplished.
6. Coordinate training policies with units represented in the training committee to ensure consistency in policy formulation.

Training Coordinators. Training coordinators may be assigned from the HRD function to each of the line departments in the organization. Training coordinators serve as the source of information for training programs currently being offered and assist in identifying needs not currently being met. They are the initial point of contact for managers wishing to enroll employees in training programs, and they provide administrative services such as program scheduling, enrollment, and record keeping within the line department. The training coordinators serve as the liaison between the line department and the HRD function.

Audio-Visual and Library Services. The administrator of HRD activities is often responsible for in-house production services for audio-visual needs in training, employee communications, and marketing. A production staff—including writers, directors, and technical personnel necessary to furnish complete preproduction, production, and postproduction services in all picture/sound media including motion picture, videotape, videodisk, slide and audiotape, and multimedia—may be part of the responsibilities of the administrator. Nowadays, an in-house cable video distribution system may fall under the supervision of the administrator.

A library of training films, in 16mm and 3/4- and 1/2-inch video formats, available for loan may also be administered by the HRD function. In addition, books, periodicals, and technical reports may be housed in the company library, with most items being loaned for a few weeks. Materials must be acquired, cataloged, and circulated. On occasion, specialized services such as reference assistance, literature searches, interlibrary loans, and translation and reproduction are also part of the library.

SUMMARY

This chapter has described the main activities of three roles that mediate between elements in a human resource development setting: HRD manager, individual career development advisor, and program administrator. These roles consist of two major parts, that of being an intermediary and that of being a manager. Both parts were shown as necessary in bringing together those resources and tasks related to improving employee productivity and development.

The manager role, that of running the HRD operation in an organization, was described and discussed in terms of the five functions of planning, organizing, staffing, directing, and controlling. The steps related to each function were treated.

The overarching goal of the individual career development advisor was discussed, namely, that of helping employees function more effectively in the intellectual, personal, social, and professional aspects of both their professional and their personal lives. The activities of diagnosis described the process of testing to identify career interests and provide interpretations of the results. Advising follows such testing and focuses on selecting approaches to achieve career goals, coping with ambiguity in the decision-making process, and strengthening the advisee's personal development.

The role of the program administrator includes determining needs, planning, implementing the plan, and evaluation.

The major mediational roles in human resource development may require specialized course work and other preparation to fulfill their requirements adequately.

REFERENCES

CHARLAND, WILLIAM A., JR. "Career Roles." *Western's World,* 12 (November–December 1981), pp. 43–44, 88–89.

CRITES, JOHN O. *Career Counseling: Models, Methods, and Materials.* New York: McGraw-Hill, 1981.

HELLRIEGEL, DON, AND JOHN W. SLOCUM, JR. *Management: Contingency Approaches,* 2nd ed. Reading, MA: Addison-Wesley, 1978.

ISAACSON, LEE E. *Basics of Career Counseling.* Boston: Allyn & Bacon, 1985.

JELINEK, MARIANN. *Career Management: For the Individual and the Organization.* Chicago: St. Clair, 1979.

MACKENZIE, R. ALEX. "The Management Process in 3-D." *Harvard Business Review* (November–December 1969), pp. 12–15.

MILES, RAYMOND E., AND CHARLES C. SNOW. *Organizational Strategy, Structure, and Process.* New York: McGraw-Hill, 1978.

OTTO, CALVIN P., AND ROLLIN O. GLASER. *The Management of Training.* Reading, MA: Addison-Wesley, 1970.

ROSE, HOMER C. *The Development and Supervising of Training Programs.* American Technical Society, 1964.

SZILAGYI, ANDREW D., JR. *Management & Performance,* 3rd ed. Glenview, IL: Scott, Foresman, 1988.

TERRY, GEORGE R., AND STEPHEN G. FRANKLIN. *Principles of Management,* 8th ed. Homewood, IL: Richard D. Irwin, 1982.

CHAPTER 9

❦ ❦

Program Areas in Human Resource Development

INTRODUCTION

The field and business of human resource development is grounded in the assumption that a person's education does not stop when he or she finds employment. As Porter and McKibbin (1988) explain about management development, "If it [management education] did [stop], such an individual would rapidly become obsolete and relegated to the 'also rans' rather than continuing to be a member of that group expected to provide leadership—at whatever organizational level—in the management sectors of our society's institutions, including, but not limited to, business firms" (p. 217).

Human resource development fosters the idea of lifelong learning and seeks to help all employees maintain relevance and avoid obsolescence so that they can provide leadership in their spheres of influence, whatever they may be in any of the institutions of society, including the families, the churches, the communities, and the businesses in which they are employed. HRD assumes that, in a period of rapidly changing markets and environments, and equally rapidly expanding information bases, a failure to provide lifelong learning for employees represents "an absolutely disastrous policy" (Porter and McKibbon, 1988, p. 218).

What are the lifelong learning needs of individuals in their roles as employees and managers in an organization? Most likely, the stages in an employee's career demand different kinds of knowledge and ability. At that, the individual

165

employee may view developmental needs differently from the way in which the organization views them. In the career of an employee—ranging from an entry-level position, to a first supervisory assignment, to managing a particular functional unit, through becoming a manager of a set of different functional units, to a position at the executive level—learning may appear differently at each stage.

Porter and McKibbon (1988) trace the changes that might occur from the perspective of the organization:

> For example, at the entry-level stage the organization would want to provide basic information about the person's job and functional area as well as about the organization and its values and ways of conducting its operations; skill building would presumably relate to those skills necessary to carry out particular functional activities (in marketing, production, finance, etc.). As the person progressed to the next level, the organization would work on broadening and deepening the person's knowledge base, probably still mostly pertaining to the particular functional area within which he or she was operating, as well as on building interpersonal skills relating to working with others as both peer and supervisor. [At the executive level], knowledge building would presumably be heavily weighted to learning about complex aspects of the external environment, and skill building would focus on such activities as the formulation of long-range strategies. Of course, at this level the distinction between knowledge and skills is often blurred, especially when the intent is to develop comprehensive perspectives as much as it is anything else. (pp. 218–219)

HRD is concerned, in a broad sense, with the total development of the individual, in knowledge, in attitude, and in skills. Most HRD roles, particularly that of individual career development advisor, address what the individual can do to develop as a total, competent person, capable of contributing in as many areas of human society as possible.

Lifelong learning may focus on either theoretical enhancement or on practical application. Given the fact that HRD practitioners generally work in organizational settings, practical applications usually take precedence in development decisions. To meet employee needs in organizations, HRD professionals are aided in their thinking by envisioning training activities in terms of program areas.

❦ Value

Program areas in human resource development are created to respond to the lifelong learning needs of members of the organization. Although the areas of need may differ somewhat from organization to organization, the basic concept of program area allows for some commonalities to emerge in the way in which HRD programs are offered.

Although the illustrations used in this chapter are primarily from business and industry, it is important to remember that all types of organizations have training needs. Productivity improvement and management skills training may be conducted for different ultimate purposes, but the actual work operations are often much the same. Secretaries, for example, need essentially the same types of operations skills regardless of the type of organization in which they work. Although the names given to different program areas across organizations may differ, what is noted relative to business and industry has application to government, education, services, and other types of organizations.

❦ *Chapter Organization*

In this chapter, the implementation of human resource development is discussed in terms of program areas, the basic format for building and offering lifelong learning activities for organization members. Various program areas are identified, analyzed, and discussed.

❦ *Learning Objectives*

After studying this chapter, you should be able to:

1. Define the concept of program area.
2. Describe how the scope of the HRD function depends on who controls training for each segment of the organization.
3. Identify and describe some appropriate program areas that might be used for lifelong learning in most organizations.

PROGRAM AREAS

To explain clearly the meaning of the concept of "program area," a brief review of the reasons why and how organizations are created is in order. Organizations are usually established, at least initially, to fulfill some purpose, often referred to as its "mission."

To accomplish its mission, an organization seeks to foster a climate that optimizes employee productivity. To proceed effectively, employees need to be clear about what tasks they are to perform and how the tasks are to be done. People are recruited to perform the tasks, and the people and tasks are arranged into work groups best suited to optimize productivity. For purposes of managing the affairs of the organization, the tasks and appropriate employees are structured into sections, departments, divisions, and strategic business units of some kind. The structural units are often portrayed in organization charts, work flow tables, and diagrams that visualize how employees relate to one another. Ongoing organizations usually follow a formal process for clarifying their missions, redefining their tasks, replacing employees, and grouping and re-grouping organization elements to ensure mission accomplishment and effective organizational performance.

Two considerations derived from the structure and operation of organizations tend to influence the creation of human resource training and development programs: (1) *the work being done* or function in the organization and (2) *the status or position held* by a particular type of employee in the organization. Thus, training is usually arranged for engineers who occupy professional, supervisory, or managerial positions. As Figure 9.1 indicates, training is available for groups of eligible employees, such as administrative assistants/secretaries, word processing operators/typists, data entry operators, and others in grades 2–7.

A program area, as illustrated in Figures 9.1 and 9.2 on the following pages, *may be defined as a cluster of courses or training activities offered to enhance the knowledge and skills of a group of employees who perform similar or comparable functions and/or who share similar or comparable positions in the organization.*

Figure 9.2, for example, identifies an executive management group, an administration group, an operations group, an engineering group, and a nonexempt group. Within three of the larger groups, three subgroups are identified: managerial, supervisory, and professional. Figure 9.2 also indicates which courses or activities are R (required), S (suggested), and A (as appropriate) for each group.

A similar pattern can be recognized in Figure 9.3 (page 171), which shows the "target audiences" and the matrix of three types of skills (basic management, secondary management, and special offerings) that are developed in a wide range of courses. Each target audience or group of employees (supervisors, managers, directors, account reps, sales reps, and others) can be advised into specific program courses that contribute most to enhancing their own productivity.

TRAINING OUTSIDE THE CONTROL OF AN HRD DEPARTMENT

In an ideal sense, from the standpoint of the HRD practitioner, every potential program area in the organization should seek and welcome the expertise of the training and development staff. In actual practice, however, many

	Administrative Assistant/ Secretary	Word Processing Operator/Typist	Data Entry Operator	Others in Grades 2-7
Beginning Typing				•
Proficiency Typing		•		
Style Training	•	•		
Statistical Typing	•	•		
Beginning Data Entry				•
Proficiency Data Entry			•	
Machine Transcription	•			
Beginning Shorthand	•			
Proficiency Shorthand	•			•
Poise and Presence				•
Number Skills			•	•
Customer Service Skills (grades 4-7)				•
Individual Development Seminar (grades 5-7)	•	•	•	•
Spelling, Punctuation, and Grammar	•	•		•
Memo Writing (grades 5-7)		•		•
Secretarial Training Program A. Forms and Procedures	•			
B. Building Communications Skills	•			

FIGURE 9.1
Sample Program Areas in Skills Development
(Groups of Employees Eligible for Available Courses)

R - Required S - Suggested A - As Appropriate	Exec Mgmt	Administration			Operations			Engineering			Non Exempt
		MGT	SUP	PROF	MGT	SUP	PROF	MGT	SUP	PROF	
Basic Project Management								A	S	S	A
Communication Skills	A	S	R	S	S	R	S	S	R	S	S
Contract Language	S	S	S	S	R	R	S	S	S	S	
Effective Presentation Skills	R	R	S	S	R	S	S	R	S	A	
Effective Terminations	R	R	R		R	R		R	R		
Effective Writing	S	S	S	S	S	S	S	S	S	S	S
Finance for Non Financial	A	S	S	A	S	S	A	S	S	A	
Interviewing Skills		R	R		R	R		R	R		
MBO	R	R	S		R	S		R	S		
Managing Human Performance	S	R	R		R	R		R	R		
New Age Thinking	S	S	S	S	S	S	S	S	S	S	S
Negotiating Skills	S	S	S	A	S	S	A	S	S	A	
Introduction to Supervision			R	S		R	S		R	S	S
Making Meetings Work	S	S	A		S	A		S	A		
Praise as a Motivator	S	S	S		S	S		S	S		
Sexual Harassment Awareness	R	R	R	R	R	R	R	R	R	R	R
Situational Leadership	R	R	R		R	R		R	R		
Technical Communications for Non-Native Speakers	A	A	A	A	A	A	A	A	A	A	A
Time Management	S	S	S	S	S	S	S	S	S	S	S
Toward Excellence	R	R			R			R			

FIGURE 9.2
Alternate Sample of HRD Programs

occupational specialties are unlikely, except perhaps on very rare occasions, to use the services of the in-house HRD function, because the actual training in such specialties is under the control of other groups such as professional associations, labor unions, and executives. Aside from some initial, general orientation to the organization, three types of personnel tend to take care of their own training:

1. *Executives.* Employees at the executive level in organizations tend to receive learning and developmental experiences from either university-based programs or from outside consultant/trainers. (Stephan et al., 1988)
2. *Professionals.* Professional employees of certain types, such as law, accounting, and nursing, tend to receive lifelong training and education from professional associations and specialized vendors.

COURSE TITLE/# Days

BASIC MANAGEMENT CORE:

Course	Supervisor	Manager	Director	Account Representative	Sales Representative	Conversion Coordinator	System Analyst	Team Leader	Support Staff
Basic Management Practices Unit 1 (2 1/2)	X	X	X					X	
Basic Management Practices Unit 11 (2 1/2)	X	X	X					X	
Performance Counseling for Results (2)	X	X	X	X	X	X	X	X	
Selection Interviewing (2)	X	X	X	X	X	X	X	X	
Time Management (1)	X	X	X	X	X	X	X	X	X
Effective Oral Presentation	X	X	X	X	X	X	X	X	X
Effective Written Communication (2)	X	X	X	X	X	X	X	X	X
Meeting Management Program (1)	X	X	X	X	X	X	X	X	X

SECONDARY MANAGEMENT CORE:

Course	Supervisor	Manager	Director	Account Representative	Sales Representative	Conversion Coordinator	System Analyst	Team Leader	Support Staff
Effective Management Program (5)	X	X	X						
Communicating for Results (3)	X	X	X						
Creating and Managing the High Performance Team (3)	X	X					X		
Managing Growth Resources: Managing Change (3)	X	X							

COURSE TITLE/# Days

Course	Supervisor	Manager	Director	Account Representative	Sales Representative	Conversion Coordinator	System Analyst	Team Leader	Support Staff
Project Management (2)	X	X	X	X	X	X	X		
Situational Leadership (1)	X	X	X						
Successful Negotiating (2)	X	X	X	X	X	X			
Managing Managers (2 1/2)	X	X	X						

SPECIAL OFFERINGS:

Course	Supervisor	Manager	Director	Account Representative	Sales Representative	Conversion Coordinator	System Analyst	Team Leader	Support Staff
Customer Satisfaction Strategies (2)				X	X	X	X		X
Persuasive Selling Skills (3)				X	X	X	X		
Women in Leadership (1 1/2)	X	X	X	X	X	X	X	X	
EEO/Sexual Harassment (1/2)	X	X	X	X	X	X	X	X	
Management Techniques for Secretaries (1)									X
Managing Conflict and Burnout (1)	X	X	X	X	X	X	X	X	X
Managing Without Interference (1)	X	X	X	X	X	X	X	X	X
Getting the Most From Your Performance Review (1 1/2)	X	X	X	X	X	X	X	X	
Data Processing for Non-Data Processing Personnel (3)	X	X	X	X	X	X	X	X	
Motivation Computer Personnel to Increase Productivity (2)	X	X	X	X	X	X	X		

FIGURE 9.3

Illustrative Program Areas in Management Training and Development
(For Use as a General Guideline for Managers to Select Appropriate Internal Training for Their Employees)

3. *Trade and Crafts.* Many employees belong to unions that provide skill training through their own organizations so that the employees can become certified and progress from apprentice to journeyman status.

THREE CATEGORIES OF PROGRAMS

An examination of potential program areas in an organization, no matter what type (business, government, etc.), suggests that most training activities may be classified in one of three categories: management training, operations training, or support services staff training, although each main category may have multiple divisions and subcategories, as illustrated above in Figures 9.1, 9.2, and 9.3. Each of the three major categories is described in the paragraphs that follow.

❦ *Management Training*

Management courses are designed to enhance managerial skills and to help participants apply contemporary management techniques in the workplace. Management-level employees engage in activities that implement the continuous functions of analyzing problems, making decisions, and communicating and the sequential functions of planning, organizing, staffing, directing, and controlling (see Chapter 8 on the managerial role).

Three general levels of management exist in most organizations: the executive level, the middle-management level, and the supervisory level. Executives manage middle managers, middle managers manage supervisors, and supervisors manage nonexempt and/or hourly employees. Because some support staff often manage other employees, such as executive secretaries who manage word processing operators and typists, the same course is frequently available to employees in different program categories. When a course such as performance appraisal, for example, appears in each program category, support materials used by the trainer emphasize applications relevant to the day-to-day functioning of individuals in a particular category. Thus, middle managers and executive secretaries may both take a course in performance appraisal, but the materials are adapted to the performance appraisal responsibilities of executive secretaries in ways that are different from the performance appraisal responsibilities of middle managers. On the other hand, each program area comprises courses that are unique to the specific group of employees. Figure 9.2 shows clusters of courses that are offered exclusively for administration and other courses that are offered exclusively for executive management. Special characteristics of the work of and demands for special program courses for each of the three levels of management are described next.

Executive-Level Programs. Executives have been seen, traditionally, as operating at a macro level, with overall concern and responsibility for organizational planning, organizing, staffing, directing, and controlling. Many have imagined, and rightfully so in some cases, that managers at the executive level have little or nothing to do with day-to-day operations. Some executives probably arrange to come and go in such a way that the average employee rarely if ever sees or has contact with them. Nevertheless, effective executives are seen and tend to challenge, by their performance, the stereotypes of the past.

Peters and Waterman (1982) have noted that some executives are aloof from the rank and file, but that increasingly the more effective executives are those who keep in close touch with the operational level by walking around (p. 122). Management by walking around (MBWA) may be a course in the executive training program area, but more likely courses such as long-range strategic planning, advanced human resource management, and corporate financial management tend to have priority in executive development programs.

Many executive development programs are tailored for executives in particular industries such as utilities, banking, and manufacturing, but courses and topics generally are more often similar for all executives. They include issues such as corporate strategy, financial analysis and economics, strategic marketing, information and decision technology, and international business. Some executive programs offer discussions of topics such as location and capacity analysis, vertical integration, technology transfer, communication skills, supplier-vendor relationships, and quality control.

Given the kinds of topics likely to be included in executive development programs and the level of treatment, executives are more likely to attend university-based programs than to participate in company-sponsored training, with courses offered by consultant/trainers a close second choice (Stephan et al., 1988). HRD staff may find that they are responsible for administering executive development programs, but only rarely do they actually present courses for executives.

Middle Manager–Level Programs. Midlevel managers are those who have responsibility for integrating policy and operations through other managers. They are usually seasoned managers with eight or more years of significant management experience. The goals of midlevel manager training and development programs is to give them a foundation in interpersonal, administrative, and conceptual skills so that they can have a positive impact on the organization and the people who work under them. In fact, skills in dealing with all levels of management should probably be explored.

Midlevel or senior manager courses are more likely to include topics such as leadership effectiveness, organizational processes, setting and achieving goals, bargaining, negotiating, and managing conflict; using power and influence, building the management team, coaching, counseling, and developing others; and managing innovation and change. Depending on the extent of training and development at the supervisory level, some middle-management programs include topics such as management styles, productivity and group processes, creative thinking and problem solving, delegation and time management, oral communication, and setting the motivational climate.

Stephan et al. (1988) discovered that middle managers are much more likely to turn to in-house training and development for assistance; thus, company training programs are also more likely to include an extensive midlevel management training and career development program. Consequently, the company HRD staff should be fully prepared and competent to handle middle-manager training programs.

Supervisory-Level Programs.   The term *supervisor* is used here to refer to the first level of management in any organization, although the exact title may range from that of foreman, group leader, or branch chief, to first-line manager (Ramsay, 1985). The single largest number of managerial employees is located at the supervisory level. They are also closest to the actual operations of the organization. Since many supervisors often enter this first level of management after having worked in some operations capacity for many years, the need for basic information about working with people is probably the greatest. At least, the period of transition is likely to be the most difficult.

The reasons why supervisory training is important have been summarized by Kirkpatrick (1983) and include at least the following:

1. The current performance of supervisors can be improved by changes in attitudes, knowledge, and skills that lead to increased personal effectiveness.
2. Technical and managerial knowledge must be updated regularly in order for supervisors to keep up with changing job responsibilities.
3. Many supervisors need to be prepared for advancement into middle-management positions.

The literature on supervision is both standard (Kossen, 1981) and uniquely adapted to special situations (in the case of Henning and Holtz, 1978, city managers; for Diekelmann and Broadwell, 1977, hospital supervisors). Kossen (1981) identifies what appear to be the most common topics that are treated in supervisory training programs: the nature of supervision, developing communication skills, perception, problem solving, decision making, planning and controlling work activities, managing time and self, the nature of stress, the employment process, organizational concepts and principles, problems of motivation, administering change, leadership skills and techniques, morale, discipline, dealing with unions, special employment groups, and dealing with higher management.

Supervisory training is the most likely managerial-type to be provided by HRD staff in the organization. In a study of HRD in *Fortune* 500 companies (Stephan et al., 1988), respondents indicated that only slightly more than 20 percent of the companies made use of outside consultants for supervisory training and only 3 percent used university-based training programs.

❦ *Operations or Technical Training*

The operations areas of an organization are those where employees produce, store, distribute, and service the outcomes of the organization. In a service organization, operations involve the service providers, such as ticket agents or case workers. In educational organizations the operations areas comprise those employees who work directly with the prime clients of the system, the students. Included are not only teachers but also counselors and any other employees whose task is to help students perform better academically. Operations training is often referred to as technical training, since operations employees usually handle the technical areas of the organization.

Organizations differ on how operations areas are set up. Manufacturing organizations have production lines and work areas, while service organizations conduct business in offices and service areas. Training in operations depends on the commitment of managers to operations training and the relationship recognized between employee skill levels and productivity. Operations training is, in effect, that part of the training activity concerned with helping employees who, in turn, work directly with the products or clients generally considered to be the prime recipients of organization activity. To illustrate the role of training in operations area, three operations categories generally associated with business and industry are discussed: manufacturing, warehousing, and distributing.

Manufacturing Training. The primary concern of manufacturing training is to satisfy certification and qualification requirements in areas such as fabrication, assembly, and maintenance. In a fabrication plant, training might involve courses in flammable liquids control, basic electronics, deburring and sanding, drilling, overhead crane and hoist operation, calibration, use of oxyacetylene equipment, optical tooling, numerical control standards, and new hire employee safety.

Warehousing Training.   Warehousing is generally concerned with the storage of materials prior to their distribution to suppliers. Training in this category of operations focuses on handling, moving, and safety procedures when working with products. One company that handles and stores chemicals has training courses in warehouse storage and receiving of hazardous materials, safety procedures for servicing tanks, control programs for hazardous materials, and transport procedures for safe passage of hazardous materials. In an industry where noise is a factor, one company has a course on hearing conservation that provides instructions for the selection, fitting, use, and care of hearing protectors.

An egg farm provides training in how to move eggs without breakage, how to store eggs so that the oldest eggs are nearest the entrance to the loading dock, and how to manage cartons for the most efficient packing of eggs.

Distribution Training.   The major training concerns in distribution tend to bear on marketing, sales, and customer service, although distribution may appropriately be considered a subcategory of marketing. In fact, marketing has dealt with the search for and motivation of buyers and the physical distribution of goods (Kotler, 1976). In this context, distribution training is a term that encompasses training in marketing, sales, and customer service. For purposes of illustration, sections on sales and customer service training are included in this chapter.

Sales Training.   Courses that provide salespeople with knowledge and skills to do their jobs are special to sales training. McCarthy (Tracey, 1985) identified ten elements that should be part of preparation and development in sales; a brief summary of each of the ten elements reveals the breadth and depth of potential sales training. These elements may be offered as separate courses, as topics within courses, or treated in more than one course.

1. *Company philosophy and the employee's role in the company's marketing function.* This element provides the new sales person with the information about the company's sales/marketing philosophy and the salesperson's place in the organization.
2. *Technical knowledge about the company's products and services.* This element includes courses about how the products are manufactured, how they function, and how they are used by customers.
3. *Product competition.* This element involves information about how the company's products relate to those of competition.

4. *Market economic and financial issues.* This element provides information about the economic and financial principles and data on which the company's marketing strategy is based. Economic information usually includes basic economics and finance, interpreting profit and loss statements, credit and collections, incentive contracting, cost estimating, and sources of economic information.

5. *Legal, governmental, political, and ethical factors that influence markets.* This element provides the salespeople with information about antitrust legislation, contract law, business ethics, and, if appropriate, international business procedures, restrictions, and philosophy.

6. *Theory, principles, and methods of persuasion.* This element provides information and skills for influencing customer decisions and includes how to manage the sales situation, psychological principles, negotiation skills, sales techniques, overcoming objections, and interpersonal skills.

7. *Planning strategies and tactics.* This element involves methods for handling accounts, preparing technical proposals, time management, maintaining records, budgeting and forecasting, and planning and organizing a sales campaign.

8. *Techniques of communication.* The key techniques for sales people are business letter writing, using the telephone, making product demonstrations, giving presentations to top management, report writing, making constructive criticisms, listening, nonverbal behavior, and creating product descriptions.

9. *Providing customer service.* This element develops an attitude and the ability to demonstrate continuing customer interest, provides ways of identifying customer needs, develops skills in handling complaints and conducting meetings with customers, and supplies information for advising on display, advertising, promotional plans, and customer buying practices.

10. *Self-development.* This element helps the salesperson prepare to meet demands that occur as career opportunities develop. Some training courses that are key for sales person self-development include public speaking, marketing management, data processing, team building, management skills, speed reading, and career paths.

Another option is to organize sales training courses into four categories: product knowledge, company policy and procedures, getting organized, and selling skills. In addition to these core elements, other special courses relevant to sales management may be important in given situations; they might include coaching and counseling, recruiting and selecting new sales people, office management, instructing and training, conducting sales meetings, and stress management.

❦ *Support Services Staff Training*

In the past, support staff training has involved primarily clerical and secretarial personnel. Nowadays, however, the information function of the office staff, including word-processing activities, and public contact employees who work directly with clients in providing services argues strongly for thinking of this category of programs in terms of support services staff training.

HRD training is particularly likely to be important as well in government and education organizations. With parent and taxpayer expectations high, and an increase in litigation brought against education organizations, organizations which heretofore appeared somewhat immune to client complaints must be more conscious of the need to appear concerned about employee productivity. As the private sector competes for a share of what used to always be government business (e.g., running penal institutions), and with continued tight budgets, such "monopolies" can no longer expect to provide less than the best service to their normal clients.

Value-Added Customer Service.   Customer service training is relevant to all support services personnel, it is a critical part of most sales training programs. The company's reputation, its investment in facilities, products, services, and staff, and especially its future prospects, are so important that a special course or even series of courses in value-added customer service are critical for not only sales but also staff support and other customer contact members of the organization (Koepp, 1987).

Value-added customer service training courses generally develop four key factors: (1) care and concern for the customer, (2) spontaneous and discretionary acts that help a customer get through the system, (3) problem-solving behaviors that handle complicated logistics and the intricacies of problematical schedules that get people on their way, and (4) behaviors that make amends to the customer and offset the negative effects of employee or organization mistakes (Albrecht and Zemke, 1985).

Value-added customer service training is set up to counteract deprivation and purchase-based climates in favor of opportunity-based ones:

Deprivation-Based Customer Service.   When employees function in an atmosphere that is oppressive, customer service is provided reluctantly and with a philosophy that the customer deserves the same kind of service that the employee is receiving from the organization. The service that is provided comes from an attitude of deprivation—that the customer should be deprived as much as the employee is deprived. The result is minimal service.

Purchase-Based Customer Service.   Purchase-based customer service responds to the demands of the job description. This kind of service involves basic customer contact skills and is regarded as part of the employer-employee contract for services. The employee sells his or her services for a price; the company or employer extracts service from the employee as part of the compensation package. The result is usually moderate customer service.

Opportunity-Based Customer Service.   Opportunity-based customer service, on the other hand, emanates from the vision that an employee has of him or herself as a fully functioning human being in society. This kind of service goes beyond providing usual customer service and finds natural expression in the four elements of value-added service: care and concern, spontaneous behavior, problem-solving behaviors, and recovery behaviors. Opportunity-based customer service training helps employees gain a vision of their own greatness in a climate where employers allow employees the freedom to serve others as a natural result of exercising the finest of human values.

Opportunity-based customer service allows employees to feel the excitement and challenge of authentic freedom of choice, to provide service beyond that which relates strictly to the purchase of a product or service; this is a true measure of value-added customer service. Opportunity-based customer service comes from the realization that offering service is compatible with one's most elegant values and endows the employee with respect, honor, peace, and, most important, freedom to give or not to give in whatever fashion the employee chooses. Opportunity-based customer service returns to the employee the dignity and regard each person deserves as a free person who can act with sensitivity and concern for others.

To enhance the four elements central to this type of training, a typical opportunity-based seminar develops at least four fundamental themes: (1) how to create a climate that allows opportunity-based service to occur; (2) how to design a physical environment for offering opportunity-based service; (3) how to deliver service that shows the central elements (caring and concern, spontaneous decisions, problem-solving behaviors, and recovery actions); and (4) how to monitor and evaluate opportunity-based customer service.

Clerical Skills Training.   Patterson (Tracey, 1985) indicates that although clerical workers may continue to have traditional responsibilities such as typing, filing, operating office machines, and taking telephone calls, new developments in automated equipment allow these workers to not only continue to perform part or all of these traditional tasks, as needed, but also to become involved in creating new and more interesting challenges. Changes in a person's level of competence in handling equipment, reading manuals and codes, and interacting with skilled technicians will increase. Training courses now have to encompass helping employees develop advanced technological skills beyond the usual clerical skills, think analytically and logically, and understand and work with a wider variety of individuals.

Secretarial Skills Training.   Since the position of secretary has changed dramatically over the years, training and development courses in a secretarial skills program tend to emphasize managerial competencies. Administrative and executive secretaries have managerial responsibilities delegated to them and need to be able to supervise others and work with integrated office systems. The development of new technologies make it essential for such employees to be knowledgeable about telecommunication equipment, microcomputers, and electronic mail.

Interpersonal skills and formal communication skills such as writing letters, reports, and memoranda encourage the development of workshops on technical writing and making technical oral presentations for secretaries.

Word-Processing Skills.   Language competencies such as spelling, grammar, and punctuation, as well as keyboarding skills, are especially important for secretarial support staff. The ability to process manuscripts quickly involves not only working with keyboards but also having the talent to proofread completed materials.

SUMMARY

In human resource development, a program area is a cluster of courses or training activities designed to enhance the knowledge and skills of a group of employees who perform similar tasks and/or who occupy similar or comparable positions in the organization.

Three broad categories of programs have been described, namely, management training (executive, middle management, and supervisory), operations or technical training (manufacturing, warehousing, distribution (marketing and sales), and support services staff training (customer service, clerical, secretarial), although each organization must identify and define its own program areas.

Continuing, lifelong learning programs help keep employees and companies competitive. The failure to have a strong lifelong learning strategy for all employees is a disastrous policy for companies in this day and age. Managerial/professional, technical/operations, and support services represent critical areas in which sophisticated courses must be provided in order to avoid obsolescence and maintain competitiveness in a world of changing markets and conditions.

Program areas in human resource development are created to respond to the lifelong learning needs of organization members in all types of organizations.

REFERENCES

ALBRECHT, KARL, AND RON ZEMKE. *Service America: Doing Business in the New Economy.* Homewood, IL: Dow Jones-Irwin, 1985.

DIEKELMANN, NANCY L., AND MARTIN M. BROADWELL. *The New Hospital Supervisor.* Reading, MA: Addison-Wesley, 1977.

HENNING, KENNETH K., AND HAROLD F. HOLTZ (EDS.). *Effective Supervisory Practices.* Washington, D.C.: International City Management Association, 1978.

KIRKPATRICK, DONALD L. *A Practical Guide for Supervisory Training and Development,* 2nd ed. Reading, MA: Addison-Wesley, 1983.

KOEPP, STEPHEN, ET AL. "Pul-eeze! Will Somebody Help Me? Frustrated American Consumers Wonder Where the Service Went." *Time* (February 2, 1987), pp. 48–57.

KOSSEN, STAN. *Supervision: A Practical Guide to First-Line Management.* New York: Harper & Row, 1981.

PETERS, THOMAS J., AND ROBERT H. WATERMAN, JR. *In Search of Excellence.* New York: Harper & Row, 1982.

PORTER, LYMAN W., AND LAWRENCE E. MCKIBBIN. *Management Education and Development.* New York: McGraw-Hill, 1988.

RAMSEY, JACKSON E. "Supervisory Development." In William R. Tracey (ed.), *Human Resources Management and Development Handbook,* pp. 968–996. New York: American Management Association, 1985.

STEPHAN, ERIC, GORDON E. MILLS, R. WAYNE PACE, AND LENNY RALPHS. "HRD in the *Fortune* 500." *Training and Development Journal,* 42 (January 1988), pp. 26–32.

TRACEY, WILLIAM R. *Human Resources Management & Development Handbook.* New York: AMACOM, 1985.

CHAPTER 10

❦ ❦

The International Setting of Human Resource Development

INTRODUCTION

Roger had spent part of his life in Asia. He relished living in that part of the world because he thoroughly enjoyed the people. Following graduation, however, he had taken a job in the HRD department of a large manufacturing company on the U.S. mainland. Now, he was ecstatic with an offer he had received to open a training office for the company in Southeast Asia. He had some reservations, nevertheless, about returning to an environment that was quite different from what he had become accustomed to on the East Coast. He wondered how, for example, one should handle employee development where confrontation was avoided and where employees showed unusual deference to supervisors. He was somewhat apprehensive as he approached this new assignment.

For Roger to succeed, he would need to rethink some of the traditional values he had assimilated during the past few years that he lived in the United States and reacquaint himself with some of the traditional values he learned during the early part of his life in Asia. In the process of reevaluation, Roger knew he would need to understand the effect of differences, among potential trainee he would work with, resulting from their social class structure, social institutions, and cultural characteristics of the society.

Most puzzling to Roger, however, was rethinking how he would approach training in light of such basic questions as, "Who is in control of one's destiny in life—the individual or fate?" "Whose needs should have priority when making decisions—the individual or the group?" In short, Roger knew that the international setting of HRD was, in most areas, much different from the one he had become accustomed to in the United States. He must rethink how his beliefs and his general approach to the theory and practice of HRD fit the social setting of another country.

❦ Value

Even a casual look at what is going on in the world of work shows that an increasing amount of HRD activity is taking place outside of the United States and that many HRD professionals have already worked, are now working, or will work at some time in an international setting. With 95 percent of the people on the earth living outside of North America, our concerns must turn eventually to cross-national contacts. With the technology of communication and transportation giving us rapid access to one another, the world is becoming more and more like a global village. The opportunities can be very exciting and rewarding, but, at the same time, they can also be stressful if not handled well. Understanding the international setting of HRD is both important and critical to being an effective professional.

❦ Chapter Organization

This chapter focuses on the international setting of HRD and the setting's implications generally for HRD practice, rather than the specific role and function of HRD in other countries. The terms *international* and *intercultural* are defined by distinguishing between the related concepts of nation and culture. The influence of both national and cultural factors on the way in which people think and react is discussed. Finally, an explanation of how national demands affect the transfer of training to work settings and to life in general is provided.

❦ Learning Objectives

After studying this chapter, you should be able to:

1. Explain the difference between international/societal and intercultural/cultural variables.
2. Explain how the concepts of *society* and *culture* help us understand HRD in an international setting.

3. Explain the objective and basic processes of HRD in an international setting.
4. Explain the problems involved in transferring knowledge, attitudes, and skills learned in training back to where international trainees live and work.

THE SETTING

Our discussions in this book, up to this point, have operated under the implicit assumption that, in HRD activities, trainers and trainees in question are from the same country and share a common culture. When HRD activities cross national boundaries, however, many new elements are introduced into the relationship between trainer and trainee, or they are, at least, activated by the international setting.

We plan, in this discussion, to limit our attention to that type of international HRD relationship where the trainer is from a developed nation and the trainees are from a developing nation. With the growing importance of Asian, South American, and African countries in the global marketplace, more and more North American and Western European HRD professionals are going to various areas of the world to conduct training, and many trainees from developing countries are coming to the United States for training.

One other common setting that has international implications is that in which a trainer from a developed country works with immigrant trainees from a developing country, such as in training given to Hispanics and Asians working for U.S. companies in America. The subcultures within which immigrants live create situations somewhat analogous to Third World training settings.

INTERNATIONAL AND INTERCULTURAL

The terms "national" and "cultural" represent related but different ideas. National relates, primarily, to differences in social structure and is equated usually with the idea of a society (the term "society" will be used generally here to refer to both concepts). On the other hand, cultural refers, essentially, to relationships or processes *within* the society, such as the types of perceptions and behaviors that exist in a specific society. International is, in the main, a concept that focuses on large or macro systems and their influence on behavior. Intercultural, in contrast, generally leads to a focus on smaller or micro elements within a society or system, such as language patterns, food habits, and verbal cues (Figure 10.1).

The roles played by HRD practitioners, when carried out *within* a given society, vary somewhat though not significantly from one part of the society to

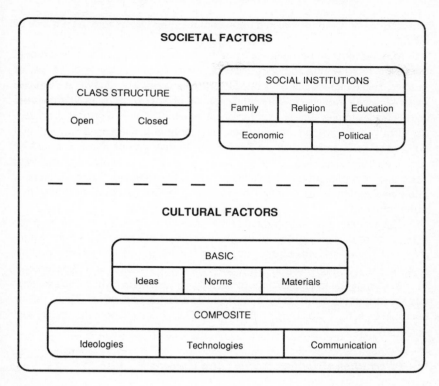

FIGURE 10.1
Selected Factors: International HRD

another. What variance exists is generally a function of different types of organizational problems or challenges. HRD practitioners analyze needs; develop strategies and accompanying instrumental materials; use these materials in individual, career, and organization situations; and mediate as needed among the various publics concerned with the overall HRD process and programs.

In an international setting, all these same factors exist, but in different configurations and with different emphases. The term "international" refers to situations in which individuals, primarily trainers and trainees in this context, have their roots in or derive their basic orientations from different societies. Rather than being able to assume conditions taken for granted by those working within and from the same societal or cultural context, the term international or intercultural presupposes operations *between* two or more different societies or cultures. Settings in which trainers and trainees come from different societies and cultures bring additional and often complicating factors into the practice of HRD.

Moving from an intranational (within the same nation) to an international (across nations) setting activates or gives greater emphasis to a wide variety of factors. These factors can be grouped for explanatory and analytical purposes into two major categories. First, the practice of HRD within an international setting brings to play the *societal* factors related to that type of setting. As noted, the term *"society"* is often used interchangeably with the term *"nation,"* and both terms refer to relatively self-contained human groups that are united by social relationships (Stark, 1989). That is, each society has a somewhat different class and social/institutional structure from other nations. These differences allow one society to be set apart from other societies by referring to it with a different name.

The second major component is that of "culture." This term refers to the way of life of those identified with a given society. Each society contains within it a set of cultural and subcultural patterns which distinguish it from other nations or societies. Although there are similarities between societies as to the elements of culture endemic to each society, differences between them allow each society, and the culture(s) within the society, to have a distinct character. These differences, in turn, have a bearing on the way HRD functions in both the society and its culture.

❦ International Setting: Society and Culture

With this initial introduction to the idea of international setting, encompassing the concepts of society and culture, we are now ready to look in greater depth at these two important concepts, their interrelationships, and the impact both have on the international practice of HRD.

The term *society* refers to relatively self-contained human groups, some relatively large and others extremely small. Societies can be distinguished from one another by geographic location, size, type of economy, and many other features, nearly all of which have some long-term impact on the practice of human resource development. Two critical factors—class structure and social institutions—will be used here to characterize a society.

Class Structure and Status.   Each society has its own class system or structure, ranging from fully open to completely closed. An open structure is one in which individuals can, if they choose, move up, down, and laterally in the system without major difficulty. Open systems are based on *achieved* rather than *ascribed* status, meaning that individuals obtain status in life primarily on their own efforts rather than on conditions related to birth. In ideal open systems, factors such as ethnic background, age, and sex do not affect opportunities to achieve in work and life. In effect, success in open systems depends on what you do or can do, not on who you are.

Closed systems, on the other hand, are conditioned much more by birth, so that opportunities and the attendant rewards are assigned to individuals based on their parents and their family standing. Upward mobility in the ideal-type closed system is not possible. Personal achievement and other attempts to succeed are likely to have little or no bearing on improvements in life-style or socioeconomic condition.

We can get a better idea initially of the impact of class structure on behavior in general, and on HRD activities in particular, by describing what might happen in a training situation where those involved are members of a closed society. Such trainees probably obtained their occupational positions primarily because of their overall social status and not because of any particular merit on their part. Until recent times, it was the practice to select military officers, for example, from the ranks of the nobility and upper-class families. Younger sons of these families would be essentially guaranteed their commissions; thus, once selected, they "owned" the position and could not be deprived easily of it.

If, then, the trainees were "owners" of their positions, there would be, in many cases, no particular motivation for the trainee to worry about improving individual job productivity because he would, in all likelihood, retain the position whether or not increased productivity resulted from the training. Conversely, those who, by prior status, did not obtain particular positions would find it extremely difficult, if not impossible, to improve their status, because such acquisition of position does not depend, in closed societies, on merit but rather on prior status. In effect, prior status, not ability, causes and perpetuates social (educational and employment, for example) differentiation.

Most nations fall somewhere on the continuum between an ideal open and an ideal closed system. Many nations, such as India, are moving toward more open systems as they industrialize and become more involved in global activities. Some nations, such as present-day Iran, appear to have moved recently toward a more closed system, resulting in, for example, more stringent sex typing of male and female roles as a consequence of Islamic fundamentalism. The effectiveness of human resource development depends, then, to a great extent on the nature of the predominant class structure of the society.

Social Institutions. The second major societal factor that distinguishes one society from another is the nature and structure of its social institutions. Social scientists have identified five primary social institutions—family, religion, education, economy, and politics—that are found in all societies (Figure 10.2). What distinguishes one society from another is not the presence or

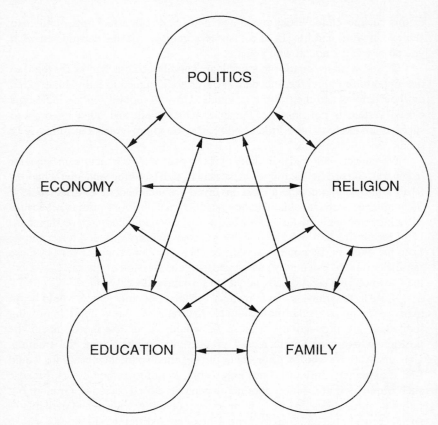

FIGURE 10.2
Society as a System of Institutions

absence of one or more of these institutions, but rather the pattern and processes within and between these institutions.

The *family* provides an interesting example of societal differences influenced by the particular nature of an institution. Families that consist of parents and their dependent children are called *nuclear families*. In the United States, there is usually limited interaction, comparatively speaking, between individuals who are related to one another by blood or marriage but who come from different nuclear families. Children are free to ignore the expectations of other, more distant relatives, such as cousins and even grandparents. Approval of grandparents, for example, is not essential when it comes to marriage, and children are not obligated by law or custom to provide financial support to uncles, aunts, and cousins—extended family relatives.

In many societies, however, *extended family* obligations override the desires and wishes of nuclear family members. In areas of China where traditional patterns are still pervasive, for instance, obligations to extended family members with regard to approval for selection of spouses are very strong. Some marriages are still arranged, family ties are very important in obtaining work, and those who are financially successful are expected to provide resources and opportunities for their extended family members.

The other four social institutions can also serve to illustrate the concept of society operating in an international setting, and definitions of each can help us understand more fully the concept of social institution.

Religion is a concept identifying a body of believers who share a particular view of the supernatural and are more or less united in their views on ultimate meaning. This body of believers carry on activities that allow themselves and others to see them as a distinct group. The particular religion in question is often seen as relating to a particular nation (for example, Jewish—Israel, Islam—Iran, Hinduism—India).

Education identifies how a given society formally transmits culture, knowledge, skills, and, attitudes to a new generation. What is transmitted, by whom, in what types of facilities, to what individuals, and at what levels (primary, secondary, higher) constitute in essence the educational institution of a particular society or nation.

The *economic* institution encompasses all those activities having to do with the production and/or distribution of goods, services, and information related to goods and services. Although many people try to type cast an economic institution as capitalistic (private) or socialistic (public), or some variant of the latter, such as communism, nations generally have economic institutions that contain elements of both public and private control of economic activity. These patterns of economic activity, as will be seen, are particularly crucial to the conduct and success of HRD activities in a given nation.

The *political* institution encompasses structures and activities related to the allocation and use of power. Another way to look at this institution is to see political activities as regulating access to resources and opportunities. Hong Kong, on one hand (at least until 1997), has a political structure that facilitates virtually unlimited access, while Albania is almost totally restrictive when it concerns access to resources and opportunity.

These five institutions, in concert with the legal structure of a given nation, comprise its institutional profile. Although specific differences can be and are often thought of as cultural differences, the total complex of these five institutions, all together, in the main represents the society or nation to the world and gives it the profile which distinguishes it from other nations.

❦ *Intercultural Setting*

The term *culture* usually refers to the way of life of a group of people. Culture consists of a system of explicit and implicit guidelines for thinking, doing, and possessing (Bierstadt, 1963, pp. 154–157). Culture is defined by Bierstadt as "all the ways of living and doing and thinking that have been passed down from one generation to another and that have become an accepted part of a society" (p. 154). The influence of culture is expressed by Bierstadt when he explains:

> people in different societies all over the world have different cultures. They think different thoughts, do different things, and use different implements and utensils. For this reason their lives run different courses and the cycles of day and year and season wear different aspects. (p. 156)

When those of one culture interact with those of another culture, or when elements of one culture contact those of another, the resulting situation can be described as an intercultural one.

The culture component encompasses three basic elements: ideas (thinking), norms (doing), and materials (having). These three basic elements can, in turn, be combined into two or more categories.

Ideas refer to what the members of a society think. When used in a culture context, ideas encompass the values, beliefs, myths, superstitions, proverbs, folklore, and other related elements as found in a given society.

Norms refer to what the members of the society do, manifest in such behavioral guidelines or terms as laws, statutes, customs, rules, regulations, mores, folkways, taboos, fashions, rites, rituals, ceremonies, conventions and etiquette, and other related elements as found in a given society.

Materials refer to what the members of the society have or use and consist of such items as machines, tools, utensils, buildings, roads, bridges, natural resources, art objects, clothing, vehicles, furniture, food and medicine, among others, as found and used in a given society.

These three basic elements can be combined to form composite compounds or concepts. Many combinations are possible, but three essential ones will be discussed and illustrated here to highlight the concept of culture and its relationship to HRD.

When an idea is supported by a norm or set of norms, it is referred to as an *ideology*. Ideologies are the ideas and accompanying behaviors which we are obligated to believe in and practice, so as to remain in good standing in a particular social group. Such ideologies are set forth not necessarily because they are true, though they might appear to be so to the individual in the society, but because they are seen as right and proper for a particular society. The statement that "all men are created equal," for example, is an ideology rather than an actual fact. Although scientifically unsupported, belief in it is taught in the United States and elsewhere as a patriotic obligation.

A second combination of these basic elements, in this case ideas, norms, and materials, produces the compound we call *technology*. This term refers to the way materials are used in a given society, how specifically one looks at their meaning and worth (ideas) and the rules set forth to act upon this understanding (norms). Questions raised relative to technology have to do with what tool is needed for a particular job, how information is to be transmitted, or goods distributed, and so on.

The third combination we will focus on in this chapter is that of communication. This combination relies also on the society's way of putting together ideas, norms, and materials. Given the centrality of communication to the practice of HRD internationally, we will explore the relationship of this particular concept to HRD in considerable depth.

For purposes of illustrating the concept of culture and its relationship to HRD, then, six critical elements come into play, namely, the basic elements of ideas, norms, and materials, and the component concepts of ideology, technology, and communication.

THE OBJECTIVES OF INTERNATIONAL HRD

The objectives of international HRD are similar in many respects to those of training and development in a simple society. In both cases, the focus is on developing individuals to be more productive, as well as to develop skills for training others. Thus, the actual impact of societal and cultural conditions on international human resource development is manifest in two different but related situations:

- *Professional:* Those situations in which trainers are preparing for HRD work, carrying out HRD activities, and seeking to coordinate and legitimize such activities with those who have control in the society.
- *Application Situations:* Those situations in which trainees return to their work and life environments and seek to apply the knowledge, attitudes, and skills acquired during training.

The essence of international HRD lies in recognizing, understanding, and dealing effectively with two fundamental realities. First, the reality that international and intercultural differences between trainer and trainee have an important bearing on the success of human resource development activities. Second, the reality that the successful application of knowledge, attitudes, and skills learned in human resource development activities depends in great measure on the ability of both trainers and trainees to take into account and overcome the challenges inherent in these differences. Although brief note was made earlier of the potential impact of each of these realities on HRD, we will take this issue farther here.

We have chosen a circular model as a means, before looking at actual HRD practices in international settings, to try and make clear the total process. In order to do this, we have selected four concepts to describe the total involvement of HRD practitioners and recipients in international and intercultural situations: structure, processes, mechanisms, and transfer.

1. *Structure.* The first step in proceeding internationally is to recognize that when people enter an international/intercultural setting, they are in a different social structure. Both their behavior and the consequences resulting from their behavior are influenced greatly by this structure. Training activities take place within social structures, which influence and in turn are influenced by the activities. A prime goal of training activities, particularly, is to help those trained to modify the structure, as needed, to allow for greater trainee productivity and personal development.

2. *Processes.* The structure is the framework in which events occur, while processes are the activities. Within each structure a set of processes develop that allow the activities that make up the core of human relationships in that culture to take place. With reference to training, the processes are those culturally influenced activities that constitute the training preparation and delivery. Such processes should be thought through and designed with great care at this stage.

3. *Mechanisms.* Mechanisms are activities or processes in action. Once the processes are set on paper, then those in a group can proceed to interact. Whereas process development is essentially an exercise of the mind, mechanisms are behavioral implementations. Relative to training, interaction results in the four role clusters explained in earlier chapters. The analytical, developmental, instrumental, and mediational roles as defined are the processes, and the actions carried out to implement these roles are what is meant by the term mechanisms. Feedback from the operation of mechanisms often leads to modifications, in the training situation, of both structure and processes.

4. *Transfer.* This is the stage in which the knowledge, attitudes, and skills that are acquired during training are "taken" by the trainee back to his or her work and life situations. It is at this stage that we see the beginning of changes in a given culture. If the skills are used successfully by the trainee and others, in work or life settings, then we are likely to see changes in the ways in which things are done in the "real world," which in turn, alters the structure of the culture.

Optimum training conditions are those in which the structure allows training to take place, in which processes are set up that allow the training to move forward successfully, in which mechanisms get underway so that the actual human resource development work takes place, and in which the trainees return to their work and living areas and successfully bring about positive changes among those with whom they work.

APPLYING INTERNATIONAL HRD OUTPUTS TO WORK AND LIFE SITUATIONS

As commented upon earlier, an assumption underlying the distinction between "intranational" (within the same nation) and "international" (across national lines) HRD is that the national context within which individuals live and work influences the nature of the trainer-trainee relationship. Whereas intranational relationships are likely to operate on the basis of shared expectations and perceptions in most areas, with fewer problems relative to differentiation and communication, international relations do not. Those who study cross-national or cross-cultural relationships limit their focus often to cultural differences. While they are important, the structural dimensions have, as well, an important and direct impact on HRD. A major issue facing human resource development is that of transferring what has been learned during the training back to the work and life situations of those who participated in the activities. How such transfer might work in a given nation will be illustrated by looking at the interplay of HRD with class structures, social institutions, and the selected cultural factors defined earlier.

❦ *Class Structure and HRD Learning Transfer*

Activities involving individuals from two different nations are subject to the influence of the structural factors existing in each society. We noted and defined previously the two major societal factors which have bearing on international HRD relationships, first, the class structure present in the country and, second, the nature of the social institutions in that nation.

Every nation has a class structure or status system unique to itself. By *class structure* is meant the relative position of individuals to one another so as to have access to and the enjoyment of power, privilege, prestige, and wealth. By *status* is meant an individual's position in the class structure. Persons are often classified by social scientists according to their socioeconomic status.

We noted that class structures range from mobile or open, where individuals can move up or down in the system, to immobile or closed, where such movement is forbidden and attempts to move are suppressed or controlled. Mobile, or open systems, are usually called *class* systems, whereas immobile, or closed systems, are called *caste* systems. The degree of openness of a system may be placed on a continuum between caste and total equality, with no societies at the absolute extremes.

Both practitioners and recipients of HRD are, to some extent, prisoners of their positions in each society's class structure. The practitioner from a developed society usually comes to his or her tasks from a background that includes a substantial amount of formal education, relationships with upwardly mobile and articulate individuals, and quite a bit of openness and independence of action. In fact, it is expected that the practitioner will be highly self-motivated, innovative, and much more results oriented rather than simply procedure oriented. What practitioners need to take into account, however, when they leave their own societal milieu and go to work in most international situations is, from a class structure point of view, that differences in class structure between practitioners and recipients, and recipients and their own class structure, are of great import.

Since it is the recipient who returns and makes the transfer of learning to the local society, the practitioner's role is limited pretty much to that of guidance and support. In many cases, the practitioner completes the training activity and leaves the scene before any transfer takes place.

Even in those situations where the practitioner is still present, too much involvement with the transfer process may create artificial conditions that do not last after the practitioner's departure. Often such support efforts raise the expectations of both recipients and others in the society to unrealistic levels and make transfer even more difficult.

The recipient is left pretty much on his own generally to cope with the challenge of transferring enthusiasm and newly acquired learning to a class structure that may or may not be eager to receive what he or she is bringing. If there are two or more recipients, the task is easier, at least in their being able to form coalitions to resist readaptation to the earlier patterns in the society. In societies characterized by openness, many avenues can be identified that may well lead to effective, self-perpetuating change. In spite of many great changes in technology, however, most developing societies are oriented more toward closed than open systems. When faced with a more closed society, the recipient has the choice of biding his time, trying to plant ideas and even advocate them by precept as well as example or, as so often happens, reverting to the way things were done before.

The effect of class structure on HRD changes depends not only on the openness of the system, but also on the skills of the recipient to introduce new ideas. If the recipients' status is lower than those they want to influence, they must seek linkages with go-betweens who may be receptive to being trained by recipients. The two might then be able to work together to produce changes in task and organizational systems.

Improvements in productivity resulting from learning in HRD programs are most likely to happen when (1) the recipient is at a sufficiently high level in the class structure to have access to power and (2) there is enough of an openness to change that new ideas may enter.

❦ Social Institutions and HRD Transfer

The second major societal or international factor related to the success of HRD activities in a given society is the institutional makeup in that society. Each society shares in common, though differs in the relative influence each exercises, the presence of the same five institutions, namely, familial, religious, educational, economic, and political. The structure and diversity of each institution and the roles played by institutional actors differ, often markedly, from one society to another. The priority given to the various institutions also differs from one society to another and serves to dictate to a marked degree whether or not that society continues to progress or be receptive to efforts to increase the productivity of its members.

Probably the single most difficult initial challenge in transferring the results of HRD is that of legitimizing in these institutions what has been learned by recipients. During the training period, trainees are as often as not in an artificial environment. They are surrounded by others who come for training, and who possess at least some level of commitment to change. Those conducting the training serve as visible role models in some instances. Others are probably present who appear to have not only acquired the learning, but are also able, because of their position, to transfer it more effectively.

To understand the problems of transferring learning back to one's regular social institutional environment, it is necessary to realize that institutional patterns, in the main, change rather slowly over time. The challenge of fostering openness to change is as critical in social institutions as it is in class structure. Moreover, the actual manifestations of the problems of transferring learning are most evident if we focus primarily on the social institutions in the society. Although most societies have an overarching social structure, in terms of actual behavior change, the results can be seen most clearly by looking at what could happen, or not happen, in the context of each social institution. Given the tremendous scope and impact of these institutions in a given society, only brief treatment of each can be made here.

Family.   One of the questions asked most often has to do with why children, even with outside educational opportunities, often end up doing pretty much what their parents do. Part of the answer lies in the nature of the family structure itself. If a society gives priority to family concerns, great progress can be made in learning and individual productivity only if the parents or elders of the extended family support such learning. In those cultures where harmony is paramount, where cooperation is stressed, and where younger family members are taught nonassertiveness, it is far more difficult for anyone in a position of nonauthority to introduce, let alone implement, changes in the family's way of doing things.

A fundamental family-related dilemma faced in implementing the transfer of HRD is the fact that many types of change tend to weaken, rather than strengthen, ties between family members. Although values and perceptions have changed markedly since World War II, there are still relatively few societal situations that make it possible for families to remain close while at the same time permitting sons and daughters to move beyond the expertise levels of their parents. American society itself has not been able to resist the individualism that comes when some become so much more productive than others in the family. If a family chooses to open the door to independence for its children, history has shown that, in many circumstances, the old, close ties and sense of harmony are greatly weakened and in some cases eliminated. It appears that, in most societal situations, changing of traditional family orientations and structures has been a precursor to the acceptance of greater changes in productivity. A challenge of developing nations is to strike a balance between maintaining optimum family institutional patterns, on one hand, and facilitating increased productivity in work and in life, on the other.

Religion.   In most developing nations or societies, religious institutions have a pervasive influence. In India, for example, there is a strong ethic of fatalism with respect to events fostered by the predominant religion. A recipient who wants to apply new-found knowledge or skills may run up against situations where no one else feels that anything of long-lasting value can be accomplished because one's life is controlled by fate.

The one answer to the question of how to work around, through, or with indigenous religious institutions has come with the advent of massive societal changes. When new technology comes onto the scene, and succeeds over time to change feelings about opportunity, materialism, and life chances, religions have either had to weaken their hold on societal members or seek some way of accommodation. HRD practitioners should be alert to the types of religions in a society and assess particularly their potential impact on HRD recipients. It may well be, if the religious institution in a given society is a barrier to innovation, that HRD practitioners and recipients in training situations may need to try and identify and involve those who are willing and able to find an accommodation with selected practices and constraints of a given religious system. On the other hand, where the religion is supportive of changes, or does not see them as threats, it would be valuable to try and extend HRD perspectives and activities to religious influentials in that society.

Education. Of all the social institutions, with the possible exception of economics, education offers the best avenue for facilitating transfer of HRD. The nature of education, generally, with some exceptions such as schooling among very conservative communal groups, is one of openness to new ideas and technologies. If teachers can be involved as potential recipients, they are probably in the best position to pass on what they have learned either to colleagues or to their students.

Teacher training is one of the most critical needs in developing countries. Most of those in teaching positions who have received initial training in improving effectiveness are not in a position to take a substantial amount of time off to retrain as the need arises. Many teachers in developing nations, moreover, have had little or no formal training. Human resource development on site is one of the best means available to help these teachers develop or polish up on their teaching skills. If school systems in developing nations could incorporate, on a permanent basis, more quality in-service human resource development, there would be a marked improvement in the skills not only of these teachers but also of their students.

The importance of HRD to educational personnel cannot be overestimated. Students, particularly younger ones, are much more open to change than are their elders. Since the students will, in turn, someday be the leaders in a given society, the success of HRD in the education institution may have the greatest impact on introducing greater productivity and effectiveness to a given society.

Economic. It is in the economic area, more particularly in business and industry, that international HRD is most visible. Being on the cutting edge of competition, many international economic organizations are looking for ways to maximize profits.

Recipients who return to these types of organizations following training experiences are faced with a mixed bag. On the one hand, the organization may welcome and appreciate the greater productivity displayed by those who have gone through HRD activities. On the other hand, an employee back from training sessions may be seen as a threat. Employees are now able to perform the tasks better, perhaps even better than their supervisor. The aura of expertise, and with it increased authority, may follow, leaving the supervisor unsure of his or her position. Unless a whole department, for example, can undergo training together, and thus advance in status together without changing relative positions, the training of one or two or even all the workers in a unit, may come to nought.

HRD continues to be a part of international settings. As both communication and transportation systems improve, greater growth in the impact of HRD on economic institutions will occur. Economic institutions, in turn, are moving toward greater openness. The prognosis is good for HRD to have more impact in economic institutions.

Political. The last social institution to be examined is the political one. Political institutions dictate who has access to power and opportunity. Any changes that are going to take place in a society depend on, at least, the acquiescence of the influentials in this institution.

HRD transfer in a political setting is also problematical. In authoritarian and totalitarian systems, the perpetuation of the status quo is seen as paramount. Anyone going into human resource development to gain knowledge, change attitudes, or improve skills is a potential threat to leaders in these types of political systems. It is expected that, for that reason, HRD which is seen by political influentials as having a potential impact on the political system will be seen as suspect.

What HRD recipients can do to allay these fears is to emphasize that the training is more "technical" than "political." Certain members of the political system, particularly those having to do with budget issues, can profit from training, and the results may be seen more in the bottom line than in changes of people's attitudes toward politics. At the same time, focusing training on technical skills still feeds people into the system who may be able, over time, to more subtly change other attitudes.

❦ Culture and HRD Transfer

Having shown how HRD relates to the concept of society, or more precisely how the societal setting influences the practice of HRD, we can now turn to the relationship between culture and HRD, and see how culture influences the success of HRD transfer. We will note briefly how five of the cultural elements identified in Figure 10.1 might influence HRD practice internationally and interculturally. We will look then in much greater depth at the relationship of one particularly critical cultural variable, that of communication, to HRD in the international setting.

We have noted that society is the framework within which human behavior takes place, while culture is the actual perceptions and behaviors. We identified earlier three basic elements of culture (ideas, norms, materials) and three components derived from these basic elements (ideology, technology, communication). Much has been written on the relationship of culture to international development. Since our intent here is to introduce the notion of culture and its relationship to human resource development, we will limit our discussion to these six cultural characteristics.

Ideas. Patterns and content of individual thought in a given culture play a significant role in what happens in HRD activity. Two particular ideas or cultural values can be used to illustrate this relationship. First, consider the relationship of humans to nature. Societies can assume three basic positions relative to this value idea, that people should be submissive to nature, should find harmony with nature, or should master nature. If, for example, a trainee comes from a background of accepting conditions as inevitable, and of seeing self and others as without recourse to do anything about these conditions (sometimes called "fate"), the trainee is not likely to be motivated to undergo training to develop new skills. People who have a "mastery" orientation, on the other hand, see themselves as able to use new skills to make a difference in productivity or effectiveness.

Second, differences can arise depending on whether the culture is oriented primarily to the present or to the future. Present-oriented individuals are much more interested in things running well now, rather than in introducing changes that may be divisive or disturbing to the status quo. Put another way, need affiliation and harmony now is seen as more critical than is need achievement, which calls for planning for the future. A strong need for immediate harmony can be a serious detriment to training in particular skill areas. Future-oriented individuals are more proactive, and look to training as a means of assuring a better condition in the future. For these people, training is much less a threat and much more an opportunity.

Norms. What one does is of course central to training. If, for example, the norms in a given cultural setting discourage any comments that may cause one to lose face, then efforts to get trainees to look critically at their present performance risk being futile. Discussions carried on under such a normative mandate may not generally allow participants to get too close to any accurate evaluation of performance on the job or the reasons why such performance may be deficient. The problems of transfer are greatly complicated, as well, when the norms in a particular cultural setting support an unwillingness to practice a new skill, if the subsequent practice is seen as one that could expose a person's incompetence in a particular area relative to the skill. Norms can, therefore, have substantial control over what can or cannot happen in training situations.

Materials. The presence or absence of some types of materials can dictate the level of success, or even whether success can occur, in a given training session. Military units in some countries, for example, train with guns that are obsolete or won't fire, or even try to learn by using sticks because there are not enough guns to go around. Frequently employees are required to train on old, obsolete equipment, even though the energy and time required to transfer skills under such conditions is greater than if the trainees had worked on the correct equipment initially.

Another situation is all too common in many developing cultures. Many rural development projects use imported materials that do not stand up under the existing environmental conditions, so that after a short time of use, the equipment breaks down and cannot be repaired. There are many instances in international settings where the materials available have little or no relationship to a specific training need. The absence of materials best suited to increase productivity presents a real hardship for both trainer and trainee.

Ideologies.   At least two noted authors, Max Weber (1958) and William Goode (1963), stress the significance of ideology in bringing about a climate where human resource development is possible. Goode argues that ideology is probably more important in fostering change than is industrialization, even though the latter element is generally accepted as the single most significant harbinger of change.

Frequently training needs run up against what is assumed as a "truth" in a given society. If, for example, the ideology reflects a belief that individuals and their abilities differ inherently by social class, training situations involving those from different social classes will probably not be successful. Individuals tend to conform to the expectations that significant others or reference groups hold for them. An ideology that holds that higher-status individuals are the only ones who can perform a particular task not only discourages those who are not of the status from trying to learn the skill, but may even prevent the trainee in question from even attempting to try.

Technologies.   The level of technology best suited to rendering a task productive may be ahead of the existing level of expertise in the culture generally. Even if the technology is present, those in the culture may see themselves as having neither the expertise nor, more critically, the temperament to use the technology properly. Technology is more than just the materials that are available. It is as well the ideas about the appropriateness of such materials, who should and can use them, and the perceived threat of such technology to the existing status structure. Examples abound of cultural situations where those from a particular segment of the population are not allowed to make use of some kinds of technology, not for practical reasons but for political ones.

An even more critical problem related to making optimum use of technology stems from the widespread hunger found in so many developing nations. Some years ago, a trainer was attempting to instruct local residents on the best ways to group particular food crops. The two-year-long training program ended without any significant impact in learning to use the requisite farming methods and related technology, when some trainees, suffering from undernourishment, harvested the crop prematurely simply to satisfy their hunger.

Lest it seem that the societal and cultural barriers to successful HRD activities are stronger than any efforts to produce change, it is important to point out that these nations, if they are to continue to develop, need the types of knowledge, attitudes, and skills that HRD practitioners can provide. Second, there are many cases where HRD efforts have been transferred. For those contemplating practicing HRD in international settings, however, it is important to be aware of those societal and cultural factors that can mean success or failure.

❦ Communication and International HRD

International HRD, thus, confronts both *societal boundaries*—class structures and institutions—and *cultural factors*—ideas, norms, ideologies, materials, and technologies. However, both societal and cultural elements require *communication* to make them operational. The levels at which communication occurs are parallel to the order of relationships in a community. An analysis of the levels of communication provides a model for understanding the factors involved in international HRD. Six levels of communication may be described (Figure 10.3).

1. Personal
2. Interpersonal/group
3. Organizational/intergroup
4. Cultural/ethnocentrical
5. Institutional/societal
6. International/intercultural

Imposed on these six levels are the media/technology of communication. The impact of media on communicative acts and processes varies by level. For example, a medium, such as a telephone, may facilitate interpersonal communication by allowing two parties to make contact over some distance. At the personal level, a hearing aid may allow an individual to pick up auditory signals, and eye glasses may facilitate clearer visual signals. At the global level, on the other hand, satellites and videotapes may be part of a distribution system for making messages available to both individuals and entire communities. Radio

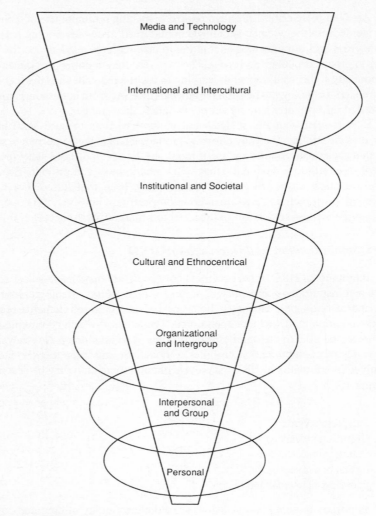

FIGURE 10.3
Levels of Communication

has long been a mechanism for sharing information in both developing and developed countries.

Individualized media, including interactive computer-video technologies and electronic mail systems, allow messages to be presented to single trainees or to large audiences. The media and technology of communication now make the concept of a "global" community possible. Individuals in all parts of the world, given the appropriate technology like a video playback machine, may view the same message at the same time, allowing for simultaneous message exposure throughout the global community.

Each level at which communication occurs builds upon the prior level; however, communication must be understood first as an act at the personal level, then it can be understood as a social process that facilitates each level in a social system.

Level 1: Personal. The word "communication" may be understood to refer to the act of *making sense out of displays*. A display represents the means by which something is put into view or made known or brought to the attention of someone. Displays consist of objects, events and actions. Objects are the concrete things around us; events are the physical happenings in our lives, and actions are the oral, written, and pictorial messages that we create to bring things to the attention of others. The process of "bringing things to one's attention" is often called "symbolizing" or using language and actions to represent the things we wish to call attention to.

The term "message" is often used synonymously with displays. In other words, when a person talks about or points to something to call our attention to it, we often say that the person is sending us a message. In reality, however, all the person is doing is making a display. The person isn't "sending" us anything. The person is talking or acting in ways that *try* to call our attention to something. If our attention is not attracted to the thing, we often say that communication did not occur, or we did not get the message.

In order for "communication" to occur in an international setting, in both a technical and a popular sense, it is necessary for the person whose attention we are trying to attract to focus on and make sense out of the displays. If the attender is unable to make sense out of what is said and the actions involved in the display, then we say that communication did not occur or that it was quite ineffective. We refer to people who are able to get our attention and help us to make sense out of what is happening as "great communicators." That is, they help us to communicate—they help us make sense out of what they say and do.

The personal level of communication consists, then, of the activities in which an individual engages in order to interpret messages or to make sense out of displays. At this level, the individual sees people and what they say and do, sees events, and sees objects and tries to make sense out of them. Communication is equal to the sense a person makes out of life. The more sense that is made, the more communication there is. All other levels of communication depend on this level, the personal level, where sense is made out of the happenings in the world.

What does it mean "to make sense" of something? In this setting, to "mean" is similar to "make sense." To mean or to make sense denotes and connotes that the person is engaged in the process of assigning significance to the person, object, or event. The significance of something results from the relationship one assigns to it in the total scheme of one's life. Thus, an otherwise harmless act on the part of a supervisor to assign you to a task that you dislike may acquire significance to you because you consider it to be an indication of distrust and a major cause or explanation for the quality of relationship between you and your supervisor. The supervisor, you reason, does not trust you, hence, the undesirable assignment. You have made sense out of the supervisor's actions. You have given the supervisor's actions meaning. They are not just actions; they are symbolic of the supervisor's distrust.

From Where Do Meanings Come? Frankl (1963) argues that "the striving to find a meaning in one's life is the primary motivational force in man" (p. 154). All other meanings come from the meaning one finds in one's own life. The most authentic and genuine aspect of existence is a person's desire for a life that is as meaningful as possible. Meaning in life is represented by one's ideals and values. Thus, a person has the most comprehensive meaning in life when he or she is able to recognize, identify, and articulate the ideals and values for which one is willing to invest the most, even to the extent of sacrificing one's life for the ideals and values.

Values and ideals, as Frankl so skillfully points out, are not forces that drive people; they "pull" a person (p. 157). With values, there is always the freedom to decide whether to behave consistent with the ideal or not, or, as Frankl says, "to fulfill a meaning potentiality or else to forfeit it" (p. 158). Thus, a person is never driven to ethical or moral behavior, but each person *decides* to fulfill his or her meaning in life or to behave ethically or morally.

It is at the personal level of communication that we are confronted most directly with the meaning of our own lives, with what we value most and with what ideals we seek to achieve. How one lives and how one dies is a function of one's meaning in life. As Frankl observes, again, "There is nothing in the world . . . that would so effectively help one to survive even the worst conditions, as the knowledge that there is a meaning in one's life" (p. 164).

Personal communication involves most deeply the process of discovering the meaning in one's life and making decisions about what other things mean in relationship to one's own life meaning. Despair, meaninglessness, helplessness, and frustration may have their basis in a lack of clear meaning in life and an inability to discover a worthy goal toward which to struggle, to overcome the meaninglessness of one's life. Without a clear meaning in life, one vacillates between distress and boredom, rather than between confidence and enthusiasm.

Different cultures hold different meanings and socialize their members to share those meanings. The success of HRD in various international settings depends to a great degree on how well the trainer understands what meanings trainees attach to symbols. Answers to questions such as, "What values does the trainer attach to his work?" "What motivates the trainee to work hard?" and "How does the trainee perceive and respond to leaders?" are important to successful HRD activities.

Level 2: Interpersonal/Group. At this level, the displays of one person are offered or presented to another or several others in a face-to-face setting or by means of media/technology in which those involved are able to respond to some personal aspects of the display of another; a conversation over the telephone is an example of a non–face-to-face interpersonal communication event.

At the interpersonal level, individuals negotiate with one another the meanings that they hold for people, objects, and events so as to arrive at shared meanings. The goal of effective interpersonal communication is to negotiate as many shared meanings as possible. Cooperation and collective action are predicated on having negotiated the minimum number of necessary shared meanings.

A prominent aspect of level 2 is the imposition of "rules" to govern meanings and decisions. As two or more people make contact with one another over time, regularities begin to occur and expectations develop. Displays become more conventional and predictable, which reduces the amount of energy necessary to interpret and understand and make sense of them. At the same time, "role" behaviors begin to appear which transform interpersonal contacts into more routine and, often, impersonal interactions. The authenticity and genuineness of the personal meaning-in-life displays and their companion understandings are often obscured by the negotiated displays and interpretations. HRD practitioners, to be effective in cross-cultural settings, need to understand and practice interpersonal communication styles that succeed in achieving basic shared meanings.

Much of the success of HRD mechanisms (processes in practice) depends on successful communication at this level. In the last analysis, it is the trainer and trainee who are at the heart of HRD practice. If there is effective communication at the interpersonal level, at least initially, the trainee will have acquired what the trainer is trying to get over.

Level 3: Organizational/Intergroup. At level 3, the conventions of interpersonal communication are formalized and reinforced by the structure, uniformities, and restrictions of organizations. Interpersonal roles are transformed into occupational positions that are accompanied by status differences resulting from differences in authority, duties, power, control, and organizational rules and regulations.

Organizational conventions evolve and solidify into what some call the "culture" of the organization. "Cultural maps" enable organization members to define situations (people, objects, and events) and develop appropriate responses. Organizational action is based on the collection of assumptions known as the "cultural pattern" of the organization (Wilkins and Dyer, 1988, pp. 523–525).

Smooth functioning of HRD-type communication at this level depends on the degree to which conditions of reciprocity or fairness are met. That is, members of the organization agree that the conditions of fair exchange and treatment have been met. Wilkins and Dyer (1988) explain that "if conditions of reciprocity are not met, groups and individuals who cannot or do not leave the organization develop countercultural or alienative orientations to the whole" (p. 524). Communication may become disruptive in organizational relationships where cultural patterns do not show reciprocity and fairness of treatment. A grasp of the culture of a given organization is a prerequisite to effective role performance, for an HRD professional.

Level 4: Cultural/Ethnocentrical.   The fourth level of communication introduces the notion of ethnocentrism or pride in the traits, distinguishing characteristics, assumptions, and customs of a group of people. The presence of a culture is revealed by such elements as language, child-rearing practices, sacred objects and taboos, behavioral guidelines, attitudes toward work and leisure-time activities, social classifications and authority structures, ideologies, common and coded law, tools and objects, and educational systems.

These characteristics both integrate the group into a whole and differentiate it from other groups. Thus, culture is the largely taken-for-granted way of life of a group that creates for it an integrated whole and differentiates it from other groups in the social system. The development of a culture depends almost entirely upon the extent to which communicative contacts are restricted to members of the group. This network of communicative links encourages a common "frame of reference" to evolve. Although all societies have activities and objects, they are essentially without meaning until the members of the culture pay attention to them and interpret them. Thus, the critical feature of any culture is the common or shared interpretations of objects, events, and people.

The most significant dimension of culture is that collective meanings or interpretations are conceptually, at least, independent of individuals in the culture and can be analyzed without reference to individual beliefs and actions. In many instances, individuals may be totally unaware that they are functioning within a culture unless someone points it out to them (Van Maanen and Barley, 1985, pp. 31–36).

Group members, nevertheless, do not have minds of their own in which to store meanings and interpretations. Culture can not be separated from the people who perpetuate it. While it takes a group to invent and sustain a culture, only individuals can perpetuate the culture. Hence, cultures endure only to the extent that they are transmitted from one generation to the next.

The concept of culture argues strongly that what people say and do are often shaped by influences far beyond their control and, of course, outside their immediate circumstances. Nevertheless, culture is about people thinking, doing, and communicating together, with resulting definitions of reality that represent collective understandings of how to think, do, and communicate. If newcomers are to work effectively in a culture, they must learn and respect the preexisting definitions and conditions.

Kohls and Riesett (1983) illustrate the dominant cultural orientations that distinguish between developed and developing countries using several issues, although over 60 such issues have been identified. A brief review of 4 of the issues reveals how culture is such a pervasive, and often detrimental, influence on efforts to work and communicate cross-culturally with others.

| | Society | |
Orientation	Developed	Developing
Who is in control?	People	Fate

Seven-eighths of the people in the world believe in the concept that fate controls who you are and what you will become. Americans, on the other hand, live their lives as if there is nothing beyond their power to achieve.

| | Society | |
Orientation	Developed	Developing
Whose needs should have priority?	Individual	Group

Although Americans, for example, consider themselves to be independent and think they should have their needs filled first, most of the people in the world feel that the groups with which one identifies are more important than individual effort or recognition.

| | Society | |
Orientation	Developed	Developing
How does a person gain respect?	Achievements	Birth

In many areas of the world, people assume that their station in life is established at birth; they willingly accept their position and seldom question those in authority. Americans, on the other hand, have relatively little respect for inherited rank and authority; they think that people should earn their right to rule by means of what they do.

	Society	
Orientation	*Developed*	*Developing*
In which direction should I be oriented?	Future	Past

The direction of one's orientation is closely related to one's concept of change. In more traditional countries, for instance, change is seen as a destructive force and one that should be avoided. Of more importance is one's ancient heritage and tradition, which produce stability and continuity rather than change. The conclusion is that one should be oriented to the past. Americans, on the other hand, tend to think of change as a good thing, associated with growth and improvement.

Since a national culture may differ from a specific organization culture, it may be insufficient in HRD practice to limit one's knowledge to the national culture or to the culture of the organization. It is important to find answers to the kinds of questions raised by Kohls and Riesett.

Level 5: Institutional/Societal.   The fifth level of communication involves and is affected by social institutions beyond that of the formal work organization. At this level, issues of politics, religion, economic philosophy, education, and family tradition influence what is said and done and how it is said and done. This level goes beyond the usual cultural determinants of interaction and involves the structures of the institutions of society, such as the law, church, and government.

The most critical long-term issue related to the effectiveness of HRD is transference of learning from the training situation to the job site and life in general. To be able to anticipate the fit between learning and the larger institutional context, and to make adjustments to heighten transferability, is likely to be the most important goal of an HRD practitioner in an international setting.

Level 6: International/Intercultural.   The sixth level of communication crosses all divisions and boundaries, physical and cultural, all systems and structures, language and social, and all events and conditions, including traditions and attitudes. This is the level at which international human resource development purports to function, crossing and encompassing personal communication, interpersonal and group communication, intergroup and organizational communication, cultural communication, and institutional communication; this level also takes into account the impact of media and technology on all levels.

SUMMARY

The purpose of this chapter has been to present a brief overview and analysis of the setting of international human resource development. Distinctions have been made between society, the international dimension, and culture, the intercultural dimension. Each of these dimensions was defined in some detail, and problems of applying HRD in society both before and after the departure of practitioners were examined.

REFERENCES

BIERSTADT, ROBERT. *The Social Order: An Introduction to Sociology.* New York: McGraw-Hill, 1963.

FRANKL, VIKTOR E. *Man's Search for Meaning.* New York: Washington Square Press, 1963.

GOODE, WILLIAM J. *World Revolution and Family Patterns.* New York: Free Press, 1963.

KOHLS, L. ROBERT, AND ROBERT F. RIESETT. "Intercultural Training: How Do You Know When You Need It?" Unpublished paper presented at the National Conference of the American Society for Training and Development, 1983.

STARK, RODNEY. *Sociology,* 3rd ed. Belmont, CA: Wadsworth, 1989.

VAN MAANEN, JOHN, AND STEPHEN R. BARLEY. "Cultural Organization: Fragments of a Theory." In Peter J. Frost et al., *Organizational Culture.* Beverly Hills, CA: Sage Publications, 1985.

WEBER, MAX. *The Protestant Ethic and the Spirit of Capitalism,* trans. by Talcott Parsons; reprinted. New York: Scribners, 1958.

WILKINS, ALAN L., AND W. GIBB DYER, JR. "Toward Culturally Sensitive Theories of Culture Change." *Academy of Management Review,* 13 (1988), pp. 522–533.

❦ ❦

CHAPTER 11

Careers in
Human Resource Development

INTRODUCTION

Human resource development, often called training and development, employee development, or personnel development, is that function in organizations concerned with improving the quantity of output or productivity and the quality of work life. Human resource development achieves its goals by employing a set of activities that prepare employees to perform their current jobs more effectively, to assume a variety of different positions in an organization, or to move into jobs, positions, and professional activities that have not as yet been identified.

A *career* is generally thought of as employment, often after a period of formal preparation, in an occupation or profession, spanning the time between entry into the career and retirement (Schein, 1978). A career is usually considered to be a person's life work. Thus, a career in government work means that a person has dedicated his or her working life to employment in a government position.

On the other hand, a career in engineering may mean that the person has made a commitment to work in the capacity of an engineer, regardless of the company in which he or she works. A career as a professional, in fact, implies that the person is willing and committed to change companies in order to continue work in the professional area if that kind of work is no longer available or is no longer satisfying in the organization where the person is employed.

Careers, therefore, may be *institutional*, meaning that the person in the career is committed to the organization and seeks continued, long-term employment in the organization, or *professional*, meaning that the person in the career is committed to the professional area and seeks continued, long-term employment in the profession regardless of the organization. Sometimes, a job embodies both the institutional and the professional elements of a career, allowing a person to function in the same professional area in the organization on a continued, long-term basis.

CAREER TYPES

INSTITUTIONAL: Primary commitment to the organization
PROFESSIONAL: Primary commitment to the profession

❦ Value

Human resource development is a professional area that allows individuals who are prepared in the roles and competencies of the field to find employment in a wide variety of organizations. Information about where opportunities are available and how to make contacts provides the potential professional practitioner with the resources to locate an entry-level position. At the same time, some understanding of the way in which a person progresses through a career, with specific application to human resource development, may help professionals make plans and recognize how they are progressing through the stages in a professional career.

❦ Chapter Organization

This chapter provides information about the location of human resource development in the complex and diverse world of work and organizational life. It indicates where entry-level positions are located and how to make contact for placement. This chapter summarizes the stages in professional careers and provides some signposts for professional practitioners to use in assessing where they are currently located on the continuum from apprentice, to colleague, to mentor, to director (Dalton and Thompson, 1986).

✌ *Learning Objectives*

After studying this chapter, you should be able to:

1. Explain what is meant by the concept of *career.*
2. Recognize where HRD opportunities exist in a variety of types of organizations.
3. Create a strategy for moving into a professional career in HRD.
4. Distinguish among the four stages in the career of professionals.
5. Devise a general plan and set expectations for what needs to be done to move systematically through each stage so as to reach a satisfying career stage at an appropriate time.

A CAREER IN HUMAN RESOURCE DEVELOPMENT

The field of human resource development has all the characteristics of a profession, and it is being recognized as a career field for professionals. As with engineers, scientists, accountants, lawyers, teachers, professors, architects, medical doctors, dentists, and social workers, HRD professionals meet all of the criteria established for classification as professional in the workplace. They have a defined area of competence, an organized body of knowledge, academic programs that are helping to control access into the profession, continuing education, research programs that support the profession, and positions in organizations where professionals function with independence.

The pressures toward professionalism are in evidence in the work of the American Society for Training and Development and other professional associations concerned with the status and standing of HRD in organizations and society. The results are being felt in the identification and institutionalization of better ways of doing the job, creating standards of quality that serve the organization, the professional, and the public interest.

CRITERIA TO BE A PROFESSION

- **Defined area of competence**
- **Organized body of knowledge**
- **Controlled access**
- **Continuing education**
- **Research programs**
- **Positions in organizations**

The ASTD Competency and Standards studies (McLagan and McCullough, 1983; McLagan, 1989), the work of the National Board of Standards for Training, Performance, and Instruction (Bratton, 1986), and the establishment of almost 300 academic programs in HRD argue strongly that the conditions for professionalism are in place. Then, add a body of literature on ethics (see bibliography on ethics, Appendix A) and journals devoted to publishing research and theory on HRD issues (see bibliography on journals, Appendix B), research councils, a Professor's Network in ASTD, and the bases of professionalism become clearer.

FOUR CAREER STAGES

Four distinct stages in the career of a professional have been identified by Dalton, Thompson, and Price (1977): apprentice, independent contributor, mentor, and director. Professionals in HRD tend to perform these functions in the same way that other professionals do. Dalton and Thompson (1986) summarize the main focal point of each stage:

> In Stage I, individuals work under the direction of others as apprentices, helping and learning from one or more mentors. In Stage II, they demonstrate their competence as independent contributors. In Stage III, they broaden and act as a mentor for others. Those in Stage IV provide direction for the organization (p. 7).

Dalton and Thompson also explain that a relationship exists between career stages and performance ratings; that is, "if one person is performing Stage I functions very well and another person is performing Stage IV functions very well, the performance of the person in Stage IV will be more highly valued because the functions are more highly valued" (p. 12).

These two observations, that careers progress through stages *and* the activities of Stage IV are more highly valued than activities of Stage I, have significant implications for career development in the lives of professionals. As Dalton and Thompson note, "Those who step forward and capably address these [organization] needs are usually recognized as having an enhanced or continuing value to the organization. Over time, those who fail to fill these needs are judged as having relatively less value" (p. 13).

To progress or "step forward and capably address" organization needs and move from one stage to another, the individual must meet two basic requirements. The individual must (1) show that he or she has the abilities and talents required of the new stage and (2) secure the confidence of those who exercise power in the organization and provide him or her the opportunity to perform at the next stage. Without both the abilities and the empowerment and support of their mentors and directors, the prospective performer will experience derailment and frustration. With their support, however, the prospect will be permitted to perform the new activities and be accepted into the new roles and experience success during the next stage in his or her career.

Career management involves many activities including choosing a particular professional specialty, such as human resource development; choosing a particular organization in which to practice the profession; accepting or declining alternative professional opportunities, such as relocations, promotions, and transfers; and ultimately leaving the organization for another position or retirement. The major goal of most professionals is to be successful, which comes in large part from progress in one's career.

❦ *A Personal Strategy*

Four key variables tend to affect how people feel about the success they are having in a career: how well they are *performing* (P), how much *opportunity* (O) they have, how *fulfilled* (F) they feel in their work, and how what they are doing meets their *expectations* (E) (Pace and Mills, 1989; Pace and Stephan, 1989). These concepts form the acronym POFÉ (pronounced "poh-fay"). The consequences of not finding fulfillment and opportunity, of not performing well, or not meeting expectations are detrimental to all careers, including HRD.

In managing a professional career, care should be taken to match your preferences and talents to an organization that allows you to experience the highest levels possible on your own POFÉ.

Seek to recognize your unique strengths and look for job assignments that allow you to devote energy to achieving the level of performance that is satisfying to you. Attempt to locate an organization or career direction that operates on the basis of values that give you a high sense of fulfillment. Look for avenues to open up opportunities so that your performance and fulfillment may be demonstrated. Discover and articulate what you expect from the organization and work to match your expectations with what the organization is able and willing to provide.

INDICATORS OF CAREER SUCCESS

- **Performance level**
- **Opportunities given**
- **Fulfillment experienced**
- **Expectations met**

❦ *Profession to Career*

Dalton and Thompson (1986), as noted previously, identified four critical stages in the life work of a professional (apprentice, independent contributor, mentor, and director). To build a career in human resource development, a person devotes his or her life work to HRD and progresses systematically through these stages. Thus, career and professional lives are closely linked together.

A key question is whether entry-level positions exist in HRD so that a person can move into and demonstrate competence in an apprentice status. A related question is whether the positions that exist allow a given person the opportunity to devote his or her life work to HRD and move from an apprentice to an independent contributor to the field to become a mentor to others coming into the profession and eventually provide direction to HRD in the organization and among professionals. The discussion to follow demonstrates a positive answer to all of those questions.

Corporate HRD, whether provided in-house, by for-profit vendors or public enterprises, constitutes almost as large a delivery system as the entire elementary, secondary and postsecondary school system. The potential employment market is astounding, providing opportunities of unparalleled importance for qualified university graduates.

EMPLOYMENT IN HRD

Employment in human resource development was reported by *Business Week* as one of the top 12 entry-level positions for this decade. *Woman's World* identified human resource development as one of the most promising career areas for women.

The variety of organizations in which an HRD professional may find career opportunities may be illustrated by the section in the Official Membership Directory of the American Society for Training and Development in which members are listed by organization. The directory contains 52 pages of listings with approximately six columns of names per page with about 200 different companies listed on each page for a total of over 9,000 companies.

The types of organizations represented in the ASTD directory is almost too diverse to classify, but just about every kind of work setting is found among the lists. Business, industry, government, health care, retailing, foods, manufacturing, transportation, utilities, finance, construction, religious, volunteer, professional and trade associations, educational institutions, accounting firms, insurance, service, research, communications, petroleum, airlines, beverages, publishing, transportation, mining, recreation, clothing, information systems, newspapers, consultants, and training vendors are all included.

HRD employment opportunities generally fall into six categories: organizational effectiveness, management development, consulting and training services, sales training, career development, and technical training.

❦ Organizational Effectiveness

Major companies are recognizing the impelling need to create work environments that promote open communication and responses based on mutual respect where personal risk taking, innovation, and individual and team participation in goal setting, problem solving, and decision making are encouraged and recognized. Methods used to achieve this new environment and culture include idea systems, focus groups, and employee and management forums designed to enhance employee involvement in improvements in the workplace.

Organizational effectiveness or "systems refinement" is an approach to organization improvement that progressively develops individuals, work teams, and systems to their maximum level of effectiveness. The process embodies a variety of team structures such as quality circles, autonomous work groups, task forces, and integrated management teams. Team members are provided with training in work methods, problem solving, project management, leadership, group dynamics, and team building. Organizational effectiveness promotes a culture of excellence by emphasizing continual improvements, teamwork, and participative management in all areas of work life.

HRD staff are assigned responsibility for the design, employee training, and implementation of the organizational effectiveness or systems refinement process.

❦ Management Development

There are more than 5 million managers in U.S. companies. Managers are the fifth most frequently trained occupational group in the work force, after technical and nontechnical professionals, technicians, and management support personnel. Most management development is provided to qualify managers for their jobs and to upgrade their positions.

Individuals prepared for HRD careers are employed to create, conduct, and administer programs for three levels of managers: supervisors, middle managers, and executives. The HRD staff may be responsible for conducting development programs in leadership effectiveness, managing conflict, communication, power and influence, team building, innovation and change, management styles, group processes, creative thinking and problem solving, bargaining and negotiating, and setting and achieving goals.

❦ Consulting and Training Services

The training industry consists of companies that provide training tailored to the needs of specific employers. Large companies buy almost 40 percent of their formal training from outside providers, midsized employers buy an even larger share, and small employers go outside for nearly all their formal training. HRD professionals are employed to perform a wide range of services in the training industry, including the design and production of materials, the presentation and facilitation of programs, and the sales and marketing of vendor products.

❦ Sales Training

Dramatic changes have occurred in the philosophy and culture of major segments of the business community regarding sales and marketing. Financial institutions, for example, are using HRD professionals to prepare employees for the transition from a product orientation to a service philosophy. HRD staff design and present programs in customer service, platform skills, office operations, management skills, and direct marketing.

Many entry-level HRD specialists are given responsibility for managing the sales training program, which often includes skills in marketing, sales, and customer service. Nearly every company that distributes products and services has a comprehensive sales training program that strengthens specific skills and prepares sales personnel for managerial responsibilities; thus, sales training and management development are often closely allied.

❦ Career Development

With increasing concerns felt and expressed about staff reductions, dislocating workers, and technological change, employees have begun to recognize that they have diminished job security and must take more responsibility for their own career progress and work vitality. In order to accept this new responsibility, employees will need new tools, more information, and access to support systems that have not been available in the past. Professionals prepared for careers in HRD train employees in the new methods, how to use information systems, and how to find and use support systems.

❦ Technical and Skills Training

In companies where technological superiority is a goal, students prepared for careers in HRD are employed to design ways and conduct programs for helping employees learn computer skills, operate computer-controlled equipment, and coordinate the use of subject matter experts in training programs, such as assisting buyers to learn automated inventory management.

Human resource development is a career area that may be for you, if you have the ability to interact with organization members at all levels, an interest in helping others develop, and the talent to conceptualize, design, and implement programs that integrate people, technology, and systems both vertically and horizontally within the organization; if you can teach people to analyze work systems, identify areas that need improvement, and assist them in acquiring the skills to refine their work systems; and if you can take a broad "systems view" of organization processes in learning and developing problem solving, decision making, leadership, and management skills so as to apply them to real work situations.

CAREER PATHS

The concept of career path can be demonstrated by examining the career progression of a professional in the Professional Education Division of Arthur Andersen & Co., one of the largest accounting firms in the country. In literature distributed to potential professional education staff members, Arthur Andersen & Co. describes its PED career path ranging from the position of professional staff to that of partner or principal in the company. As Figure 11.1 shows, the path moves from a staff position to that of senior staff, then to education manager, followed by senior education manager, and ultimately to partner or principal in the company.

❦ Career Path When HRD Is an Independent Unit

In most organizations, a professional's career path follows the order of promotion. Depending on the complexity of the organization, a professional in HRD begins as a training specialist and rises to vice president of human resource development. On the way, the professional may have technical responsibilities in HRD, working in such areas as program planning, program design, materials development, administrative support, or delivery of training programs. On the other hand, the professional may have administrative responsibilities over one or more program areas, such as management development, technical training,

PED Career Path

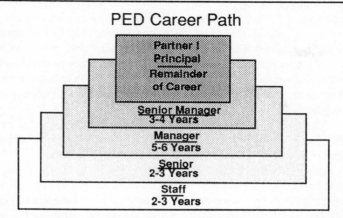

Guidelines for Your Professional Development

STAFF	You will develop a solid foundation in training problem analysis and the application of instructional design to business training needs.
SENIOR	You will begin to supervise and teach others as you continue to develop your own business and design skills.
EDUCATION MANAGER	You will develop project management and other managerial skills as you broaden your scope of concern to curricula and business trends.
SENIOR EDUCATION MANAGER	You will refine your managerial skills and apply a broad perspective that will establish you professional reputation within both PED and the firm.
PARTNER/ PRINCIPAL	For the balance of your career with the firm, you will continue to develop your skills and add to your reputation. You will exercise your independent judgment in supervising teams of professionals in the business community and in civic and professional organizations. You will be the beneficiary of the high standard of excellence set by principals before you.

FIGURE 11.1
PED Career Path, Arthur Andersen & Co.

sales training, or support staff development. As a training representative or coordinator, the professional in HRD may have responsibilities that involve advising operations managers about the full range of training services available and how to make full use of divisional or corporate staff, programs, and facilities.

In large organizations, an HRD professional may proceed on a career path that leads to managerial or administrative responsibilities over a technical or a program area, or possibly supervising and working with apprentices and other entry-level staff.

The next position in an HRD professional career path is usually that of manager of a training and development or HRD department that includes a number of technical specialists and several program areas.

Beyond being a local manager, the HRD professional may move to a position as regional director of HRD with some policy-making authority and responsibilities for liaison and coordination among several local units.

The next move is usually to the corporate HRD staff where strategic planning and key policy decisions are made. This level may also be represented by the position of director of a corporate training center.

The final move is to the position of vice president or corporate director of HRD, training, or education. This professional has primary responsibility for the direction and management of the entire HRD functionin the organization.

❦ Career Path When HRD Is Commingled with Personnel

In some organizations, the human resource training and development function is administered by personnel, and HRD specialists are called personnel specialists. The career path follows the structure of the personnel department in those cases. From the position of personnel generalist, an employee may move to a specialist's position in one of the personnel areas, such as compensation, labor relations, employment, safety, or training.

From a specialist's position, an employee may move into the role of manager of training. Advancement beyond the position of manager requires the employee to move into personnel positions at the plant, divisional, or corporate levels. Because of the limited number of positions in human resource training where HRD is commingled with personnel, a person would need to move into some other area or relocate.

A personnel department may have as few as three levels: the lowest level is personnel specialist, then the assistant manager level, and finally the manager of personnel level; in some cases, personnel may include a position at the vice presidential level, although the person's title may more often be that of vice president of industrial relations.

Included within the personnel department, however, may be a fairly large number of activities. In a medium-sized company, for example, personnel may include coordinators or directors of employee services, cafeteria, and recreation; medical services such as first aid; employee communication involving the company newsletter and newspaper; safety; wage and salary services; employment; employee benefits, insurance, retirement, and savings; and training services, including technical training and management development.

Career paths in personnel, beginning with training services, may include lateral experience in one or more of the allied services, with possible promotion to the position of assistant manager, and eventually to manager of personnel or industrial relations.

CAREER MOVEMENT FROM HRD TO OTHER PROFESSIONS

Preparation in human resource development provides perspectives and skills that can be used in a wide variety of career areas. HRD specialists can assume line responsibilities with relative ease because they have breadth of understanding that comes with exposure to analytical, developmental, instrumental, and mediational role clusters and the associated knowledge, attitudes, and skills. For that reason, many HRD professionals make career shifts, moving into line management, private business, and consulting activities.

For individuals who are competitive and like a challenge, there are many management positions available, in such diverse areas as commodities trading, real estate development, and property management. Preparation in HRD lends itself particularly well to applications in public relations, marketing, sales, and counseling. Health administration and recreation management are popular career areas for HRD students because they make high demands on analytical and interpersonal skills.

CAREER PLATEAUING

HRD careers, whether positioned as independent or commingled with personnel, are staff-type positions. Staff influence is exercised through advisory channels and, as such, has little formal power relative to decisions about products and services. Line management positions are, therefore, often seen as more desirable than staff positions because they have not only more power, but they also have a larger number of vertical opportunities that allow for more promotions and a longer career path. When a person's career shows a likelihood of no further promotion up the hierarchy of the organization, he or she is plateaued. The level at which an employee plateaus is the last step in the career path (Slocum et al., 1985).

Most employees seem reluctant to reveal to others that they are plateaued, or they may not be able to recognize or they are not willing to accept plateauing, but it is estimated that as many as 60 percent of the managers in a company are plateaued (Near, 1980). All managers, nevertheless, reach plateaus in their careers. If plateauing is widespread and the plateaued managers or employees are performing poorly, the organization and the individual may have a serious problem. For example, Near (1985) reports that plateaued managers were absent more frequently from their work, reported poorer supervisory relationships, and suffered more health problems.

Career paths in all areas of a company, including HRD, may lead to earlier plateauing than most college graduates expect. The consequences of early plateauing may suggest that individuals entering the work force in the future may need to have in mind alternate strategies for coping. For example, employees who have plateaued need to be provided meaningful work on a continuing basis, they should be involved in decisions, and they should be encouraged to teach and coach other employees (Lorsch and Takagi, 1986).

SUMMARY

This chapter has defined the concept of career and distinguished between an institutional career and a professional career. It has described a professional career in human resource development and identified alternative career paths where HRD stands alone and where training is part of personnel. The characteristics of four stages in the career of a professional were discussed, and four variables—performance, opportunity, fulfillment, and expectation—that affect career success were introduced. Some types of organizations where a career in HRD is possible were mentioned.

The next chapter will continue the treatment of HRD as a profession in more detail, focusing primarily on how one might prepare to enter HRD as a career.

REFERENCES

DALTON, GENE W., AND PAUL H. THOMPSON. *Novations: Strategies for Career Management*. Glenview, IL: Scott, Foresman, 1986.

DALTON, GENE W., PAUL W. THOMPSON, AND RAYMOND L. PRICE. "The Four Stages of Professional Careers—A New Look at Performance by Professionals." *Organizational Dynamics* (Summer 1977), pp. 19–42.

LORSCH, JAY W., AND HARUO TAKAGI. "Keeping Managers off the Shelf." *Harvard Business Review* (July–August 1986), pp. 60–65.

MCLAGAN, PATRICIA A. "Models for HRD Practice." *Training and Development Journal* (September 1989), pp. 49–59.

MCLAGAN, PATRICIA A., AND RICHARD MCCULLOUGH (EDS.). *Models of Excellence.* Alexandria, VA: American Society for Training and Development, 1983.

NEAR, JANET P."The Career Plateau: Causes and Effects." *Business Horizons,* 23, No. 5 (October 1980), pp. 53–57.

PACE, R. WAYNE, AND GORDON MILLS. "Career Plateauing." Paper presented at the ASTD annual conference, Boston, June 1989.

PACE, R. WAYNE, AND ERIC STEPHAN. "Work Vitality." Paper presented at the annual conference of Region 8, ASTD, Monterey, California, September 1989.

SCHEIN, EDGAR H. *Career Dynamics: Matching Individual and Organizational Needs.* Reading, MA: Addison-Wesley, 1978.

SLOCUM, JOHN W., JR., WILLIAM L. CRON, RICHARD W. HANSEN, AND SALLIE RAWLINGS. "Business Strategy and the Management of Plateaued Employees." *Academy of Management Journal,* 28, No. 1 (1985), pp. 133–154.

CHAPTER 12

❦ ❦

How to Prepare for a Career in Human Resource Development

INTRODUCTION

The status of any profession is, in part, related to how well its practitioners are prepared to perform relevant roles and to work in the field. This chapter addresses the issue of securing an academic degree as preparation for a career in human resource development. Although lifelong learning is one of the most important factors affecting a person's income (Carnevale, 1989, pp. 28–29), it takes more than a desire to learn or even learning itself to have a successful professional career. Academic preparation is, nevertheless, a vital ingredient for most people hoping to start a successful career.

In Chapters 1 and 11, we pointed out that employees usually take one of two approaches to careers: institutional or professional. Assignment to an HRD position as part of an institutional career path usually means that an employee has been asked to assume some responsibilities in HRD on a short-term basis, after which the employee takes an assignment in some other area of the organization. Neither the organization nor the employee intends for the assignment to be permanent.

If the employee performs well or spends an appropriate period of time, he or she receives a transfer to another position in the organization. In most cases, the transfer, it is hoped, represents an advancement and provides a form of preparation for an ultimate position, usually in upper management. This process is often called "cross-training," meaning that the employee is crossing professional boundaries, getting experience in a variety of areas, but without being required to have the academic preparation in the professional area necessary to function successfully as a professional.

Professionals in the field, those who have this prior preparation in HRD in this case, may feel that the person in "training" is infringing on their domain and lacks the background to work effectively. Professional employees should, however, view the cross-training as an opportunity to inform potential managers about HRD and the contributions that professionals can make to helping the organization meet its goals.

Cross-training in HRD is accomplished by having the employee observe, engage in developmental activities under the supervision of experienced professionals, and take responsibility for self-directed learning in the form of reading, attending workshops, and completing projects on a trial and error basis.

Line managers and supervisors may also engage in activities that develop employees over whom they have responsibility; initially, such managers will participate in some form of cross-training, both formal and informal, by being sent to workshops or by engaging in their own self-directed learning. HRD professionals should feel a strong obligation to assist in making HRD cross-training as effective as possible.

Much of the work of professional organizations, such as local chapters of the American Society for Training and Development (ASTD) and the National Society for Performance and Instruction (NSPI), is devoted to the development of individuals who receive organizational assignments in HRD for more or less temporary periods, and whose orientation is essentially an institutional one.

The professional in HRD is prepared, however, in quite a different way. The professional intends to remain in the field, to work in HRD over his or her lifetime, in whatever location is promising to enter the field as one who has been prepared as a professional, and to contribute to the profession over a long period of time by being active in professional associations like ASTD and NSPI. Professionals identify with the field and enhance it through their own efforts.

Entry into professional areas is determined, generally, by successful completion of occupationally related academic programs. As human resource development acquires more characteristics of a professional area, greater demands will be placed on faculty in HRD academic programs to prepare and certify those allowed entry into HRD jobs.

Philosophies that underly the design of different types of academic programs influence decisions about the type of educational preparation that leads to work in human resource development. The number of academic programs is increasing yearly, giving more people the opportunity to prepare for careers in HRD (ASTD, 1986). At the same time, many academic programs may claim to provide preparation to enter the field of HRD, but lack the courses and resources necessary for satisfactory preparation (Pace, Peterson, and Porter, 1986).

❦ *Value*

The preparation of professionals is of major concern to a wide range of individuals and organizations, including students, parents, administrators, managers, universities and their faculties and trustees, and employers. Each group has its own goals to achieve, such as finding a job, budgeting and staffing a university department, getting a satisfying return on an investment in education, and admissions policies and accrediting standards.

The overriding question or issue is, however, how can we best educate and prepare individuals who now have, or who will likely have in the future, responsibility for the development of employee talents, skills, and abilities? The remainder of this chapter outlines a way to prepare high-quality HRD professionals.

❦ *Chapter Organization*

This chapter provides a brief overview of five slightly different ways that most colleges and universities approach the challenge of educating students. Although some argue that just going to college is adequate and even the best preparation for entry into the work force, we shall reason that professional areas, such as HRD, require practitioners to make their knowledge useful. The case is made that human resource development is a professional career field that requires specific entry-level educational preparation. Finally, this chapter describes the levels at which HRD professionals learn and work, and how HRD knowledge relates to careers in other helping professions.

❦ *Learning Objectives*

After studying this chapter, you should be able to:

1. Recognize and characterize five ways in which colleges and universities approach the task of educating students.
2. Explain why HRD is a professional area and how a career approach to curriculum design and other aspects of HRD academic programs is the best way to prepare individuals to enter the field.
3. Explain the different levels at which HRD professionals learn and work.
4. Distinguish between HRD and other careers, and point out the strengths gained in the academic preparation of HRD professionals that can complement other professions.

5.   Design a program of study which offers adequate academic preparation for work in human resource development.

WHO STUDIES HRD?

A college or university program in human resource development tends to attract students of two general types. The first type is a person who already has a temporary job in HRD and who would like to complete a degree in order to fulfill more clearly the requirements for becoming a professional. This group of students may tend to look for more direct and immediate applications of course materials in the workplace. Course projects may need to be more practical or related to specific organizational practices.

The second type is a person who has little if any background or experience in HRD, but who wishes to prepare for an entry-level professional position in the field. This group tends more often to be regular, full-time students attending a college or university with the purpose of receiving general preparation for broad categories of career opportunities, of which HRD is one of the potential entry points.

Although both groups may benefit from the same courses, some aspects of the total academic program need to be adjusted to accommodate the real differences in the two groups of students. If you, the reader, are a student in either group, or if you are an educator who is interested in establishing an academic program in HRD, the information that follows provides you with guidelines for selecting or creating courses or, even, college programs that give the best possible preparation for a career in HRD.

It may be, as many may argue, that there is no single, right way to prepare HRD professionals, or that there is even a commonly agreed-upon core of skills and knowledge for HRD practitioners, and that there are wide variations in the skills used by practitioners in different organizations; nevertheless, the monumental work of ASTD and NSPI in completing national studies of HRD competencies do provide a basis for curriculum development in this field.

WHAT IS IMPORTANT TO LEARN IN COLLEGE?

Most people who enter the field of human resource development in the future will have completed at least a bachelor's degree from some accredited college or university. Much has been written about what is important and even essential for a person to learn during his or her college days (Boyer, 1987). Although the differences of opinion will not be resolved here, an understanding of what the differences are may allow you to decide what kind of academic program provides the best preparation for a career in human resource development (Friedrich, 1982).

What is presented here are ideal types. In actual situations, each approach either acknowledges or tries to combine some elements of the others. A benefit in distinguishing them analytically here is to alert one to the underlying philosophy and operational emphasis of a given educational organization or unit.

FIVE WAYS TO WISDOM

- **Learn about civilization**
- **Learn how to think**
- **Prepare for a career**
- **Discover who you are**
- **Learn morals and ethics**

❧ *Learn About Civilization*

One goal of higher education is to pass on to each new generation of students the core of knowledge that best represents "civilization." Civilization is the total culture of a people, nation, or period. The concept of advanced civilization is associated, generally in the minds of most people, with countries and peoples who have reached a high stage of social and cultural development. Thus, a college education should provide the essential background necessary to understand one's culture and to help each person reach this higher stage of social and cultural development.

In most colleges and universities, the "general education" program is comprised of courses designed to transmit critical aspects of one's civilization. Although not typical, Friedrich (1982) described the corpus of knowledge some people believe should be part of general education in this way:

> a list of 130 great books drawn heavily from the classics and philosophy but also from the ranks of modern novelists like Faulkner and Conrad . . . four years of math, three of a laboratory science, two of music and two years of Greek and French. . . . [It] includes no such novelties as psychology (except what can be learned in the works of Freud and William James) and no sociology (except perhaps Jane Austen). (p. 69).

On most campuses, the civilization component of a general education program usually includes psychology and sociology, as well as the humanities, natural sciences, fine arts, physical sciences, communication and mathematics, and offerings from the rest of the social and behavioral sciences.

Academic majors that extend and elaborate upon this basic core of general education courses combine major offerings with this core to represent the ideal university education from this point of view.

❦ *Learn How to Think*

A second goal of higher education is to teach people to think. This means, generally, producing graduates who not only have some understanding of their civilizing roots but also of the ways in which decisions are made. When a person is able to "think," he or she is able to analyze, draw reasonable conclusions, and determine the goodness or badness of something. Thinking is a process or method of handling information rather than of learning any particular bit of information. Thinking in this sense, thus, depends on having some idea about how knowledge is gained and organized. Accordingly, it doesn't matter particularly what one studies, as long as the methods of inquiry and knowledge building are understood and applied.

In the learning-how-to-think approach, having a core or a common body of knowledge is distinctly secondary. The methods of each discipline are more important. The consequence for someone taking this approach to learning usually results in the pursuit of a diverse, elective-type curriculum.

❦ *Discover Who You Are*

A third goal of higher education is helping individuals discover who they are and aiding them in developing their own potentialities. Given the premise that individuals differ from one another, a curriculum grounded in the need to discover self is largely designed by and for each individual. Courses are offered and selected because they allow each person to discover something of the truth of existence and to evolve a meaning in life. Faculty are present for the purpose of helping students find their own way and discover the wonders of who they are and where they fit.

Academic programs that seek to free individuals from personal background and traditional modes, and help them to become what they can, regardless of the great ideas or the processes involved, have this goal in mind.

❦ *Learn Morals and Ethics*

The primary goal of some universities and colleges is to cultivate students who can recognize and deal with the moral and ethical issues involved in living.

Students are taught, for example, moral philosophy and theology along with and sometimes rather than psychology. Courses in applied ethics in business reflect an effort to introduce this type of moral/ethical dimension into specific university curricula.

Those who urge that this goal be the dominant one of college and university education argue that engineers should never learn to build highways without being taught a concern for the lives of people whose homes they displace. The study of standards of conduct and moral judgments and the principles of right and wrong as they apply to daily living and interaction with others are central to this approach to education. Appendix A contains a bibliography on ethics in HRD that provides basic information on ethics issues.

🌳 Prepare for a Career

The fifth approach to higher education emphasizes preparing individuals to contribute to society in a practical way. The main force of career education is to develop competent individuals who can perform tasks and make knowledge effective in society. The message here is that a college or university education should provide exposure to all the foregoing, but should exist primarily to prepare individuals to be useful.

A career approach to education, if related properly to the other four approaches, can be the most effective way to make a college or university a place where students become educated in the finest sense possible. A professional curriculum allows research and teaching, studying and learning to be organized around the substance of living—the world in which we live—while integrating and capturing the strengths of the other approaches.

Knowledge of civilization is not, for example, something separate from what we do and how we live. Thinking is not something done in the abstract and separate from what we do and how we live. The self is a function of what a person does and how a person lives. Ethics and morals are not abstractions separate from what we do and how we live. By having clearly defined programs of study that lead to areas of application, we, in fact, can have curricula that help create the truly well-educated person.

Boyer (1987) explained that "all students, regardless of their major, are preparing for productive work. As with engineering, business, and computer science, a student who majors in English or biology or history will, it is assumed, someday become employed and use what he or she has learned for some useful end" (p. 109).

Education for work in human resource development is accomplished best by following curricula designed to prepare students for careers. Students who have mastered the principles and methods of a professional curriculum acquire aspects of civilization, learn to think for themselves, discover ways to develop and be self-actualizing, and recognize some of the moral and ethical issues of life.

Human resource development academic programs are found in at least eight different academic administrative units across the country: adult education, behavioral sciences, business, communication, counseling, curriculum and instruction, human services/education, and vocational/occupational education (Pace, Peterson, and Porter, 1986). Most of these units tend to organize knowledge around areas of application or have strong interdisciplinary inclinations. Thus, degree programs in HRD may have a somewhat common "driving force," regardless of the administrative unit in which they are located. Most of these academic departments offer "professional" degree programs and consider professional degrees as compatible with what they are currently doing or have done traditionally.

CHARACTERISTICS OF A PROFESSION

As a professional area, human resource development academic programs are designed to meet the eight characteristics of a profession (Marston, 1968).

1. *A Defined Area of Competence.* The definition of HRD indicates that its area of competence has to do with helping employees acquire, expand, and develop their knowledge, perceptions, and skills so as to be productive and contributing individuals. The specific goal is that of preparing members of the work force to improve the quality of their work.

2. *An Organized and Important Body of Knowledge.* Human resource development academic programs represent an effort to organize knowledge around an area of application. In the case of HRD, the curriculum is designed to prepare students to perform the key roles performed by HRD practitioners, the professionals in the field. The 11 roles identified by an ASTD task force (McLagan, 1988, 1989), and discussed extensively in Chapters 5 through 8, are:

Administrator	Marketer
Evaluator	Materials developer
HRD manager	Needs analyst
Individual career development advisor	Organization change agent
Instructor/facilitator	Program designer
	Researcher

Although not everyone agrees on the relative importance of each of the roles, it is apparent that the best curricula include courses that treat the content and methods of most of these roles.

Knowledge involved in preparing for and performing the roles in HRD comes from recognized, legitimate, and important sources. This knowledge is associated with the modes of operation, methods, and skills of human resource development and is organized and presented in textbooks and other publications, making it available for study and use.

3. *Identified with a Career Field.*   Those prepared to be HRD practitioners actually use their knowledge in identifiable organizational and institutional positions. The professionals are represented by an association or associations dedicated to supporting the best interests of the field and those in the field. The American Society for Training and Development (ASTD) is the primary organization representing the career field of human resource development.

4. *Competent Individuals Enter the Profession by Controlled Access.* Those who are employed in the field have learned the theory and methods and have acquired the skills in ways that allow them to qualify legitimately for the positions. This implies that curricula are accredited and professionals who successfully complete HRD academic programs based on roles are certified to enter the profession.

5. *Principles and Practices Supported by Research.*   The most common way to make research available is through publication in professional journals. The field of human resource development has faculty members and other professionals who are engaged in research and who publish in the *Training and Development Journal, Training, The Journal of Management Development, Performance and Instruction, The Human Resource Development Quarterly,* and in other sources. Although more research needs to be done, the field of HRD has established itself as one in which research is being done.

6. *Involvement of Working Professionals in Academic Programs.*   The best academic programs involve HRD professionals in advisory committees, as guest speakers, and as adjunct faculty. In addition, professionals provide access to their work locations by encouraging field trips by students and by placing students on compensated internships.

7. *Program of Continuing Education.*   The best academic programs share their research and ideas with working professionals through conferences, joint projects, and seminars.

8. *Graduates Who Exercise Independent Judgment.*   Those who are admitted to HRD academic programs are selected on the basis of intelligence, technical competence, and maturity. HRD academic programs should be designed and managed so as to attract individuals of the highest caliber. The best programs use both scholarly and personal criteria in the selection of candidates for entrance into the degree program.

PRINCIPLES OF CURRICULUM DESIGN

In looking for a professional program of study that has the potential for high-quality preparation, look for a program that meets five important principles of curriculum design.

1. The courses have a "center that holds." The curriculum has a core of courses that define the content of the major and the focus of the program. These courses are not just a collection of topics, but they are geared to help students learn to perform effectively the key HRD roles.
2. The courses are structured in a hierarchical sequence of knowledge, skills, methods, and products that show progression through some pattern. The courses are ordered with prerequisite knowledge and skill in which some knowledge and skills precede other knowledge and skills.
3. The courses represent a "lean" curriculum with clearly defined "essential" courses and relevant elective courses, rather than topical courses that reflect the preferences and whims of individual faculty members.
4. The courses are driven by the "force" of *application* or making knowledge effective and useful. Each course in the curriculum results in clearly defined end products or projects that demonstrate that the skills and competencies have been acquired by students.

Preparation for work in human resource development shares some similarities with preparation for work in other helping professions. As a result, you will recognize that it is likely that some movement occurs across boundaries of many of the allied helping professions. For example, social work, although focusing primarily in business and industry on employee assistance, has aspects of its preparation that provides opportunities for those in social work to move into positions in human resource development. In fact, in one chapter of ASTD, several of the officers and many of the chapter members now working in HRD had formerly been in social work.

Some of the helping professions that commonly provide preparation in roles that are relevant to human resource development include teaching, social work, counseling, selling, legal affairs, public administration, recreation, psychiatry, and urban and community development. Although each, including HRD, has a set of technical skills unique to basic performance in the professional area, the cluster of helping professions share a couple of aspects in common.

The most apparent connection, but not always the most obvious to observers, is that the helping professions share a common "driving force," that of "enhancement" or *improving the lives of their clients*. A driving force is the energy that comes from the fundamental concept of what the professional area is attempting to accomplish. In the case of some professional areas, the driving force is "artistry" or "entertainment." For others, it is "maintenance" or "profit." For some, the driving force is "service" and for some it is "action." The helping professions have a driving force that impels them to make the development of people their main priority, although the way in which the driving force is manifest may differ widely among them.

Each of the helping professions has a particular way of helping its clients. Selling, for instance, develops people by helping them purchase products and services, social work develops people by helping them secure life support systems, counselors and psychiatrists develop people by helping them take control over their own lives and find meaning in living, teachers develop people by helping them learn about ideas and acquire skills, and lawyers develop people by helping them manage formal relationships in society that are governed by laws and conventions.

HRD specialists develop people by helping them to acquire the skills, perceptions, and knowledge to perform their jobs, to do better in their organizations, and to make progress in their own careers. Human resource development helps people where they work, although the results may also help people where they play, where they worship, and where they serve the community.

Second, the helping professions share some methods, such as interviewing, and have a common interest in improving the way in which people communicate. The foundation of nearly all helping professions is communication theory (Ruesch and Bateson, 1963; Combs, Avila, and Purkey, 1971; Pace, 1983).

5.   The program offers auxiliary support activities, such as field experiences and internships, student professional associations such as ASTD, and conferences and other continuing education activities for students and professionals in the field.

These five guidelines can be used in the selection of an academic program that has the promise of providing excellent preparation for entry into the HRD field. The quality of faculty is, naturally, an important consideration, but, if the curriculum and support activities are in place, the reputation of local faculty members is of less concern. A very good program can be offered to the credit of the college.

The size and location of the college are, also, of minimal concern when the academic program is well designed. The two illustrative programs that follow are from a small, private college in the Pacific Islands and from a large, state university in a southwestern state. They are excellent programs located in different academic units and in quite different types of institutions. The direction and emphasis of academic programs are usually revealed through the "program description."

PROGRAM DESCRIPTION: BACHELOR'S DEGREE IN HUMAN RESOURCE DEVELOPMENT

The major in human resource development offers students an interdisciplinary blend of courses in the behavioral and organizational sciences that prepare them for careers in personnel development, corporate education, management and supervisory training and development, and technical training, as well as work in personnel, employee and industrial relations, and general management.

The HRD major provides for breadth of scholarship in the liberal arts and depth in the applied behavioral sciences. As an undergraduate major, HRD is appropriate preparation for graduate work in human resource development, instructional science, organization development, and other behavioral and organizational sciences.

PROGRAM DESCRIPTION: MASTER'S DEGREE IN INSTRUCTIONAL DESIGN AND HUMAN RESOURCE DEVELOPMENT

This program is intended to prepare participants to improve human performance and productivity in business, industry, government, military, and educational environments.

Essential to the program are areas of study which emphasize human resource development, instructional design, instructional strategies, instructional delivery systems, educational technology, evaluation, and program management. A broad theoretical base is integrated with laboratory and applied experiences producing a comprehensive program that prepares graduates for work in the rapidly expanding instructional design and human resource development field.

In addition to courses offered within the department, students are encouraged to select relevant offerings in adult education, information science, communication, and business. Maximum effort is made to tailor programs to the needs and experience of students. To accommodate working students, many courses are offered in the afternoons and evenings and on weekends.

PLANNING YOUR ACADEMIC PROGRAM

Both these programs explain that they provide preparation for careers in human resource development; both use the terms "human resource development" in their titles; both purport to offer courses that prepare students to perform the roles of HRD professionals. Both these programs appear to provide specific preparation in HRD.

You may wish to evaluate how completely an academic program prepares a person for work in HRD. How could that be done? One way would be to take the courses listed in the class schedule of the college program being evaluated and compare them with the HRD roles. The matrix represented in Table 12.1 demonstrates how this process might be accomplished.

Study the matrix to discover the relationship of courses to the content of HRD roles. The matrix lists courses that are well suited for preparing individuals to perform HRD roles, some of which are drawn from the HRD programs described earlier. If possible, of course, you should examine the content of the courses and match them with the definitions of each of the HRD roles. The matrix indicates which courses offer preparation for each of the roles. If your college or university does not offer a major in human resource development, it may be necessary for you to identify courses like those listed in the matrix from various departments throughout your college or university; this can be done by consulting your local college or university bulletin.

A number of other courses may be available in the more extensive HRD programs, including an introduction to the field of HRD, learning theories, management development, leadership, and organizational communication.

❦ *Internship or Field Experience*

The culminating experience for HRD majors should be an internship where students apply what they have learned in real organizations under the supervision of human resource development professionals. The internship is a cooperative arrangement between an organization and the university on behalf of the student. Every human resource development professional should arrange to place an HRD major in his or her organization not only as a benefit to the organization but as a professional obligation to contribute to the education of new professionals.

Preparation for the internship experience should begin early in a student's academic career. Materials that can be used in a "portfolio" to demonstrate skills related to HRD roles should be assembled. As term papers or research papers, for example, are completed in other classes, neat copies should be made to include in the portfolio as indications of research and writing skills. Each project

TABLE 12.1
Matrix for Selecting Courses for an Academic Program

HRD Roles	Courses Often Included in HRD Academic Programs*
1. Administrator	Principles of Management
2. Evaluator	Evaluation in HRD
	Program Design
3. Career development advisor	Career Planning
	Interviewing
4. Instructor/facilitator	Instruction in HRD
	Group Process
5. Manager	Principles of Management
6. Marketer	Introduction to Marketing
	Public Relations
7. Materials developer	Media in HRD
	Instructional Materials
8. Needs analyst	Analysis in HRD
	Microcomputer Operations
9. Organization change agent	Organizational Behavior
	Theories of Change
10. Program designer	Strategies of HRD
	Instructional Design
11. Researcher	Social Research Methods
	Statistics

*Courses with these titles or their equivalents tend to provide the theory and skills related to the roles.

completed in a class should be packaged and displayed so as to reveal competencies and capabilities.

❦ Student Society

Students should be able to affiliate, where possible, with professional organizations in the field (Pace, 1983a). Chapters of the American Society for Training and Development are located in most population centers. Some schools have chapters of ASTD for students; Ohio University and Brigham Young University are two that have had active student-only chapters. Other schools have affiliated associations or special organizations in the field. Brigham Young University–Hawaii, for example, has a student organization called The Society for Human Resource Development (SHRD) for majors in the field.

ASTD has published papers about academic programs that are available from its press (see Pace, 1981). ASTD also has information about HRD academic programs in a directory that it publishes.

SUMMARY

In this chapter we have identified and characterized five goals associated with higher education: (1) learn about civilization, (2) learn how to think, (3) learn who you are, (4) learn morals and ethics, and (5) learn to apply knowledge in a career. Education in human resource development is best achieved when curricula are designed to prepare students to apply knowledge in a career. Eleven roles performed by HRD professionals were listed for purposes of matching educational programs with role preparation. Eight characteristics of a professional field were described in terms of the career field of human resource development. Some similarities between HRD and other helping professions were cited, especially the commonality in "driving force." Finally, how to build an academic program for you was discussed, characteristics of effective HRD academic programs were reviewed, and some illustrative programs were cited.

REFERENCES

AMERICAN SOCIETY FOR TRAINING AND DEVELOPMENT. *Academic Directory of Programs in HRD*. Arlington, VA: ASTD, 1986.

BOYER, ERNEST L. *College: The Undergraduate Experience in America*. New York: Harper & Row, 1987.

CARNEVALE, ANTHONY P. "The Learning Enterprise." *Training and Development Journal* (February 1989), pp. 26–33.

COMBS, ARTHUR W., DONALD L. AVILA, AND WILLIAM W. PURKEY. *Helping Relationships: Basic Concepts for the Helping Professions*. Boston: Allyn & Bacon, 1971.

FRIEDRICH, OTTO. "Five Ways to Wisdom." *Time* (September 27, 1982), 66–72.

MARSTON, JOHN. "Hallmarks of a Profession." *Public Relations Journal* (July 1968).

MCLAGAN, PATRICIA (ED.). *ASTD Competency and Standards Project*. Alexandria, VA: American Society for Training and Development, 1988.

MCLAGAN, PATRICIA. "Models for HRD Practice." *Training and Development Journal*, 43 (September 1989), pp. 49–59.

PACE, R. WAYNE. "Organizational Communication: Foundations for Human Resource Development." *Models and Concepts for T&D/HRD Academic Programs*. Washington, D.C.: American Society for Training and Development, ASTD Research Series, 1981.

———. "ASTD Student Chapters: The Integrating Force of Successful HRD Academic Programs." *Academic Programs and the World of Work*. Washington, D.C.: American Society for Training and Development, ASTD Research Series, 1983(b).

———. *Organizational Communication: Foundations for Human Resource Development*. Englewood Cliffs, NJ: Prentice Hall, 1983(a).

PACE, R. WAYNE, BRENT D. PETERSON, AND W. MARC PORTER. "Competency-Based Curricula." *Training and Development Journal* (March 1986), 71–78.

RUESCH, JURGEN, AND GREGORY BATESON. *Communication: The Social Matrix of Psychiatry*. New York: Harper & Row, 1963.

APPENDIX A

❦ ❦

Bibliography on Ethics in HRD

AMERICAN SOCIETY FOR TRAINING AND DEVELOPMENT. "Code of Ethics." *ASTD Who's Who in Training and Development.* Adopted November 1975, 1981, pp. 30–31; 1982, pp. 418–419.

BECKER, STEVEN P. "The Trainer's Changing Ethics." *Training,* 13 (November 1976), p. 20.

CARROLL, ARCHIE. "Linking Business Ethics to Behavior in Organizations." *S.A.M. Advanced Management Journal,* Summer 1978, pp. 4–8.

CLEMENT, RONALD W., PATRICK R. PINTO, AND JAMES W. WALKER. "Unethical and Improper Behavior by Training and Development Professionals." *T&D Journal,* 32 (December 1978), pp. 10–12.

DEWINE, SUE, AND ANITA JAMES. "The Hippocratic Oath and Standards for Organizational Consultants." *ERIC Document,* ED 165 217 (1978).

DONALDSON, JOHN, AND MIKE WALLER. "Ethics and Organization." *The Journal and Management Studies* (February 1980), pp. 34–55.

DUBINSKY, ALAN J., AND JOHN M. GWIN. "Business Ethics." *Journal of Purchasing and Materials Management* (Winter 1981), pp. 6–7.

ERDLEN, JOHN D. "Ethics and the Employee Relations Function." *Personnel Administrator,* 24 (January 1979), pp. 41–43.

FAGOTHEY, AUSTIN. *Right and Reason: Ethics in Theory and Practice.* St. Louis: C. V. Mosby, 1976.

FRANKENA, WILLIAM. *Introductory Readings in Ethics.* Englewood Cliffs, NJ: Prentice Hall, 1974.

GOLDHABER, GERALD M. "Ethical Considerations of Consulting." In *Organizational Communication,* pp. 374–377. Dubuque, IA: W. C. Brown, 1974.

HARMOND, GILBERT. *The Nature of Morality: An Introduction to Ethics.* New York: Oxford University Press, 1977.

HOSPERS, JOHN. *Human Conduct: Problems of Ethics,* shorter version. New York: Harcourt Brace Jovanovich, 1972.

JOHANNESEN, RICHARD. *Ethics in Human Communication.* Columbus, OH: Charles E. Merrill, 1975.

KRAMLINGER, THOMAS. "If You Have Questions About Ethics, Why Not Ask an Ethicstition." *Training* (May 1977), pp. 40–41.

LOSITO, WILLIAM F., AND ROBERT MAIDMENT. "Ethics and Professional Trainers." *Eric Document,* ED 186 980 (January 1980).

MAIDMENT, ROBERT, AND WILLIAM F. LOSITO. *Ethics and Professional Trainers.* Madison, WI: ASTD, Organization Development Division, 1980.

NEWSTROM, JOHN W. "Ethical Considerations and the Supervisor." *Supervisory Management,* 20 (November 1975), pp. 16–21.

NEWSTROM, JOHN W., AND WILLIAM RUCH. "Managerial Values Underlying Intraorganizational Ethics." *Atlanta Economic Review* (May–June 1976), pp. 12–15.

OAKS, DALLIN H. "Ethics, Morality, and Professional Responsibility." *BYU Studies,* 16 (Summer 1976), pp. 510–575.

PACE, R. WAYNE, BRENT D. PETERSON, AND M. DALLAS BURNETT. "The Ethics of Using Communication Techniques." In *Techniques for Effective Communication,* pp. 9–11. Reading, MA: Addison-Wesley, 1979.

PAHEL, KENNETH, AND MARVIN SCHILLER. *Readings in Contemporary Ethical Theory.* Englewood Cliffs, NJ: Prentice Hall, 1970.

PERRY, LEE T., AND JAY B. BARNEY. "Performance Lies Are Hazardous." *Organizational Dynamics,* 20 (Winter 1981), pp. 68–80.

PINTO, PATRICK R. "Your Trainers and the Law: Are They Breaking It in and out of the Classroom?" *Training,* 15 (October 1978), pp. 71–76.

SCHWARTZ, LOIS. "Ethical Issues in Consulting." *NSPI Journal,* 25 (February 1980), pp. 40–43.

VELASQUEZ, MANUEL. *Business Ethics.* Englewood Cliffs, NJ: Prentice Hall, 1982.

VON GLINOW, MARY ANN, AND LUKE NOVELLI, JR. "Ethical Standards Within Organizational Behavior." *Academy of Management Journal,* 25 (June 1982), pp. 417–436.

WALTON, RICHARD E., AND DONALD P. WARWICK. "Ethics of Organization Development." *The Journal of Applied Behavioral Science,* 9 (1973), pp. 681–698.

ZAKRAINSHEK, EDWARD A. "How Unethical Are We?" *Supervision,* 40 (March 1978), pp. 1–3.

APPENDIX B

ɞ ɞ

Bibliography of Journals on HRD

Academy of Management Journal
Academy of Management
P.O. Drawer KZ
Mississippi State University
Mississippi State, Mississippi
   39762-5865

Academy of Management Review
Academy of Management
P.O. Drawer KZ
Mississippi State University
Mississippi State, Mississippi
   39762-5865

Adult Education
Adult Education Association
810 18th Street, N.W.
Washington, D.C. 20006

Adult Literacy and Basic Education
Commission on Adult Basic Education
Auburn University
Auburn, Alabama 36830

Communication Education
Speech Communication Association
5105 Blacklick Road
Annandale, Virginia 22003

Confluent Education Journal
Confluent Education
P.O. Box 30128
Santa Barbara, California 93105

Education + Training
MCB University Press, Ltd
62 Toller Lane, Bradford
West Yorkshire, England BD8 9BY

*Exchange: The Organizational Behavior
   Teaching Journal*
Organizational Behavior Teaching
   Society
Bureau of Business Research and
   Services
Box U-41 Br
Storrs, Connecticut 06268

Group and Organization Studies: The International Journal For Group Facilitators
University Associates
8517 Production Avenue
P.O. Box 26240
San Diego, California 92126

Human Performance
Lawrence Erlbaum Associates, Inc.
365 Broadway
Hillsdale, New Jersey 07642

Human Resource Development Quarterly
Training and Development Research Center
University of Minnesota
1954 Buford Avenue
St. Paul, Minnesota 55108

Industrial and Commercial Training
MCB University Press, Ltd
62 Toller Lane, Bradford
West Yorkshire, England BD8 9BY

Journal of Business Communication
Association for Business Communication
608 South Wright Street
Urbana, Illinois 61801

Journal of European Industrial Training
MCB University Press, Ltd
62 Toller Lane, Bradford
West Yorkshire, England BD8 9BY

Journal of Management
Southern Management Association
College of Business Administration
Texas Tech University
Lubbock, Texas 79409-4320

Journal of Management Development
MCB University Press, Ltd
62 Toller Lane, Bradford
West Yorkshire, England BD8 9BY

Lifelong Learning: The Adult Years
Adult Education Association
810 18th Street, N.W.
Washington, D.C. 20006

Organizational Behavior and Human Performance
American Psychological Association
1200 17th Street N.W.
Washington, D.C. 20036

Performance and Instruction Journal
National Society for Performance and Instruction
1126 Sixteenth Street N.W.
Suite 102
Washington, D.C. 20036

Personnel Administration
American Society for Personnel Administration
19 Church Street
Berea, Ohio 44017

Training and Development Journal
American Society for Training and Development
1630 Duke Street
Box 1443
Alexandria, Virginia 22313

Training Magazine
Lakewood Publications, Inc.
731 Hennepin Avenue
Minneapolis, Minnesota 55403

Name Index

Subject Index

definition, 85
formative, 86
of results, 161
summative, 86
Expected outcomes of research,
identifying, 82
Experiential activities, 117

Facilitating learning, 118
activities, 96
analysis, 125
Facilities and equipment for
training, 108
Factory schools, historical
importance of, 28
Family, as social institution, 188,
195
extended, 189
nuclear, 188
Fishbowl format for group
analysis, 126
Flip chart and newsprint, 123
Forecasting, as step in planning,146
Format of training materials, 105
Form of information presentation,
119
Fractured puzzle exercise, 120
Future research, planning for, as
step in research project, 83

Getting an idea, 78
Global economic marketplace, 41
Goal:
accomplishment, 47
ownership, 47
Government:
efforts in training, 29
workforce programs, 31
Group size, 107

Guilds, historical importance of, 27

Habit formation, as step in
training, 128
Hierarchical order, as characteristic
of bureaucratic organization,
134
Human resource activity areas, 4
Human resource development
(HRD):
analytical roles, 68
assumptions, 8–9
Bachelor's degree, 235
definition, 2, 6, 10
development, philosophy of, 2
forces, 37–45
goal, 2, 5, 52
history of, 19
importance, 10
indicators of effectiveness, 47
line function, 11
line personnel, 11
manager role, 145
Master's degree, 235
materials developer role, 101
in the organization, 9
organization charts, 54, 56, 57,
58, 59
physical resources, 60
profession (HRDP), 16
reporting relationships, 11
role in the 1990s, 48
role combinations, 15
roles, 63
specialists, 9
staff function, 11

Ideas, importance of recognizing in
international HRD, 190, 199

Thinking and fooling around, as
  element in research project, 78
Third party intervention, as
  element in integrative
  decision making, 131
Time blocks and periods in training
  session, 94
Trainee:
  impact on, of training process,
    measures of, 87
  preparation for practice, 128
  satisfaction, 87
Trainer, effectiveness of, 86
Training, 152
  clerical skills, 179
  committees, 162
  coordinators, 163
  craft, 27
  distribution, 176
  executive, 30
  institutes, 28
  management, 172
  manufacturing, 30, 175
  materials, personnel required to

  develop, 108
  materials, value of, 86
  operations or technical, 175
  resources, 162
  sales, 176, 217
  secretarial skills, 179
  sequence, 94
  services, 217
  session, 94
  support services staff, 177
  teacher, 197
  technical and skills, 218
  warehouse, 176
Training room, equipment for
  ideal, 61
Turbulence, societal, effect of on
  HRD, 43

Visualization step, 108

Word processing skills, 180
World War II HRD programs, 31
Written methods for presenting
  information, 125